*Real Fake News*

To Ross and
the team
Best wishes

T.J. Coles

# Real Fake News

Techniques of Propaganda and Deception-based
Mind Control, from Ancient Babylon to
Internet Algorithms

Red Pill Press
2018

Red Pill Press
An Imprint of Quantum Future Group
295 Scratch Branch Rd.
Otto, NC 28763
redpillpress.com

# Contents

Acknowledgements                                                    7

Introduction: 'Control exactly what people think'                   9

Part I: Fake news in history                                       31

1  History: 'Keep the people ignorant'                             33

2  Empire: 'Harshness is the greatest humanity'                    49

3  Indoctrination: 'Making minds'                                  57

4  Science and medicine: 'Fictionosis'                             75

5  Film and photography: 'Seeing isn't always believing'          85

Part II: Fake news goes to war                                    101

Introduction                                                      103

6  Iraq: 'Psyops on steroids'                                     113

7  Libya: 'The British people are very humane'                    137

8  Syria: 'A dead body can't tell you anything'                   159

Part III: The battle                                              175

Introduction                                                      177

9  Mainstream: 'News is a way of making money'                    181

10 The internet: 'Content will be opinion-based'                  203

11 Algorithms – 'The Harvey and Irma of journalism'          217

Conclusion: Some personal reflections          249

Index          267

About the author          281

# Acknowledgements

I sent a draft of the manuscript out for endorsements. Professor Richard Keeble at Lincoln University gave it a thorough going over, pointing out errors and making suggestions for improvements. I'm indebted to Richard for that. Errors and shortcomings are, of course, entirely my own.

# Introduction: 'Control exactly what people think'

Since candidate and later President Donald J. Trump came along, fake news has been a hot topic. It will continue to be a significant subject of debate for years to come.

How do we define fake news? How do we detect and counter it? Do we want to counter it or merely reinforce our beliefs? Who's to say that the given piece of counter-fake news is 'real'? What criteria for 'truth' exist and what can be formulated? Information is power, so is there a danger that, by the mere fact of claiming that something is fake news, the claimer implies that they have the 'real' news? If so, does this create conflict between two or more groups?

This book doesn't pretend to have the answers. Rather, it presents some criteria for what is and is not fake news. It analyses cases in ancient and recent history, as well as recent hi-tech developments, such as social media.

## A THREAT TO 'DEMOCRACY'?

US President Barack Obama criticized fake news as a threat to democracy. But this falsely presupposes that our Western governments are 'democracies'. Public opinion polls regularly show that most people are disenfranchised and feel excluded from the political system; that Washington or Whitehall has too much power, local authorities have too little and that members of the public are excluded from the policymaking process. Obama's statement is also hypocritical, given his administration's fake news about ethnic cleansing in Libya, which turned out to be a pretext for another illegal war.

Obama's successor, Trump, as well as Trump's alternative media supporters, spread all sorts of fake news about their rival, Hillary Clinton. Clinton herself, as US Secretary of State, spread fake news; that the US was working with 'moderate rebels' in Syria, when emails published by WikiLeaks show that Clinton knew full-well that the 'moderates' were terrorists. But even more interesting, Trump and his supporters spread fake news about Clinton while condemning the mainstream media in its entirety as fake news. The mainstream did itself no favours, with liberal-centrist MSNBC anchor, Mika Brzezinski, stating: '[Trump] is trying to undermine the media and trying to make up his own facts ... [H]e could have undermined the messaging so much that he can actually control exactly what people think. And that is our job'.[1]

Just to confuse things, Brzezinski denied this on Twitter, writing: 'To-day I said it's the media's job to keep President Trump from making up his own facts, NOT that it's our job to control what people think'. The fact that she is on record saying it doesn't count.[2]

Fake news will also last as a topic of debate because very powerful groups and individuals on all sides—politicians, corporations, enemy states, internet entrepreneurs—have something to sell: ideologies, prod-ucts, services. Sometimes the individuals and groups move in the same direction, as in the case of repeatedly bombing Iraq (1991–present). Other times, they pull in the opposite direction, as in the case of Trump v. Clinton. Either way, ordinary people bear the brunt during times of elite cooperation and non-cooperation. Another element that will make

---

[1]On Libya, the UK government which, along with France, was instrumental in the bomb-ing, later conceded: 'policy was not informed by accurate intelligence. In particular, the Government failed to identify that the threat to civilians was overstated and that the rebels included a significant Islamist element. By the summer of 2011, the limited intervention to protect civilians had drifted into an opportunist policy of regime change. That policy was not underpinned by a strategy to support and shape post-Gaddafi Libya. The result was political and economic collapse, inter-militia and inter-tribal warfare, humanitarian and migrant crises, widespread human rights violations, the spread of Gaddafi regime weapons across the region and the growth of ISIL in North Africa'. (House of Commons Foreign Affairs Committee, 'Libya: Examination of in-tervention and collapse and the UK's future policy options', Third Report of Session 2016–17, HC 119, 6 September 2016.)

The Clinton-Blumenthal emails are analysed in my *Britain's Secret Wars* (2016, Clairview Books), pp. 31-33. NTK Network, 'Mika Brzezinski: "Our Job" to "Control Exactly What People Think"', YouTube, 22 February 2017, https://www.youtube.com/watch?v=OJ9ce-yMEfc.

[2]Mika Brzezinski, *Twitter*, 22 February 2017, https://twitter.com/morningmika/status/834463604531404 800?lang=en.

fake news a hot topic over the next few years is the growth of the internet. Most of us now have unprecedented access to information—including false information. We also have the ability to self-publish and generate advertising revenue potentially with fake news, via paid content and monetization of social media.

## ABOUT THIS BOOK

It would be naïve to think that fake news and post-factualism began with the internet and Donald Trump. As this book documents, fake news has always existed and will continue to exist. The demon is not the alternative right and its messages of hate. That is a symptom of a much deeper problem: one of 'info dominance' (as the US Pentagon calls it) and the exclusion of ordinary citizens from the information gathering and formulating process. Western media, both corporate and state-owned, have a duty to provide a public service. But we need much more than that. We need a people's media. One in which the views, experiences and wishes of non-elites, i.e., the majority, are not merely aired, but one in which stories are selected, shaped and broadcast by ordinary people.[3]

*Part 1.* Chapter 1 is about the history of fake news. It covers the earliest empires and the many ways they deceived their populations. Chapter 2 is about the later-period empires of Europe, particularly the UK, and how fake news blamed colonial-era famines on the victims. Chapter 3 is about the education system in Britain and America: how it limits thought and makes children vulnerable to accepting lies told to them by authority. Chapter 4 looks at the history of fake news in science, particularly travelling medicine shows and pharmaceutical companies. Chapter 5 is all about advances in technology, particularly film and photography and how the new mediums enabled manipulators to deceive news consumers.

*Part 2.* Chapter 6 is about the invasions of Iraq (2003–present). It is less about the well-debunked lies concerning weapons of mass destruction and more about the post-invasion lies told by elites about Islamic State

---

[3]Info dominance is a phrase used by the US Space Command in 'Vision for 2020', February 1997. See also David Miller, *Information Dominance: The Philosophy of Total Propaganda Control*, January 2004, http://www.coldtype.net/Assets.04/Ess ays.04/Miller.pdf.

and other factions. Chapter 7 deconstructs the lies that attempted to justify NATO's decimation of Libya (2011). Chapter 8 is about Syria and the chemical weapons attacks, how numerous experts reason that several videos purporting to show victims of sarin gas (2013) were possibly staged.

*Part 3.* Chapter 9 is about the decline in trust—as opposed to ratings— of the mainstream media: how it happened and what this means for the internet. Chapter 10 is about the rise of so-called alternative sites: who funds them, who shares their stories and what narratives do they sell? Chapter 11 is about the battle being waged between social controllers (like the UK Ministry of Defence and US Pentagon, which have weaponized social media), alternative sites (including self-professed debunkers of 'fake news', like Snopes), and the mainstream, which are also guilty of hosting sponsored content by clickbait advertisers.

The overall message of this book is: believe neither the mainstream nor the alternative media. Assess and evaluate all evidence—including the evidence presented here—and draw logical conclusions, especially when they conflict with your existing prejudices.

## SOCIAL CONTROL...

Before looking at fake news, let's examine the purpose of so-called real news. In doing so, we find that governments and businesses alike— including those of so-called democratic societies—consider news and infor- mation tools of social control. Many journalists (and even editors) really believe that their work is adversarial and opposed to power, even if the outcome of their work doesn't reflect their beliefs. Others are shameless supporters of the state and of big business.

Numerous public opinion polls show that most people in Europe and America do not believe they live in a democracy. Most people believe that government acts in the interests of powerful private organizations and that individual needs are seldom met. Government itself, however, is convinced that we live in a democracy. But its understanding of democracy is a system in which the public chooses between two parties (usually left and right) which share similar interests. The public should not be involved in running, in the public interest, the corporations in which they work, but for the good of shareholders. Wealth should not be shared, it should flow to a minority. People should leave policy formation and implementation to 'experts'. They should sit back and ratify decisions every few years at the ballot box. For government, this is what 'democracy' means.[4]

That so-called democratic governments believe in social control and not in being controlled by the public is easy to prove. Let's look at some examples.

On the so-called left, Cass Sunstein, an advisor to Barack Obama, co-authored a book called *Nudge* (2008), in which he argues that the role of government is to control the public (through what the authors call 'libertarian paternalism'), not to respond to their wishes. The public is best manipulated by being 'nudged' in certain directions through creating bounded choice ('choice architecture'), rather than having free choice. The authors write: 'The false assumption is that ... people ... make choices that are in their best interest or at the very least are better than the choices that would be made by someone else'. The truth, as far as the authors are concerned, is that they know what's best for you.[5]

In 2009, the so-called left-wing New Labour government in the UK published a paper called *MINDSPACE: Influencing behaviour through public policy*. The introduction is signed by Sir Gus O'Donnell (Head of the Home Civil Service) and Sir Michael Bichard (director of the Institute for Government). They write: 'Influencing people's behaviour is nothing new to Government, which has often used tools such as legislation, regulation or taxation to achieve desired policy outcomes'. If we go back in history, for instance, to the 1819 Peterloo Massacre, we find that government control extended as far as the murder of 15 demonstrators. But now, the public is so well controlled, say the authors, that social engineers can move to comparatively bland forms of social control, such as saving money on the health service and sanitation by 'nudging' people to eat better and pick up their rubbish (and yes the report uses the language of Sunstein). '[M]any of the biggest policy challenges we are now facing – such as the increase in people with chronic health conditions – will only be resolved if we are successful in persuading people to change their behaviour, their

---

[4]For extensive polling results, see Chapter 9.

[5]Cass R. Sunstein and Richard H. Thaler, *Nudge: Improving Decisions about Health, Wealth, and Happiness* (2008, Yale University Press).

lifestyles or their existing habits', say O'Donnell and Bichard.[6]

The report itself says: 'Influencing behaviour is central to public policy. Recently, there have been major advances in understanding the influences on our behaviours, and government needs to take notice of them'. It goes on to note that '[i]f we provide the carrots and sticks, alongside accurate information, people will weigh up the revised costs and benefits of their actions and respond accordingly'. As this book will show, what constitutes 'accurate' information is highly selective. For instance, it may save the government money on the health system by getting people to quit smoking via 'nudge' manipulation, but if people don't know that most smokers smoke because they are poor and stressed, they are not going to get to the root of their poverty and stress, namely the government and its socioeconomic policies which favour the wealthy and perpetuate social privilege (as government reports acknowledge). Notice also that absent from the report is any serious questioning of the moral *right* of governments to influence behaviour. That's because they really believe they have the right. Totally absent is the idea that government serves people: in fact, the psychology of people in power is that government knows better than the public what is good for them ('libertarian paternalism').[7]

What about the right-wing? In 2010, the British Tory government established an organization called the Behavioural Insights Team (BIT), in collaboration with Oxford University. BIT boasts of working to cut poor people's benefits and getting them 'back into work' as well as influencing international institutions, including the World Bank and the UN Development Programme. Their work includes psychological pressuring, such as texting benefit claimants to 'remind' them to turn up to job interviews. These measures are designed to be 'cost effective', says the report. Notice that BIT does not use psychological techniques to empower benefits claimants to fight for a more just society in which major benefit claimants (like banks and the oil industry) have to pay their fair share of taxes.[8]

---

[6]David Halpern, Dominic King, Ivo Vlaev and Michael Hallsworth, *MINDSPACE: Influencing behaviour through public policy*, 2 March 2010, https://www.instituteforgovern ment.org.uk/sites/default/files/publications/MINDSPACE.pdf.

[7]Ibid.

[8]Owain Service, Michael Hallsworth, David Halpern, Felicity Algate, Rory Gallagher, Sam Nguyen, Simon Ruda, Michael Sanders, Marcos Pelenur, Alex Gyani, Hugo Harper, Joanne Reinhard and Elspeth Kirkman, *EAST: Four simple ways to apply*

This kind of mind manipulation works in concert with the privately-owned tabloid press, which appeals to working class readers by promoting sports, sex, gossip and celebrity. Such papers are notorious for assaulting social security recipients with anti-welfare propaganda. This is an example of how newspapers owned by wealthy people turn the poor (e.g., working people) against each other (e.g., benefits claimants) through demonization. By pitting poor against poor, the wealthy seek to perpetuate their privilege. As Tory-led fiscal austerity literally put thousands of Britons in the grave, a study co-authored by researchers at the University of Kent found that 'media coverage of benefits in national newspapers from 1995 to 2011 ... contain[ed] both positive and negative representations of claimants, [though] the content of press stories is indeed skewed towards negative representations'. It concludes that 'both the language and content of "negative" coverage have changed substantially over time. While [alleged benefit] fraud remains very important in negative coverage, articles are much more likely now to refer to lack of reciprocity and effort on the part of claimants than they were previously'.[9]

## ... & 'REAL' NEWS

So where does so-called real news fit into the social control agenda?

In America in the 1920s and '30s, the Chicago School received grants from wealthy businessmen (all of them men), such as John D. Rockefeller. The school emerged in a period when anti-union violence in the USA was extreme. It included the Ludlow Massacre 1914, in which 19 or more people (including women and children) were shot by the Colorado National Guard and Colorado Fuel and Iron Company. The land was owned by Rockefeller. People like Rockefeller sought to use the emerging science of social control as a more PR-friendly way of hobbling organized participation by workers and their families. Social control researcher Dario Melossi writes that '[t]he neo-Chicagoans expressed a new situation of normative pluralism and a vision of democracy as conflict and competition among

---

*behavioural insights*, BIT, July 2015, http://www.behaviouralinsights.co.uk/wp-con tent/uploads/2015/07/BIT_Update-Report-Final-2013-2015.pdf.

[9]Turn2Us, 'Benefits stigma in Britain', Elizabeth Finn Care and University of Kent, no date, circa 2014, https://wwwturn2us-2938.cdn.hybridcloudspan.com/T2UWebsite /media/Documents/Benefits-Stigma-in-Britain.pdf.

unevenly powerful groups', like Rockefeller and his labourers. In a book on social control sponsored by the Spanish government, Colin Sumner writes that 1930s' America saw 'a growing need for conscious planning and social control to sustain social order'. Prior to WWII, 'American sociology was concerned to do empirical research into various forms of social control to determine which were the most effective in enabling social groups to regulate themselves'.[10]

After WWII, the US sought to influence media in Europe in the interests of American corporations and 'values'.

The Trilateral Commission was established in the early 1970s by major North American, European and Japanese corporations, whose directors were worried about the social activism of the late-1960s. Members include(d) the Bank of America, Barclays, Lehman Bros., Lloyds, Wells Fargo, and numerous energy, manufacturing and media companies. A report by the group published in 1975 explains that 'journalists possess a crucial role as gatekeepers of one of the central dimensions of public life ... If journalists can create events, they have a structuring impact on public and social life'. Those 'values' include consumerism, respect for law and authority, conformity and the atomization of individuals. Gatekeepers must protect elites because 'a pervasive spirit of democracy may pose an intrinsic threat ... [T]he effective operation of a democratic political system usually requires some measure of apathy and noninvolvment', the authors explain. A disinterested and ignorant population poses no threat to decisions made by rulers.[11]

Numerous studies suggest that in Britain and America, mainstream media portray the powerful favourably and the powerless unfavourably. Muslims are less of a threat if they identify with their nation (Britain or the USA, for instance) more than with their religion. The free market is the best system we have and while it excludes some people from success, it benefits the majority. There is still scientific debate about whether

---

[10]Dario Melossi, 'The law and state as practical rhetoric of motives' in John Lowman, Robert J. Menzies and T.S. Palys (eds.), *Transcarceration* (1987, Gower Publishing). Colin Sumner, 'Social Control: the History and Politics of a Central Concept in Anglo-American Sociology' in Roberto Bergalli and Colin Sumner (eds.), *Social Control and Political Order: European Perspectives at the End of the Century* (1997, Sage).

[11]Michel J. Crozier, Samuel P. Huntington and Joji Watanuki, *The Crisis of Democracy* (1975, New York University Press).

humans are driving climate change. War is always waged either to defend ourselves or human rights abroad, anti-war demonstrators are weird, unpatriotic and/or conspiracy theorists. In general wealthy people are the paragons of achievement, welfare recipients are undeserving. Public spending is a failure, privatization a success. Corporate crime is an exception, lower class crime is the norm. Some black people are successful and progressive, most are criminals. Latinos and Hispanics who are integrated into the free market system have adopted American values, immigrants are a threat.[12]

Class is a significant issue when it comes to media. The wealthy are disproportionately represented and most editors and executives in the US and Britain come from wealthy backgrounds. This structure means that any 'balanced' reporting is undermined by the fact that the given issue has been selected and framed by elites. A report (2016) headed by British MP Alan Milburn, Chair of the Social Mobility and Child Poverty Commission, finds that 7% of the British public attends a private school. Yet those graduates make up 54% of top media professionals. In print media, 43% of columnists attended a private school. Of the top media professionals, 74% attended Russell Group Universities as did 68% of columnists.[13]

The internet therefore represents more of a 'people's media' than the mainstream, particularly through its ability to allow 'self-disclosure'. On the internet, issues and framing are selected and designed by individuals with their own concerns. Naturally, this is a threat to the powerful, hence their inclination to lump 'fake news' together with alternative news websites.[14]

Private ownership is a major factor influencing media content and output. It is not surprising, then, that the quality of media content is low. The internet allows people to look for information more relevant and sympathetic to their lives, status, values and beliefs, even when those beliefs are regressive and underpinned by mainstream media. Because most peo-

---

[12]See Chapter 9, notes 6 to 7.

[13]Philip Kirby, 'Leading People 2016: The educational backgrounds of the UK professional elite', Sutton Trust, February 2016, http://www.suttontrust.com/wp-content/uploads/2016/02/Leading-People_Feb16.pdf.

[14]Natalya N. Bazarova and Yoon Hyung Choi, 'Self-Disclosure in Social Media: Extending the Functional Approach to Disclosure Motivations and Characteristics on Social Network Sites', *Journal of Communication*, December 2013, doi:10.1111/jcom.12106.

ple are not rich and the media are owned by rich people, most people don't trust the media because they don't reflect their interests or experiences. The Media Reform Coalition notes that two billionaires—Rupert Murdoch and Jonathan Harmsworth (4th Viscount of Rothermere)—own more than 50% of the British print media market. Three companies control 71% of the British newspaper market. Five companies control 80% of online mainstream news. The Coalition also notes that 80% of local newspapers are owned by six companies. The conglomerates Bauer and Global Radio own 40% of local analogue licenses and 65% of digital stations.[15]

## CASE STUDY: BAD NEWS ABOUT BANKS

Let's look more closely at how financial institutions—asset managers, banks, hedge funds, insurers, liquidity firms, savings and loans—were portrayed during the global financial crisis, which started in 2007, peaked in 2008, was bandaged by central banks in 2009 and whose reverberations are still felt today.

In 2014, Reuters Institute for the Study of Journalism at Oxford University published a report by Picard et al. into media coverage in the US and Europe over the banking and financial crisis. The authors find that one of the goals of business, which it seeks to attain through PR firms, is to perpetuate a 'narrative of normality', in which their non-philanthropic works are kept out of public view for as long as possible. As the authors put it, 'no news is good news'. When a crisis breaks, the task is perception management. '[S]tories originate from six main categories of sources', say the authors: from journalists, corporations, analysts, authorities and politicians and shareholders. Notice that unions, activists, alternative currency purveyors and dissident academics are not included. They can be found in the alternative online media and are thus at risk of being labelled 'fake news' by the powerful.[16]

---

[15]Media Reform Coalition, 'Who Owns the UK Media?', October 2015, http://www. mediareform.org.uk/who-owns-the-uk-media.

[16]Robert G. Picard, Meera Selva and Diego Bironzo, 'Media Coverage of Banking and Financial News', University of Oxford, Reuters Institutes for the Study of Journalism, April 2014, https://reutersinstitute.politics.ox.ac.uk/sites/default/files/Media %20Coverage%20of%20Banking%20and%20Financial%20News_0.pdf.

The authors go on to note that, '[w]hen excluding the 'default category' of journalists, most of the information in news stories about the banking crisis comes from banks themselves'. Indeed, more than half came from financial institutions. 'On average 52% of all information comes from banks, another 18% from analysts/experts'. The authors note that prior to the crisis, 'banks themselves were the initiators of 62% of coverage. By 2013, this figure had fallen to 47%'. However, when factoring in parroting by journalists, the percentages change. Negative coverage of financial institutions was surprisingly low, given the severity of the crisis. The authors find that the 'average level of coverage ... is about 25% negative, 48% neutral, and 24% positive coverage. 3% of coverage was classed as ambivalent'. Predictably, the authors found that 'even during the crises, most of the coverage about banking did in fact retain a neutral tone'.[17]

Another factor in the pro-banking or neutral coverage was the professional proximity of journalists to the institutions. 'While it was impossible to ignore the bad news, ... the close contact between reporters and public relations officers meant that much newspaper coverage in Britain contained background and context'. As a result, the tone remained neutral-to-positive in most stories. Most journalists 'adopted a neutral or ambivalent tone' in the 2007–08 coverage. In the US, 'even the most critical of the journalists, Julia Werdigier at the *International Herald Tribune* and Christine Seib at *The Times*, were not that negative. Only 33% of Werdigier's coverage was classed as negative, an equal amount to her coverage classed as positive. Thirty-five percent of Seib's is classed as negative and 22% is positive'.[18]

The mainstream's news about banks is not blatantly fake (i.e., directly lying), but it tries to shape perceptions that are not real (e.g., by omission of crucial contexts and facts).

## THREE BROAD PROPAGANDA TYPES

What do we mean by fake? Scholars frequently identify three types of propaganda. Usually these are engaged in by governments and related agencies (such as secret services) with the aim of satisfying particular ob-

[17]Ibid.
[18]Ibid.

jectives. They target both home and foreign audiences, depending on the given situation. They are different from profit-driven advertising objectives, for instance, which crudely seek to encourage consumption. They are also different from generic corporate public relations, which usually attempts to humanize business, particularly during periods of negative publicity (e.g., after an oil spill).

The three broad types of propaganda are black, white and grey.

*Black propaganda* is where agencies invent stories. One example is the British Conservative government's invention of former social security claimants (actors in reality) who appeared to make statements of gratitude concerning how benefits sanctions helped them find employment (in reality scripts written by Department for Work and Pensions employees). The objective was to portray benefits sanctions and reductions in social security as being in the best interests of the people hurt by the policies.[19]

*White propaganda* is where the given party simply states its objectives. For example, Michael Walker, executive director of the Frazer Institute, said that all common land should be privately owned because private interests can best look after global resources (tragedy of the commons fallacy). Such outrageous statements evoke knee-jerk oppositional reactions from sane human beings and therefore require other forms of propaganda (such as PR) to make them marketable.[20]

Finally, *grey propaganda* means statements of confusion, where audiences are unsure who is making them or what the motives are. For instance, the alleged Osama bin Laden tapes post-2004 (to which we shall return) featured a man who didn't look like bin Laden threatening more

---

[19] A CIA report into covert actions against Salvador Allende in Chile states: 'assets manufactured "black propaganda," material falsely purporting to be from Allende and his supporters, and intended to discredit them' (James A. Barry, 'Managing Covert Political Action', Center for the Study of Intelligence, 36(3), https://www.cia.gov/library/center-for-the-study-of-intelligence/kent-csi/vol36no3/h tml/v36i3a05p_0001.htm.)

BBC, 'DWP admits using 'fake' claimants in benefit sanctions leaflet', 18 August 2015, http://www.bbc.co.uk/news/uk-politics-33974674.

[20] Another CIA report analysing WWII says that white propaganda 'tended to be related to American policy'. CIA, 'Study in "Black"', https://www.cia.gov/library/reading room/docs/CIA-RDP80R01 731R003600010 034-9.pdf.

Walker cited in Dierdra Reber, *Coming to Our Senses: Affect and an Order of Things for Global Culture* (2016, Columbia University Press), p. 281n3.

terrorism in a poorly produced video, whose frames stuck and jumped. The tapes were so poorly produced that two theories emerged: either the CIA or related agencies were keeping the bin Laden myth alive to justify perpetual war, or al-Qaeda was keeping the bin Laden myth alive to make itself seem like a functioning organization.[21]

In cases of black propaganda, mass media are particularly susceptible and often directly culpable.

## FOUR CATEGORIES OF FAKE NEWS

Like any ideology or theoretical system, fake news is a broad spectrum. Its features are manifold, sometimes contradictory, sometimes confluent, often overlapping and not easy to categorize into neat taxonomies.

1) *Fake news for social control.* This is where the establishment (whatever it may be at any particular time and in any particular location) lies and/or exaggerates news with the express aim of manipulating the attitudes, opinions and ultimately course of affairs among the public. This can be for purposes of war (e.g., invasion of Iraq), demonization of domestic threats to elite control (e.g., unions, activists), reinforcement (e.g., pro-monarchic propaganda) or denial of alternative systems (e.g., keeping off the mainstream agenda the fact that European countries with tighter state controls over jobs and the economy have higher social indicators than the USA or UK, with their 'free markets').

A) A subcategory or at least feature of this mode is omission. Take the regular mainstream media reports in the UK about the state of the health service: the one crucial piece of missing information is usually that, yes, the health service is in decline, but this follows a dedicated course of privatization. B) A second feature of 1) is and can be accidental fake news, such as erroneous beliefs on the part of elites or dedication to particular ideologies at the expense of others. This is sometimes called the god that failed.

---

[21] The CIA's forerunner, Office of Strategic Services, says: 'Grey propaganda is the most mysterious of all because the source of the propaganda is never identified'. (OSS, 'Morale Operations Branch', https://www.cia.gov/news-information/featured-story-archive/2010-featured-story-archive/oss-morale-operations.html.)

2) *Revolutionary fake news.* Grassroots organizations can and have spread fake news exaggerating the crimes of government or corporations with the aim of implementing or stopping particular policies, even up to the point of revolution. For example, People for the Ethical Treatment of Animals (PETA) is a worthwhile, dedicated organization which has done much to raise awareness and shape the popular mood towards respecting minimal rights for animals. However, their methods and the methods of some of their activists have included lies. In 2017, it was revealed that PETA paid a PR firm to create a CGI cat realistic enough to appear to be being abused in an effort to raise awareness about cruelty. The aim was laudable but the means dishonest.

A) A subcategory includes agitprop, wherein elite intelligence organizations plant fake stories among target populations in order to elicit political agitation against target governments (see Black Propaganda and the endnote about the CIA in Chile, above). B) Over the last decade, revolutionary fake news has been generated by multimillionaires and billionaires whose targets are Washington, DC and the 'crony-capitalism' from which they are excluded. Certain billionaires have financed their own 'nationalistic' revolutions *à la* Trump and Brexit by promoting a particular form of nationalism via web-based proxies, including news sites and forums.

3) *Fake news for profit.* Long before so-called rebel political leaders working within the establishment provoked concerns about fake news, the general public did not trust the tabloids because of their poor reputation for accuracy. A tabloid will sell on the basis of attention grabbing, often inaccurate headlines. This overlaps with point 1, concerning the limits of fake news between outright lies and exaggerations.

A) Tabloids and broadsheets alike have engaged in this behaviour (e.g., 'Jeremy Corbyn sparks HORROR with plan to turn Britain into North Korea', *Express*, 27 Sep. 2017. This overlaps with social control, i.e., demonizing social progress). B) Corporations do it all the time to sell products (see Patent Medicine in Chapter 4). For example, Naked Juice (owned by Pepsico) claimed that its juices were 'all natural'. However, it was discovered that some contained genetically-modified foods. How is advertising news? Advertising is news because PR companies frequently give local and national media news promos for products like orange juice or medicine in the form of video news releases. C) In the internet age, clickbait is the latest form of fake news, where so-called respectable news sites raise revenue by hosting advertising content targeted to your region (by your IP address, that's why you'll often see an advert appearing to relate to your location, even though it is often for a national company), age (based on the average age of the average webpage viewer (as determined by polling and algorithms) products can be targeted) and emotion (such as a fake picture of a child about to be eaten by a lion with the headline, 'What happens next is heartbreaking'). Clickbait embedded in so-called respectable sites is just as a bad as PR-supplied video news releases; though, at least with clickbait you can roll over the thumbnail and see a URL which indicates that the location to which you are being directed has nothing to do with the advertised story.

4) *Fake news for merriment/notoriety.* Examples include Orson Welles's radio broadcast in 1938 of H.G. Wells's *War of the Worlds.* The broadcast was so realistic that supposedly millions of Americans believed that an alien invasion had occurred. (The idea that the broadcast caused mass panic has subsequently been disputed. It is an interesting example of the evolution of fake news: from a hoax broadcast to possible exaggerated media claims of resultant mass panic.) In the 1990s, the BBC broadcast *Ghostwatch* (1992) as a purported live documentary about hauntings. It was a spoof and only later did the BBC confirm and apologize. These are elite-driven instances of hoaxes as fake news. There are non-elites who seek profit and attention by perpetrating hoaxes (e.g., the couple who faked incest for the Channel 4 documentary *Daddy's Girl* (1998)).

## SUSCEPTIBILITY TO FAKE NEWS

Here are four broad principles of media *susceptibility* to reporting fake news:

1) *Ignorance.* Due to a number of factors, many journalists and editors are ignorant of facts and broader context. These include, particularly for journalists: A) working conditions (long hours, low pay, low job satisfaction). B) Taking 'easy info' (such as hand-outs from PR companies) as a consequence of *a.* C) Rewriting wire reports (from Reuters, AP, etc.) and claiming them as their own. D) Editorial control, which confines many journalists to the desk and newsroom. E) Government secrecy and

corporate privacy laws can work against journalists. Often, important revelations concerning the internal workings of business and government are not revealed for years. F) Embedding does not only take place abroad: many journalists rely on close access to politicians in order to get scoops. This creates a mutually-beneficial and thus reinforcing relationship between media and government.

2) *Incompetence.* Some journalists and editors (as a result of incompetence, greed for a scoop, or both) report and re-report stories that are either false or contain a degree of falsification and exaggeration. More than a decade ago, Cardiff University was commissioned by award-winning journalist Nick Davies to study major newspapers in the UK for two weeks. The researchers studied 2,207 articles published by the *Daily Mail, Daily Telegraph, Guardian, Independent* and *The Times.* The researchers concluded that, based on this sample, 70% of all mainstream print sources are uncorroborated. Just 12% are 'thoroughly checked'. The Cardiff University researchers note that 'meaningful journalistic activity by the press is the exception rather than the rule'. So much for the mainstream pointing fingers at the internet over 'fake news'.[22]

3) *Conspiracy.* Not all conspiracy theories are real, but many are. We shall later examine British journalists and their connection to the deep state. Other conspiracies include instances of editors and journalists taking bribes for favourable coverage of bribers. The Ethical Journalism Network published a report entitled, *Untold Stories: How Corruption and Conflicts of Interest Stalk the Newsroom* (2015–16). The work was financed by the Norwegian Ministry of Foreign Affairs. The report covers journalists and editors in the Balkans, Colombia, Denmark, Egypt, India, Malaysia, Mexico, Nigeria, the Philippines, Turkey, Ukraine and Britain. The report cites cases of bribe-taking, but more importantly: a 'growing dependence on political and corporate power'. It acknowledges the structural threats emanating from '[g]overnments, unscrupulous politicians, ... the overweening power of corporations, ... cuts and restructuring of the media economy', but adds that many wounds are 'self-inflicted'. If they ever were, journalists and editors are no longer working along ethical guidelines. Examples cited by the authors include journalist Peter Oborne leaving the *Telegraph* over alleged censorship of stories critical of HSBC,

---

[22]Nick Davies, *Flat Earth News* (2008, Vintage).

then embroiled in a tax scandal. The report mentions growing corruption in journalism across the world, including bribery.[23]

4) *Convenience.* A combination of factors, including those mentioned in points 1, 2 and 3, interact to make it easy and convenient for journalists and editors to publish stories without checking them, pull stories from the wires/rewrite them and take freebies from PR companies or wealthy patrons in exchange for favourable coverage.

## SEVEN PRINCIPLES OF FAKE NEWS

Can fake news be defined and analysed in a systematic way? This book identifies seven guiding principles of fake news.

1) *Historical.* There is a rich historical record of fake news, from religion to elite-making mythology to deception as a method of war. Rulers invented stories about their own greatness, divine right to rule, magical powers, etc., to cement rule over domestic populations and justify hegemony over foreign ones. Those on both sides—authority and opposition—are consciously or unconsciously following deep-rooted patterns laid by professional propagandists and public relations experts of bygone centuries.

2) *Social control.* One of the striking facts about fake news, to which we shall return, is that the intellectual class usually defines and describes fake news as a threat emanating from the grassroots, both by far-right extremists and progressive leftists. Without spelling it out, they condemn fake news as countering the establishment. What makes their position striking is that it ignores the lies and crimes of the establishment. Throughout history, fake news has been used as a tool of social control: to limit thought and perpetuate a status quo favourable to select elites. Those who condemn fake news today often do so in an effort (probably subconscious) to reinforce the given system which has privileged them.

3) *Profit-making.* Many critics of fake news point to the obvious business model. In the mainstream, if you want to sell newspapers, you must invent or exaggerate stories and grab attention with provocative headlines. Usually, our instinctive response to an outrageous proposition is

---

[23] Aidan White (ed.), *Untold Stories: How Corruption and Conflicts of Interest Stalk the Newsroom*, Ethical Journalism Network (2015-16), http://ethicaljournalismnetwork .org/wp-content/uploads/2016/08/untold-stories-full.pdf.

to learn more about it in case it is a threat of some kind. In the entrepreneurial alternative (usually web-based) media, it is much easier to get webpage hits with crazy or provocative headlines because editorial filtration and censorship are unlikely. The mainstream media are not just about profit-making: they also serve to reinforce the given political and economic structure. Many clickbait sites on the other hand are concerned solely with profit. Others, like Breitbart, also have a political agenda.

4) *Echo-chamber.* The internet has become a marketing tool. Websites collect data on visitors in order to target information to them. This is now true of the BBC's news website, which (at the time of writing) is encouraging (soon forcing, it says) users to sign in, in order to market personalized data to the user. People's natural bias towards information that supports their values and outlook, coupled with new technologies, are freezing out alternative views, evidence and opinions. But the trend cannot be blamed on the internet. Talk radio in particular has been identified by scholars (especially Jamieson and Cappella) as a format and medium in which users are susceptible to hearing opinions that reinforce their beliefs. It matters not if stories are outlandish and false, it chimes with a person's world view and is therefore accepted as fact.[24]

5) *Snowball.* In the next chapter, we give the example of lies about Christian artefacts (the Holy Lance) spreading to mainland Europe through letter-writing. Today, it is the newswires, such as Reuters, which spread mis- and dis-information. For reasons expressed above (such as long hours and incompetence), many journalists pick up the false stories and report them as fact. Currently, information sharing—literally at the click of a button on PCs and mobile devices—via social media like Twitter and Facebook, has made the snowball effect of fake news even more pervasive; but again, nothing new.

6) *Counter-narrative.* Related to echo-chamber is counter-narrative. Information from established, powerful and wealthy sources, such as state-owned television and radio and corporate-owned mass media by their very structures do not and cannot reflect the diverse wishes, needs and opinions of everybody. People with 'extreme' views, be they progressive or regressive will be marginalized by the mainstream; even though 'extremists' may

---

[24]Kathleen Hall Jamieson and Joseph N. Cappella, *Echo Chamber: Rush Limbaugh and the Conservative Media Establishment* (2008, Oxford University Press).

be in the majority. For instance, Labour Party leader Jeremy Corbyn ran on a platform of nationalization. Poll after poll suggest that a significant majority of Britons want public services renationalized. Corbyn and his supporters have been labelled extremists by the mainstream media which also keeps nationalization off the agenda of news and analysis—in most cases, at least. This is why alternative websites like *The Canary.co* are becoming so popular: they offer a counter-narrative to the mainstream. Others, like Drudge Report, represent the regressive far-right, but for the people who consume their stories, Drudge et al. offer an alternative to the marginalizing mainstream.[25]

7) *Context-dependence.* News can be fake or real depending on the context. Leaving aside satirical websites like *The Onion,* mainstream newspapers like the *Washington Post* can spread fake news, e.g., that certain websites are actually Russian front agencies, cite no evidence whatsoever in support of the claims, issue minor retractions and still maintain credibility among most readers and other news agencies. This fake news was spread in the context of Russia-bashing, so it was acceptable to most American audiences. However, when Russia's state-propaganda outlets, like *Pravda* and RT, criticize America, often with genuine but targeted information, they can be dismissed as fake by outlets like the *Washington Post.*[26]

## PARADOXES: THE *DAILY MAIL*

As various surveys (detailed later) have demonstrated, most people do not trust mainstream media, particularly print in the UK and television in the US. So when people like Trump condemn the mainstream as 'fake news', he is not only right to say so, his words resonate with a majority of

[25]Matthew Smith, 'Following Labour's manifesto pledge to nationalise (or renationalise) several industries, YouGov looks at who the public thinks should run 13 different industries and companies', 19 May 2017, https://yougov.co.uk/news/2017/05/19/national isation-vs-privatisation-public-view/. Will Dahlgreen, 'Nationalise energy and rail companies, say public', 4 November 2013, https://yougov.co.uk/news/2013/11/04/nat ionalise-energy-and-rail-companies-say-public/.

[26]Glenn Greenwald, 'WashPost is richly rewarded for false news about Russia threat while public is deceived', *The Intercept,* 4 January 2017, https://theintercept.com/2017/01/04/washpost-is-richly-rewarded-for-false-news-about-russia-threat-while-public-is-deceived/.

Americans; even though the majority may not like Trump on other issues. The irony is that Trump himself has spread fake news, as various organizations have documented. The battle commences when one side (Trump) uses fake news to attack the other and vice versa (the mainstream) and people reflexively believe Trump because they hate the mainstream. This is the dialectic.[27]

The British newspaper, *Daily Mail*, exemplifies the complexities of fake news. The paper is one of the UK's biggest sellers and most viewed online, yet it gains some of the lowest levels of trust among readers. It is a striking fact that British newspapers with the highest circulation gain the lowest levels of trust. This suggests that the paper (and others, like the *Sun* and the *Mirror*) is bought by most readers for the sports section, celebrity gossip and erotica. The newspaper also spreads fake news homogeneously via frequent negative portrayals of Muslims, ethnic minorities and social security claimants. This creates a false impression that said groups are threats to white middle class values.[28]

Yet here is the paradox: the newspaper often contains important revelations. In order to attack the supposedly left-wing New Labour government, the *Daily Mail* was the only newspaper in Britain to report Aidan Hartley's important findings in Somalia: that the famines of 2006–08 were caused by government policy. Further, Britain was involved, as Hartley documents. When Britain trained and armed terrorists in Libya *before the Arab Spring*, the newspaper was the only one to report the facts. It did so in patriotic praise of our brave SAS.[29]

## MISTAKES VS. DISINFORMATION

Honest mistakes can lead to fake news. In two books of mine, *Britain's Secret Wars* (2016, Clairview Books) and *Human Wrongs* (2018, Iff Books), I

---

[27] For example: David Leonhardt and Stuart A. Thompson, 'Trump's lies', *NYT*, 21 July 2017, https://www.nytimes.com/interactive/2017/06/23/opinion/trumps-lies.html and *PolitiFact*, 'Donald Trump's file', http://www.politifact.com/personalities/donald-trump/.

[28] Jill Rutter, 'Are our media threatening the public good?', February 2010, https://www.instituteforgovernment.org.uk/sites/default/files/publications/Are%20our%20media%20threatening%20the%20public%20good.pdf.

[29] See my *Britain's Secret Wars* (2016, Clairview Books).

discuss the Military Reaction Force (MRF). The MRF was a secret British Army unit established in Northern Ireland whose purpose was to target enemy republicans. The MRF not only murdered militant republicans but also unarmed civilians. In both books I erroneously name several Northern Irish people 'murdered' by the MRF, when many were in fact alive, though not all of them well.

Upon learning of my mistake, I immediately told both publishers. Clairview agreed to make the corrections for the second edition and Iff Books agreed to make the changes straight away, meaning that the first circa 100 copies of *Human Wrongs* printed contain the error. Overzealous readers could easily conflate my sloppy mistake with purposeful disinformation. This ambiguity adds an extra layer of complexity to how to assess 'fake' news and 'real' news. In such cases, an assessment can be made based on the response of the individual or organization that made the given mistake. If the individual or organization denies their error in the face of evidence or absolute proof, or ignores the issue altogether, it could then be reasonable to consider that they are spreading disinformation. Consider the BBC and Reuters:

Shortly after 9/11, the BBC published a list of the alleged hijackers. Around two weeks later, the BBC reported:

> Saudi Arabian pilot Waleed Al Shehri was one of five men that the FBI said had deliberately crashed American Airlines flight 11 into the World Trade Centre [sic–Center] on 11 September.
>
> His photograph was released, and has since appeared in newspapers and on television around the world.
>
> Now he is protesting his innocence.[30]

Never mind 'protesting his innocence'. If Al Shehri is able to do anything at all it means he's still alive.

This hasn't stopped the BBC from continuing elsewhere at much later dates (e.g., the latest edition of its *9/11: Conspiracy Files* (BBC 2) episode) from including Al Shehri's image among the alleged hijackers. The BBC's refusal to offer a retraction and correction, coupled with its continued use of Al Shehri's image (i.e., still accusing him years later), goes beyond error and enters the realm of disinformation.

---

[30]BBC News Online, 'Hijack "suspects" alive and well', 23 September 2001, http://news.bbc.co.uk/1/hi/world/middle_east/1559151.stm.

Consider now Reuters. In October 2016, a car bomb was detonated in Al-Hurriyah, a Shia-majority district of Baghdad, Iraq. Leaked CCTV footage clearly shows that *after* the explosion, crisis actors run onto the scene and play dead and injured. Even the Western media- and government-approved Bellingcat analysis website (which frequently targets Russia for criticism) acknowledges that the event was a hoax and draws no firm conclusions as to why it was perpetrated. But this didn't stop international news agencies, including Reuters, from reporting it as real. Not only that, but Reuters refuses to offer a retraction and also refuses to enter into a discussion about the case, indicating that the event is being used for some obscure disinformation agenda.[31]

A lot is written about propaganda. Less is written on whether propaganda is effective. Each chapter ends with a brief summary on the likelihood of the effectiveness of the fake news being examined.

---

[31]Christiaan Triebert, 'The remarkable case of an Iraqi car bomb', Bellingcat, 4 November 2016, https://www.bellingcat.com/news/mena/2016/11/04/remarkable-case-iraqi-car-bomb/ and Reuters, 'Car bomb kills at least eight in Baghdad market – police, medics', 30 October 2016, https://uk.reuters.com/article/uk-mideast-crisis-iraq-blast-idUKKBN12U0KE.

# Part I: Fake news in history

# Chapter 1

# History: 'Keep the people ignorant'

*Power uses information as a weapon against foreign and domestic citizens. This chapter shows that fake news is as old as empire. The earliest known fakery began with the self-aggrandizing myths spread by Babylonian rulers. As art and literature got more sophisticated, it entered the realms of medicine and prophesy, giving power to seers and doctors like those in ancient China. Crucially, it is the intellectual class who must, in any system of power, be indoctrinated to believe in their own greatness because they are social managers. Ordinary citizens have always been less susceptible to lies and exaggeration.*

Social control is one of the main objectives of elite-driven fake news. Dr Bill Ivey is an expert in fantasy: how people respond to it, how it influences culture and crucially how it affects thought. It is through his connections with the Democratic National Committee (DNC), the organization of the US Democratic Party, that Ivey sought to spread folklore and fairy tales to what he considers to be a childlike public.[1]

Leaked emails from Ivey to John Podesta, chief strategist of presidential nominee Hillary Clinton, reveal the Democratic Party's long-term attempts to, in their words, 'conspire to produce an unaware and compliant citizenry. The unawareness remains strong but compliance is obviously fading rapidly'. The Democrats are so transparently in the pocket of big business that they failed in 2016 to win enough Electoral College votes to secure a Clinton presidency. The children were no longer complying with the adults. Many were simply not voting, others were mobilized by the hate-speech of Clinton's rival, Donald Trump.[2]

---

[1]Bill Ivey, Global Cultural Studies, http://globalculturalstrategies.com/.

[2]Bill Ivey, 'From Bill Ivey', WikiLeaks, 13 March 2016, https://wikileaks.org/podesta-emails/emailid/3599.

The Ivey emails were not the only ones to suggest that the public should be prevented from participating in the political process. Jeremy Berns was a researcher for the DNC. Kelly Roberts was a staffer involved in shaping CNN's coverage. The sticky issue of Clinton's close relationship with Wall Street was raised in a series of questions and answers between Berns and Kelly. With regards to Clinton's presidential debates with then-Republican nominee Trump, Clinton—according to the leaked emails—'doesn't want the people knowing about her relationships on Wall Street. She wants to achieve consistency and the best way to do that is to keep the people ignorant'.[3]

The emails generated disgust on the alternative internet news sites that carried them. The mainstream television and print media barely covered these specific emails. We cannot be surprised that wealthy elites actively 'conspire' to keep people 'compliant' and 'ignorant': that has been the strategy of the ruling classes for millennia. Even left-liberal governments and advisers understand 'democracy' quite differently from most people. Most people think of democracy as rule by the people via elected representatives. Elites think of democracy as non-participation by passive majorities.

The aim of this chapter is to sketch a broad history of fake news and related propaganda. Propaganda in ancient Egypt and ancient Greece was aimed primarily at elites. It was essential that the political class be indoctrinated to believe in the moral righteousness of the given empire. As far as controlling the masses goes, elites had numerous methods: violence, criminal justice, economics, religion and private ownership. Whether the 'masses' believed the propaganda or not was of secondary importance to the ideological shapers, who often used brute force.

## ANCIENT BABYLON: DIVINE RIGHT OF KINGS

The Babylonian empires (in modern-day Iraq) lasted for about 900 years, before the Egyptians came to prominence. Between 2100 and 1200 BCE, the city of Ur underwent significant urban and political developments, with the construction of temples and money mints; often the two were

---

[3]Jeremy Berns, 'Video Request: Ben Carson on MSNBC', WikiLeaks, 13 May 2016, https://wikileaks.org/dnc-emails/emailid/4788.

connected. Propaganda was one of the many tools of social control, the others included worship, money and punishment.

The legend of Gilgamesh originated in ancient Sumer and Akkadia and is best known as an epic poem. In it, Gilgamesh, a man-god, builds the walls of Uruk. Gilgamesh was likely a real historical figure, but very unlikely a man-god. Ur-Nammu (circa 2047 BCE) founded the eponymous Dynasty, governed the city of Ur and was king of neighbouring Uruk. Ur-Nammu spread the fake news that he was the brother of Gilgamesh. He also claimed that his huge infrastructure project was undertaken in service to the gods. Since the 3rd millennium BCE, the rulers of ancient Babylon 'fostered an image' of themselves as 'good shepherds'.[4]

By the time of Hammurabi, the most famous Babylonian king, this was 'already an ancient strategy', writes archaeological historian, Marlies Heinz. Hammurabi (1810–1750 BCE) and those before him spread fake news, that the god of the world (Enlil) had given Hammurabi the right of kingship. This divine right was accompanied by impressive violence for the doubtful, including the flooding of rebel villages. Hammurabi projected himself as a caretaker of the natural world, as well as temples and irrigation systems. Hammurabi also spread fake news via 'texts of self-praise', a technique adopted by the Egyptian pharaohs in the coming centuries.[5]

Local and regional tribes and villages were conditioned to admire their new king on account of his supposed devotion to the gods and genius for creating 'flourishing landscapes'. Meanwhile, the rulers got down to business, opening trade routes with Cyprus, the Indus Valley, Levant and Persian Gulf. The Kassites of the ancient Near East took over Babylonia when the old empire fell, between circa 1531 and 1155 BCE. They made the god Enlil, who was familiar to Babylonians, the main deity over the later-generation god, Marduk.[6] This appeased the majority of worshippers. As the new regional powers, the Hittites and especially the Egyptians, came to prominence, the Kassites continued the economic or-

---

[4]Stephanie Dalley (trans.), *Myths from Mesopotamia: Creation, the Flood, Gilgamesh, and Others* (2000, Oxford University Press). Marlies Heinz, 'The UR III, Old Babylonian, and Kassite Empires' in D.T. Potts (ed.), *A Companion to the Archaeology of the Ancient Near East, Vol. 1* (2012, Wiley-Blackwell), p. 721.
[5]Ibid.
[6]Ibid.

der of centralized control and vast trade.

Historian Phil Taylor writes that 'it is only really with the organization of violence' in the city-state system, 'that we can begin to talk properly of warfare and of war propaganda'. News fakery, including lies and exaggeration, is a core element of propaganda. Public opinion, even crudely managed, 'was an important factor in early political life', judging from the early Sumerian images on pots and tablets. These depicted professions, indicating that subjects had to know their social place. Exaggerated achievements in battle are to be found in the *stela* of Eannatum of Lagash (c. 2550 BCE), a slab depicting the god of Lagash (Nin-girsu) capturing his enemy in a net and chariot. The images are fake in that they depict success in battle, with no indication of losses on the winning side.[7]

Sargon I (c. 2276 BCE) conquered the Akkadians and absorbed the tribes into Sumerian city-states. Both he and grandson Naramsin (c. 2196 BCE) made the false claim that they were divinely ordained by placing the name of a star before their names. The visual propaganda of the strategically placed *stelae* reminded subjects and enemies alike of the kings' alleged powers. Taylor notes that the Assyrians also spread fake news via poetry about the victories over the Kassites, the later-rulers of Babylon. The poem of King Tukulti-Ninurta I (c. 1250 BCE) 'glorifies the king's military accomplishments and magnanimity towards the Kassites'. Taylor concludes that 'the events depicted in the poem were largely fictitious, that it was designed for public consumption and intended for oral recitation before large and illiterate [crowds]'.[8]

## ANCIENT EGYPT: SECRET ALLIES

Between 1182 and 1176 BCE, the administration of Ramesses III spread fake news by exaggerating its victories over Libyan invaders. The battles 'had been nowhere near as conclusive as the official propaganda suggested', writes Toby Wilkinson. The intellectuals of the day reported that Ramesses III successfully transformed captured Libyan prisoners of war into fully-fledged Egyptians: 'He makes their speech disappear and

---

[7]Philip M. Taylor, *Munitions of the Mind: A History of Propaganda* (4th ed., 2003, Manchester University Press), pp. 20-23.

[8]Ibid.

changes their tongues, so that they set out on a path they have not gone down before'. In reality, enculturation was 'superficial', writes Wilkinson, and 'sizeable concentrations' retained their Libyan identity.[9]

Sometimes, propaganda was honest but used ultimately to reinforce fear and awe in the minds of the governed.

The First Dynasty of the Pharaoh Narmer (3100 BCE) and predecessors gained power by force 'and would not hesitate to use violence to retain power', Wilkinson continues. 'The visual propaganda employed to promote the monarchy—king as a lion, a giant scorpion, a fierce catfish, a wild bull or mace-wielding superhero—was unashamedly brutal. It was both a promise and a warning'. As the empire spread, the Pharaohs maintained the fiction of Egyptian identity. As the military established outposts, laying the basis for international trade in southern Palestine, local pottery was transformed into 'Egyptian' pottery for importation. At En Besor (modern-day Gaza), the Egyptians established revictualling trade caravans. Foreigners were portrayed as the enemy. But 'in the real world ... xenophobic ideology masked the practical reality' of trade, or more accurately plunder. Artwork in tombs showed foreigners, like Palestinians, cowering in awe of the Egyptian king.[10]

The despotic Senusret III (1836–1818 BCE) used 'a new vehicle for projecting royal power: portrait sculpture'. The poets and scribes of the age competed for the most laudatory texts. The Cycle of Hymns, for instance, spread the fake news that all of Egypt loves the great king: 'the common people rejoice in your counsel', 'How your young conscripts rejoice: you have made them flourish', etc. Wilkinson points out that as the texts were aimed at the few literate Egyptians, the aim was to convince the policy elite of the king's greatness. Below, we shall see how the Greeks used the same principle.[11]

By the end of the Egyptian empire, Antony had allocated Roman territories to Egypt, allowing Cleopatra 'to pose as an imperialist pharaoh, a ruler who had restored some of the lustre to her forebears' once great empire'. To achieve this, she proclaimed her sixteenth year on the throne by changing the dates, issuing '[p]hony title deeds' and a collection of books

---

[9] Toby Wilkinson, *The Rise and Fall of Ancient Egypt: The History of a Civilisation from 3000 BC to Cleopatra* (2010, Bloomsbury Paperbacks), p. 50.
[10] Ibid.
[11] Ibid.

from the largely destroyed Alexandria Library.[12]

## ANCIENT GREECE: ELITES KNOW BEST

In the ideal state proposed by Socrates-Plato in *The Republic*, it is argued
that the philosopher-kings instil creation myths in the young, that Earth
is Mother and that metals developing within the bodies of the young
determine their fate and place in society. Catherine Rowett notes that
lie translates as *pseudos* or 'falsehood'. 'Socrates suggests using falsehood
and asks how we might get the citizens to believe a myth which, in some
sense at least, is acknowledged to be untrue'. Rowett comments that '[i]t
seems surprising, then, that lying should be required in a perfect society'.
But this assumes that it is a 'perfect' society.[13]

It may be perfect for elites, but not for ordinary Greeks. Perhaps the
most important element in Socrates-Plato is the idea that rulers themselves should be taught to believe the noble lie, that without indoctrination of the ruling class, the auxiliaries will undermine their interests. The
elites, then, also need a unifying doctrine, namely that of their own superiority. By connecting farmers to the land through Earth-Mother creation
myths, the Socratic rulers hoped to instil a belief in workers that they are
bonded to the land and in that way are willing servants. The metal origin
myth is also a mechanism for enforcing class. 'How exactly you become
prone to absorb silver rather than bronze is under-specified in the myth,
except that the work is attributed to 'the god'', says Rowett.[14]

Historian Jon Hesk writes about the 'valorisation of *metis* ('cunning
intelligence') in a wide range of [ancient Greek] texts spanning centuries
from Homer down to Oppian'. Hesk goes on to note the 'many positive
evaluations of deceit in certain contexts'. What makes this research all
the more interesting is its placement in the so-called cradle of democracy. This suggests that 'democracy' has always gone hand-in-hand with
the manipulation of public opinion. Thanks to the revelations of former
US National Security Agency contractor, Edward Snowden, the public at

---

[12]Ibid.

[13]Catherine Rowett, 'Why the philosopher kings will believe the noble lie', *Oxford Studies in Ancient Philosophy*, Vol. 50, 2016, DOI: 10.1093/acprof:oso/
9780198778 226.001.0001.

[14]Ibid.

large has learned of the massive, hi-tech surveillance culture in the USA. However, Hesk notes that Greece, too, was a 'surveillance culture'. He notes 'a strong and persistent ideological construction of deceit and trickery' in Athens. In the great city-state, 'deception was a crucial strategy'.[15]

In the Introduction, I quote Sunstein's opinion that deception is a crucial part of the functioning of a democratic state because the beneficent patriarchy knows best. Hesk writes of the 'democratic and civic culture of Athens in the fifth and fourth centuries' and notes that Greek rulers considered 'deceptive communication as inimical to its very existence'. Hesk reminds us that in the classical period, military service merged with the civic organization. The Spartans were not only seen as duplicitous, but their very duplicity was at odds with the Greek ethos of honour.[16]

The Greek intellectuals of the day (Pericles in this case) spread fake news about the Spartans and their military-training practices, which allegedly involved training boys as young as seven, starving them, issuing only one cloak, and subjecting them to the lash. The playwright Euripides described Sparta as 'wild and intricate', compared to the supposedly more relaxed Greece. In *Supplices*, Spartans are portrayed as 'changeable and slippery in terms of both character and rhetoric'. Aristophanes in *Lysistrata* alleges that Laconian men 'can no more be trusted than can a ravening wolf'.[17]

Lisa Crowley in an interestingly titled article, 'Ancient Advertising', notes that art in the form of sculpture in the ancient world gave viewers a 'tangible legitimation' of rulers' authority. These works of art were fake news in their attempts to associate the rulers with gods, 'and to broadcast the reach and breadth of their power over their people'. Alexander the Great, a student of Aristotle, spread fake news about himself via commissioned artwork. 'In order to achieve the god-like status he aspired to have, he associated himself in art with numerous gods'.[18]

---

[15] Jon Hesk, 'Deception and the rhetoric of Athenian identify' in Hesk (ed.), *Deception and Democracy in Classical Athens* (2000, Cambridge University Press), pp. 20-64.

[16] Ibid.

[17] Ibid.

[18] Lisa Crowley, 'Ancient Advertising: Political Propaganda in Ancient Art of the Mediterranean Basin', Art of the Mediterranean Basin 319, Section 1, 3 May 2008, http://www.endicottuniversity.net/~/media/Endicott/home/Undergraduate/Writing-at-Endicott/Student-Writing-Samples/PDFs/LisaCrowleyPaper.pdf.

# ANCIENT CHINA: THE ART OF DECEPTION

Sun Tzu (544–496 BCE) was born prior to China's unification, at a time of war between seven nations, which fought for control over Eastern China. Qin Shi Huang, the First Emperor of unified China (reigned from 220–10 BCE) credited Sun's *The Art of War* as one of the great military texts. *The Art of War* is full of useful tips on how to spread fake news and beliefs: 'All warfare is based on deception'; 'when able to attack, we must seem unable'; 'Hold out baits to entice the enemy. Feign disorder, and crush him'; 'Pretend to be weak, that he may grow arrogant'; '[do] certain things openly for purposes of deception'.[19]

Like Babylon's, China's rulers portrayed themselves as crucial and unique mediators between heaven and earth. The Emperors claimed that elements ruled their destinies, as did the Greek in the Socratic 'noble lie' strategy. The Han Dynasty (206 BCE–220 CE), for instance, associated itself with the colour red, hence the symbolic importance of the colour. As the Han Dynasty faltered, court intellectuals believed that the Mandate of Heaven was changing. For a brief time (until 23 CE), Wang Mang, a court official, founded the Xin (or renewed) Empire from the Liu family. *The Cambridge History of China* notes that the Wang Clan's supposed genealogy connecting them with the Shun and Yellow Emperor (Huang-ti) was 'fabricated'. Like the claims of Ur-Nammu of Babylon (that he was related to Gilgamesh), '[f]raudulent geneaologies were ... common in China'.[20]

Wang's task 'was to persuade the general public by skilful propaganda that the moment of change had come'. Wang spread fake news via 'the fabrication of auspicious omens'. This was easy because the rulers and their intellectuals were 'masters of applied psychology'. Throughout history, then, propaganda has gone hand-in-glove with psychology. In the Intro, I note the use of behavioural psychology on the part of British rulers today to influence social decisions. Later, we shall see how Trump's fake news pushed all the right buttons to reinforce his supporters' hatred

---

[19]Sun Tzu (trans. Lionel Giles), *The Art of War* (2002, Courier).

[20]Denis Twitchett and Michael Loewe, *The Cambridge History of China: Volume 1: The Ch'in and Han Empires, 221 B.C.-A.D. 220* (1986, Cambridge University Press), pp. 224, 230-31, 363.

of the corrupt Hillary Clinton.[21]

The masters of psychology in ancient China 'interpreted prophecies in the classical and apocryphal texts to their advantage, invented prognostications, manufactured auspicious omens, and circulated political songs against their enemies'. Wang even went as far as writing fake inscriptions in stones which he then 'discovered' and readied for interpretation. Heavenly messengers were said to have visited him in dreams. A bronze casket containing envelopes were also 'found' and the meaning interpreted. When those who overthrew Wang installed the Han Dynasty, they employed the same methods.[22]

Above I argued that propaganda among elites themselves is of prime importance. It is essential that the ruling class believes in its own motivations and superiority. The same was true in ancient China. The Hans 'came to believe their own propaganda'. As a result '[f]abricated prophecies changed into true messages from Heaven'. One spectacular accolade to the Hans celebrates their victory over Liu Pei and Tung Cho. It gloats that 'Heaven is … showing regret for the disasters it caused to imperial Han'. Toward the end of the great Chinese period, the intellectual propagandists of the day scrambled to write histories portraying 'continual Chinese unity, based on a single cultural heritage and purged of uncivilized or savage activities'.[23]

Literary inquisitions, where scholars and artists were imprisoned or worse, were common throughout Chinese dynastic history. Not only was fake news spread through poetry and pictures, information was censored. China was ruled by the Qin Dynasty (beginning 221 BCE), during which time Confucian texts were burned *en masse*. The scholars who had memorized the texts attempted to restore them during the Han Dynasty (206 BCE–220 CE).[24]

Towards the end of the Chinese imperial age, writes Michael McCarty, Confucian scholars selectively edited the official valedictories of Emperor Kangxi (1661–1722 CE). They 'removed references to Kangxi's human weaknesses and added depictions of his Confucian piety and dignified ritual role'. The alterations took place, 'despite his instructions to leave

---

[21] Ibid.
[22] Ibid.
[23] Ibid.
[24] Ibid.

his final words untouched'. McCarty notes that this kind of censorship shows 'how institutional the propaganda system had become, ... [with] never-ending rivalry between scholar and emperor'.[25]

## ANCIENT ROME: BARBARIANS & GENTLEMEN

Historian Jane DeRose Evans defines the purpose of ancient propaganda as 'making the audience take a particular course of action or conform to a certain attitude desired by the organized group'. Julius Caesar (100–44 BCE) spun stories about his military successes and combined them with domestic terror tactics. Coins were used to spread the message of Caesar's greatness. Without spelling it out, the propaganda suggested that Caesar was a descendant of Venus. His strategists thought up *veni, vidi, vici*: 'I came, I saw, I conquered'.[26]

Between 50 BCE and 50 CE, imperial Rome employed an increasingly sophisticated propaganda system to justify rule over its subjects. The wide geography of empire necessitated a 'highly visible, centralized government', write Jowett and O'Donnell. The Roman rulers spread fake news about their power and brilliance by spending on architecture, art, coinage and literature. Their propaganda were akin to 'modern-day advertising plans, which projected the image of an all-powerful, omnipresent entity'. The Romans mass-produced their propaganda in a more vulgar fashion than the Greeks'.[27]

Geographical representation was and remains an important tool in perception management. Where is east and west on a near-spherical world? Where north and south lie from point $x$ or $y$ is of propagandistic significance to cartographers. This was not lost on the imperial Romans.

Fabienne Michelet notes that ancient Britain was considered by the Romans to be a northern border delineating savages and civilization. In *The Gallic Wars* (58–49 BCE), Julius Caesar suggested that as one travels further north, the less civilized 'the world becomes'. For Caesar, '[t]he

---

[25] Michael McCarty, 'The historical roots of Chinese communist propaganda', *The Pulse*, 3(1), pp. 1-17.

[26] Jane DeRose Evans, *The Art of Persuasion: Political Propaganda from Aeneas to Brutus* (1992, University of Michigan).

[27] Garth S. Jowett and Victoria O'Donnell, *Propaganda and Persuasion* (4th ed., 2006, Sage), pp. 54-56.

most civilized people among the Britons are found in the south'. Part of Caesar's measure of distinction is the similarity between Kentish Britons and Gauls. 'Distance is here the mark of what is wild and outlandish'. Michelet writes that '[t]he evaluation of distance does not rely solely on scientific measurement: its appreciation varies depending on the context and on the author's particular agenda'.[28]

Strabo (63 BCE–24 CE) was a Greek philosopher who lived under the rule of imperial Rome. He started writing *Geographica* around 20 BCE. In it, he describes Britain as wooded and hilly, with rich potential in gold, silver, iron, slaves, cattle and hunting dogs, all of which were exported. The Britons were taller than Romans and Celts, but their 'habits ... in part more simple and barbaric'. Caesar Augustus transformed 'the whole island virtually [into] Roman property'. Strabo had little respect for Britons, but even less for the inhabitants of Ierne island. Solinus (200 CE) 'suggests that Britain is separated from the rest of Europe, not only geographically, but also by its very nature: it is a radically different place'.[29]

# ISLAM

Islamic PR dates back to the origins of the religion itself, says Sharif Ikbal of the People's University of Bangladesh. Sharif notes that Muhammad 'used extensively communication and public relations' to introduce Islam to the heathens of the Kureish and Arabic regions. In the Kureish region, Muhammad and his follows engaged in '[a] huge work of persuasion'. By promoting community values, the objective of Islamic propaganda was 'to help establish the perfect Umma of believers'. Citing verse, Muhammad spread fake news by telling kings and community leaders alike that Allah 'guides' whoever accepts his rule and that he protects them from 'mischief'. There is no suggestion that Ikbal considers Muhammad's work fake news.[30]

Part of Muhammad's PR strategy was to use the art of persuasion over offensive dogmatism. In Islam, propaganda and proselytizing are

---

[28]Fabienne L. Michelet, *Creation, Migration, and Conquest: Imaginary Geography and Sense of Space in Old English Literature* (2006, Oxford University Press), pp. 119-24.

[29]Ibid.

[30]Sharif Ikbal, 'The Islamic roots of modern public relations and corporate social responsibility', *World Vision*, 9(1), November 2015, pp. 160-68.

interconnected. The 10th century Ismaili Fatimid rulers of North Africa employed a *da'i*, or propagandist, to convert other Muslims to the school of Ismail.[31]

The Umayyad family supposedly descended from the biblical Ismail and ultimately Abraham. Tradition divides Arabs into northerners (from Arabia) and southerners (descendants of Noah through Qahtan). Muhammad's tasks was to purify the city of Ka'ba, which had been corrupted by polytheistic Arabs. Like the Umayyads, Muhammad was supposedly descended from Quraysh. By 624 CE, the Umayyads were the leading family in Mecca. Their leader, Abu Sufyan, declined to battle the pagans of Mecca. His image was then used as a symbol against Muhammad.[32]

In the story, Muhammad takes Mecca without spilling blood. The enslaved Umayyads are freed by the benevolent Muhammad and choose Islam of their own accord. Muhammad used persuasion over violence— in the mythology—and bestowed gifts on his former enemies. For the Syrians, things were not so pleasant. Muhammad supposedly dispatched troops, led by Abu Sufyan's sons, to depose of the Byzantine rulers of Syria. Historian G. R. Hawting regards much of this anti-Umayyad propaganda as fake history concocted by Muhammadians. Simultaneously, the propaganda favours the Umayyads, after their conversion. It was alleged that Abu Sufyan 'aroused the spirit of Muslims at a crucial time in the conquest of Syria'.[33]

Abd al-Hamid ibn Yahya al-Katib (c. 749) was the secretary of Marwan II, the last Umayyad Caliph. Prose served as toolkits for Caliphs, addressing issues of posture, oratory and military conduct. Abd al-Hamid's prose advocated fake news with the aim of winning wars: 'propaganda, subversion and the incitement of enemy troops to assassinate their leader are the best tactics', write historians, A.F.L. Beeston et al. Like returning to the Socratic ideal, that leaders should believe their own propaganda, the general should 'exhort the troops with descriptions of Paradise'. It was important that the general believed in the paradise they preached.[34]

---

[31] Farhad Daftary, 'The Ismaili da$^c$wa Outside the Fatimid dawla', The Institute of Ismaili Studies, http://iis.ac.uk/academic-article/ismaili-da-wa-outside-fatimid-dawla.

[32] G. R. Hawting, *The First Dynasty of Islam: The Umayyad Caliphate AD 661–750* (1986, Routledge), pp. 20-22.

[33] Ibid.

[34] A.F.L. Beeston, T.M. Johnsone, R.B. Serjeant and G.R. Smith, *Arabic Literature to*

# HOLY ROMAN EMPIRE

This final subchapter takes us into the era of European empires, most of which had a Catholic basis until the Reformation. In fact, the word propaganda (which is so central to understanding the principles of fake news) derives from the modern Latin, meaning to propagate. As late as 1622, the church created *Congregatio de Propaganda Fide*, or Congregation for Propagating the Faith; typically in non-Catholic countries.

Historian Janet L. Nelson notes the impossibility of historical personage. Based solely on written accounts of contemporaries, is it feasible to 'know' Charlemagne the man? From this we learn that the image of Charlemagne has been constructed from biased material. It might not be fake news in the sense of black propaganda (inventing lies to favour one narrative over the other) but amounts to grey propaganda in that uncomfortable facts are suppressed and favourable ones exaggerated to the limits of credibility.[35]

Nelson notes the 'absence of substantial writings produced by Charlemagne himself'. Over the king's sixty-five years, the written record ranges from solid to 'even'. Nelson criticizes the standard biographies of Charlemagne as ignorant to these facts and thus as revealing more about the idiosyncrasies of the biographers than of Charlemagne. This can help our contemporary approach to fake news in that first-hand evidence must be identified if possible, contrasted with counter-narratives and finally divorced as far as one can from personal biases. Nelson adds the element of nationalism to the propaganda question. For contemporary British historians biased in favour of presenting ancient rulers as leaders of neatly defined nation-states, Charlemagne is distinctively 'French'. But in the real world, arguments could be made in favour of his Germanic origins (Karl der Grosse). It suits the modern historian to confine the loose, tribal 'nations' of peoples to imagined, modern geographical areas; despite the fact that modern France and Germany did not exist as nation-states. Fake news analysis must also be sensitive to cultural nuances.[36]

At the time, it was novel that a ruler lived to the age of sixty-five. Charlemagne's propaganda team had to therefore justify his being fit to

---

the *End of the Umayyad Period* (1983, Cambridge University), p. 172.

[35] Janet L. Nelson, 'Charlemagne the man' in Joanna Story (ed.), *Charlemagne: Empire and Society* (2005, Manchester University Press).

[36] Ibid.

rule. This led in part to 'major changes in the way public affairs were conducted'. In an effort to appease all sides, Charlemagne 'gave his contemporaries a sense of partnership ... and reconstructed Frankishness in terms of it'.[37]

PR specialist Simon Moore writes that Middle Age instability enhanced the value of bards, skalds and other poets and forms of poetic expression. Rome's historic legacy was deeply entrenched in the Frankish kingdom. Poets including Venantius Fortunatus reportedly manipulated patrons' self-images in line with more established models. Such poets avoided swearing political allegiance to any one particular faction.[38]

In 1095, Pope Urban II launched the Crusades at the Council of Clermont. He did so by reading what specialists now regard as the first example of atrocity propaganda: a letter condemning alleged attacks on Christians by Persians. The gory details make the letter one of the earliest examples of a call for humanitarian intervention: to invade Jerusalem and defend innocents against barbarity. Such calls are made by blood-thirsty politicians in modern times, who cite sometimes real, sometimes false and sometimes exaggerated atrocities as pretexts to invade other countries, including Serbia and Libya.[39]

Urban II said: 'The sad news has come from Jerusalem and Constantinople that the people of Persia, an accursed and foreign race, enemies of God ... have invaded the lands of those Christians and devastated them with the sword, rapine, and fire'. Rapine refers to the theft of land. Urban II continues: 'Some of the Christians they have carried away as slaves, others they have put to death. The churches they have either destroyed or turned into mosques. They desecrate and overthrow the altars. They circumcise the Christians and pour the blood from the circumcision on the altars or in the baptismal fonts'. The kind of dehumanization of Middle Eastern peoples continues today, with endless media stories about the atrocities of Islamic State and not a word about what happens to a child when a US-made missile hits them.[40]

---

[37] Ibid.

[38] Simon Moore, 'Building certainty in uncertain times' in Burton St. John, Margot Opdycke Lamme and Jacquie L'Etang (eds.), *Pathways to Public Relations: Histories of Practice and Profession* (2014, Routledge).

[39] Oliver Thomson, *Mass Persuasion in History* (1977, Paul Harris Publishing), p. 71.

[40] Urban II, Speech at the Council of Clermont, 1095, http://media.bloomsbury.com/

Urban II continued: 'Some they kill in a horrible way by cutting open the abdomen, taking out a part of the entrails and tying them to a stake; they then beat them and compel them to walk until all their entrails are drawn out and they fall to the ground. Some they use as targets for their arrows'. He went on: 'They compel some to stretch out their necks and then they try to see whether they can cut off their heads with one stroke of the sword. It is better to say nothing of their horrible treatment of the women'. Next comes the call for humanitarian intervention. Jerusalem, he said, 'asks aid especially from you because, as I have said, God has given more of the military spirit to you than to other nations. Set out on this journey and you will obtain the remission of your sins and be sure of the incorruptible glory of the kingdom of heaven'.[41]

The story of Jesus of Nazareth is an example of how news can become fake. Over the centuries, the crucifixion of an anti-imperialist Rabbi by the Roman occupiers of Jerusalem somehow became a tale of virgin birth, healing lepers and walking on water. A thousand years later, the Spear of Longinus (or Holy Lance), which was supposedly used to check if Christ was really dead, ended up in the folklore of the Crusaders during the Holy Roman Empire:

The Crusaders captured Antioch in 1098. The exhausted troops were immediately threatened by the governor of Mosul, Kherboga. Miraculously, crusader Peter Bartholomew received a vision of where to locate the Holy Lance. In Bartholomew's fake news, the Apostle Andrew visited him to bless the crusade. Like the fictions of ancient China, this was an omen. But unlike the Chinese alchemical magic, Bartholomew was not asserting his right to rule, but rather using a story as a psychological weapon designed to rouse the embattled troops. Soon after Bartholomew's revelation, he was trotting off to the church of St. Peter to dig up the Holy Lance.[42]

Soldier Anselm of Ribemont wrote to the Archbishop of Rheims: 'when this precious gem was found it revived all of our spirits'. Historian David S. Bachrach notes that 'it would be difficult to overstate the importance of the discovery of the Holy Lance for rebuilding the morale of the Chris-

---

rep/files/Primary%20Source%205.3%20-%20Urban%20II.pdf.
[41] Ibid.
[42] David S. Bachrach, *Religion and the Conduct of War c. 300-c.1215* (2003, The Boydell Press), pp. 110-17.

tian soldiers battered by fatigue, hunger, and despair'. For our modern
purposes, this event confirms the importance of fake news when it comes
to rousing support for otherwise unpopular or losing wars and battles. Of
equal importance is the use of image and iconography. In contemporary
Western media propaganda, a bearded Arab or Pakistani signals terrorist.
A photo or film of a uniformed police officer signals authority and protection. No matter how inaccurate and falsely stereotypical such images
are, they affect perception. Before the fight against Kherboga, the Holy
Lance was held up to the Catholics by Bartholomew as they confessed
their 'sins'. Just like today, where fake news spreads across the wires (like
Reuters and the Associated Press) and gets reported by the 'respected'
broadsheets and gutter tabloids alike, the heartfelt testimonies of crusad-
ing soldiers were based on fake news and made their way to mainland
Europe in the form of letters to the authorities.[43]

## CONCLUSION

Organized religion was and continues to be an excellent source of fake
news, making people believe, often (though not always) in fantastical
things, and thus in the brilliance of their own culture, leaders and political
systems. History is a rich template of deception-based social control.

---

[43]Ibid.

# Chapter 2

# Empire: 'Harshness is the greatest humanity'

*This chapter concerns the crimes and lies of empire. It documents the privately-owned media's portrayal of imperial foreign policy, particularly during times of genocidal levels of death. The two main examples are Ireland and India. The media portrayed the famines as either exaggerations, the fault of the victims or the responsibility of mother nature. The chapter demonstrates how media can act as an accomplice to crimes against humanity.*

Historians continue to make absurd, widely-debunked claims about the greatness of the British empire: how it brought civilization to backward peoples, introduced constitutional laws (omitting the fact that Britain itself has no written constitution) and praising the imposition of representative, parliamentary 'democracy' over direct rule, as many peoples had enjoyed prior to conquest.

Tory MEP Daniel Hannan writes that the British are superior to the Spanish because Britain's values 'exist on a higher plane'. 'Settled at around the same time, the two great landmasses of the New World serve almost as a controlled experiment', says Hannan, referring to South America conquered (mainly) by the Spanish and North America conquered (mainly) by the British. 'The north was settled by English-speakers, who took with them a belief in property rights, personal liberty and representative government', Hannan continues. 'The south was settled by Iberians who replicated the vast estates and quasi-feudal society of their home provinces'. Hannan concludes that, '[d]espite being the poorer continent in terms of natural resources, North America became the most desirable living space on the planet, attracting hundreds of millions of people with the promise of freedom'. Hannan's is one of the more impressive cases of genocide denial. The other omission is theft. When referring to the exportation of property rights, Hannan presumably means the rights granted the British by themselves to steal Native American land.[1]

Let us turn now to ye olde media and its complicity in imperial genocide.

## NATIVE AMERICANS

Prior to conquest, 70 million Americans lived in the North and South. Contrary to still-pervading false histories, the peoples of the continents had developed complex societies, laws, customs and trade routes.

In the 18th century, the Whig newspaper, the *Observator*, spread fake news about Mohawk Indians terrorizing Londoners on their visit as part of a Jacobite Tory plot. Meanwhile, in America:[2]

During the War of Independence, the Founding Fathers, notably Benjamin Franklin, regularly wrote fake news, including under the pseudonym, Mrs Silence Dogood. When Britain realized it was losing the War and became more open to negotiations, Franklin sought to 'make them a little asham'd of themselves' by spreading propaganda, as he confessed to John Adams. Franklin even went as far as creating a fake newspaper supplement, the *Boston Independent Chronicle*. To make the hoax seem real, Franklin included fake adverts for land sales and missing horses. Franklin erred only in including French instead of English typeface.[3]

Franklin signed the letter John Paul Jones. He wrote the letter from the point of view of Britons receiving money from an expedition. But the bounty contained 'SCALPS of our unhappy Country-folks, taken in the three last Years by the Senneka Indians from the Inhabitants of the Frontiers of New-York, New-Jersey, Pennsylvania, and Virginia, and sent by them as a Present to Col. Haldimand, Governor of Canada, in order to be by him transmitted to England' (Franklin's emphasis). To add realism to his lies, Franklin included two letters (forged), supposedly written by shipmates. One of which told of '43 Scalps of Congress Soldiers killed

---

[1] Daniel Hannan, *How We Invented Freedom and Why It Matters* (2013, Head of Zeus).

[2] Evelyn Lord, *The Hell-fire Clubs: Sex, Satanism and Secret Societies* (2008, Yale University Press).

[3] Founders Online, 'Supplement to the Boston Independent Chronicle [Before 22 April 1782]', National Archives (US), https://founders.archives.gov/documents/Franklin/01-37-02-0132.

in different Skirmishes'. Other packages supposedly contained dozens of heads, numbering into the hundreds. Some victims were 'Farmers killed in their Houses'. Some women 'had their Brain[s] beat out'.[4]

Franklin's aim was to demonize both the British and their Native American allies. One of the fake letters in the supplement reads: 'We wish you to send these Scalps over the Water to the great King, that he may regard them and be refreshed; and that he may see our faithfulness in destroying his Enemies, and be convinced that his Presents have not been made to ungrateful People'. Franklin's is an early example of what became known as atrocity propaganda.[5]

## POTATOES. REALLY?

The Protestant Reformation in England gave new impetus to controlling Catholic Ireland. John Derrick's history of supposedly brave military conquests, *Image of Irelande* (1581), contained a number of fake illustrations depicting the Irish defecating in the street, cooking children over a fire and dancing drunkenly. Cromwell led an invasion in 1649 to crush the pro-Catholic King, Charles I. This was one of the many factors that led to the war of 1689–91 between James II and his Protestant successor, William of Orange. In Ireland, fake testimonies were deliberately leaked to English Protestant media in the 17th century to rouse support for a Cromwell-led humanitarian intervention, the real aim of which was to crush Catholics.[6]

A few years ago, Trinity College Dublin led a project to digitize the 1641 Depositions. These were the eyewitness statements, many of them based on hearsay, gathered from 1,559 Irish men and women, most of whom were Protestants. Dr Mark Sweetnam, who led the project, comments:

> One of the iconic narratives that comes up in hearsay evidence is reports of atrocities against pregnant women who were said to have been ripped open, had their babies pulled out and beaten against rocks ... That image is drawing on biblical prophecy ... and contemporary accounts of European massacres ... It's very striking that it

---

[4] Ibid.

[5] Ibid.

[6] University of Edinburgh, 'The Image of Irelande, by John Derrick (London, 1581) – Plates', http://www.docs.is.ed.ac.uk/docs/lib-archive/bgallery/Gallery/researchcoll /ireland.html.

crops up regularly in hearsay accounts but I never came across an
example of it in eyewitness evidence ... While these depositions were
being taken, they were being leaked and published in London with
the clear intention that they would elicit the sympathy of English
Protestants.[7]

Dr Barbara Fennell, who also examined the texts, says: 'The more lurid
and appalling the 'atrocity' was, the less reliable the evidence'. There
are contemporary parallels, with Western-spun stories about Muammar
Gaddafi's Viagra-fuelled plans for mass rape in Libya (2011) and Bashar
al-Assad's supposed use of chemical weapons (2013). Returning to 17th
century Ireland and allegations of the rape of Protestants by Catholics,
Dr Nicci MacLeod comments:

> [t]he atrocious acts committed against women and children are a cen-
> tral image of the rebellion as it was reported in London and propa-
> ganda texts of the period ... We have been able to show that there are
> significant differences between the use of words and phrases mean-
> ing 'heard' as opposed to 'saw' when it comes to the worst atrocities
> reported within the depositions, such as an act of cannibalism and
> many of the more infamous events.[8]

Two centuries later, more than a million Irish civilians perished in the
famine.

The causes of the Irish famine are understood, yet today most Britons
still think that potato blight was the sole cause. Nobel Prize–winning
economist Amartya Sen writes that 'the famines of the 1840s that devastated Ireland ... kill[ed] a higher *proportion* of the population than any
other famine anywhere in recorded history' (emphasis in original). He
goes on to note that '[t]he small Irish growers of potatoes were severely
hit by the blight, and through the increase in the price of food, others
were too'. Sen also notes that, 'far from there being a systematic import
of food into Ireland to break the famine, there was ... the opposite movement: the export of food from Ireland to England (especially of food of a
somewhat higher quality)'. The same thing happened in British colonial

[7]Owen Bowcott, 'How lies about Irish 'barbarism' in 1641 paved the way for
    Cromwell's atrocities', *Guardian*, 18 February 2011, https://www.theguardian.com/
    world/2011/feb/18/1641-irish-rebellion-anti-catholic-propaganda.
[8]Ibid.

India. Because of neoliberal globalization, the same thing is happening today in food-producing regions, including India: people starve as their food is exported for international markets.[9]

Continuing with food exports, Sen writes: 'This did happen on quite a large scale in Ireland in the 1840s, when ship after ship—laden with wheat, oats, cattle, pigs, eggs, and butter—sailed down the Shannon bound for well-fed England'. Sen goes on to note that '[m]arket forces would always encourage movement of food to places where people could afford to pay a higher price for it ... [I]t is hard to think that famines like those in Ireland in the 1840s would have been allowed to occur in Britain'. On fake news, Sen concludes: 'the Irish taste for potatoes was added to the list of the calamities that the natives had, in the English view, brought on themselves'.[10]

How was the famine reported in the British press? A study by Christophe Gillissen of one of Britain's leading newspaper, *The Times*, holds journalists and editors partly responsible for the famine. They emphasized that Ireland was richer than England. They also claimed that workers' taxes had to finance poor relief in Ireland because the Irish were too stupid to manage their own affairs. Just as the Romans reported the ancient Britons and Celts as being hapless and in need of civilizing, *The Times* stated: 'there are ingredients in the Irish character which must be modified and corrected before either individuals or Governments can hope to raise the general condition of the people'. And that is the least offensive. Another *Times* article said of the Irish and Ireland:

> Never let anyone pretend to be satisfied that he knows the worst of that country. Depend on it, there is worse still in store. It has been called an incubus, a burden, a millstone, a chaos, a ditch, a slough of despond, a Maelstrom. Alas! these are feeble expressions. They are much too finite. Under the heaviest burden you can only fall to the ground. A ditch, a bog, a Charybdis itself has a bottom. Not so Ireland. Of all human things it presents the nearest approach to an infinite idea. Each year opens to the awe-struck soul a perpetual increasing vista of misery, trouble, animosity, expense, mismanagement, and ingratitude.[11]

---

[9] Amartya Sen, *Development as Freedom* (1999, Oxford University Press), pp. 170-77.
[10] Ibid.
[11] Christophe Gillissen, 'The Times and the Great Irish Famine 1846–47', *Cahiers du*

In the fake news of the day, England could not afford to spend money saving lives. The press also inferred that the problem was not the famine, the severity of which was minimized in the opinion columns. The problem, said the editors, was the nature of the Irish and their 'astounding apathy' (*Times*). Ultimately they were responsible for their own misery. As for charity, or better yet withdrawing and letting the Irish manage themselves, *The Times* wrote that sometimes 'harshness is the greatest humanity'.[12]

More fake news held that Britain was a righteous nation defending against unjustified foreign and domestic political opposition and sometimes violence. *The Times* also championed an England-style Poor Law for the Irish, where landlords would be obliged to pay for the poor to prevent mass deaths and rioting. This was merely a way of maintaining the status quo power dynamics instead of getting to the root of the problem, which was British imperialism.[13]

Gillissen draws the devastating conclusion that, '[b]y constantly questioning the reality of the famine, *The Times* undermined feelings of empathy and charity among its English readers'. We can draw parallels today between the way the media portray refugees as scroungers, rapists and extremists and the waning levels of support in America and Europe. In October 1847, the British government proposed another round of aid for Ireland. The newspaper opposed the measure: 'We do not ... fear the imputation of inhumanity when we say that public opinion is decidedly averse to this repeated 'begging' for Ireland'.[14]

## INDIA: 'A LOT OF BLACK FELLOWS'

In colonial India, Britain's Vernacular Papers Act 1878 sought to prevent local Indian newspapers from reporting on the famines ravaging the country. The aim was to prevent villages, towns and provinces from uniting in opposition to the colonial government.[15]

In the 2,000 years prior to British rule, the region that we now call India experienced seventeen famines, according to the *Journal of the Statistical*

---

*MIMMOC*, Vol. 12, 2015, https://mimmoc.revues.org/1828.

[12]Ibid.

[13]Ibid.

[14]Ibid.

[15]Mike Davis, *Late Victorian Holocausts* (2002, Verso).

*Society.* During 120 years of British rule, thirty-one major famines were recorded. Before the British, Indians enjoyed sophisticated methods of food and water storage in times of drought. Due to a number of factors, the British Empire changed India's internal political and subsistence infrastructure to suit its own interests. This resulted in the deaths of at least 29.3 million Indians from famine, dehydration and murder in the last half of the 19th century alone.

Factors included divide and rule, forcing the gold standard onto a silver-backed currency, turning subsistence farmers into labourers for other industries, privatizing and selling land, restructuring wages, taxation, irrigation (which drove up water prices), exporting grain during famine and London-based financial speculation which benefitted from high prices. Not all the news in Britain was fake. Henry Fawcett MP wrote in *The Times*: Indians were hitherto capable of 'storing rain and diverting the torrent to the first necessities of man', not the international market. The *Manchester Guardian* reported: 'In the name of liberty we have made the individual a bond slave'. On the eve of Victoria's death, journalist William Digby wrote: 'the British Empire in the nineteenth century ... [caused] the unnecessary deaths of millions'. But these were exceptions.[16]

Historian Mike Davis writes that 'starvation deaths were being deliberately misreported as cholera or dysentery mortality in order to disguise the true magnitude of the famine'. The media suppressed famine reports, instead lamenting the problems of Boer suppression in South Africa. Lt. Col. Ronald Osborne wrote: 'The journals of the North-West were persuaded into silence. Strict orders were given to civilians under no circumstances to countenance the pretence of the natives that they were dying of hunger'.[17]

The colonial administrator Trevelyan chastised 'the selfish, perverse and turbulent character of the people'. The biologist Alfred Russel Wallace called the famines failures, not crimes: 'the most terrible failures of the century'. The *Economist* weighed in on the moral aspects of Indians dying under colonial rule: '[it is not] the duty of the Government to keep them alive'. Civil servants lamented the 'mistake [of] spend[ing] so much money to save a lot of black fellows'. The worst condemnation that Reuters'

---

[16]Ibid.
[17]Ibid.

famine report could muster was that 'the famine in the Central Provinces was grossly mismanaged'.[18]

In the real world, the Empire's own famine report states: 'supplies of food were at all times sufficient [between 1899–1902], and it cannot be too frequently repeated that severe privation was chiefly due to the dearth of employment in agriculture'. The fake news, which downplayed the famine and misattributed it to disease, undermined the efforts of resistance in England, which came from John Bright (Quaker and Liberal), Sir Arthur Cotton (Gen. and engineer), Henry Hyndman (an Oxbridge politician and founder of the Social Democratic Federation), Sir William Wedderburn (civil servant and reformer) and Florence Nightingale, who wrote letters to the press.[19]

Others privately acknowledged some of the factors contributing to famine. The Dufferin Enquiry (1887) found that 'forty million of the poor go through life on insufficient food'. The Duke of Buckingham commented: 'It was apparent to the Government that facilities for moving grain by the rail were rapidly raising prices everywhere'. In 1879, insurer Cornelius Walford wrote: 'with her famines on hand, India is able to supply food to other parts of the world'. During the famines, the railways transported grain from drought-stricken areas to storage depots. By 1880, the Empire's death estimate for the Deccan and Mysore regions was 5.5 million. Viceroy Lord Elgin acknowledged that 4.5 million had starved to death in the late-1870s to early-90s. In 1901, the *Lancet*'s epidemiological study estimated that nineteen million Indians had died in the previous decade.[20]

## CONCLUSION

Imperial propaganda is most effective among elites in making them believe their own lies concerning their own benevolence and the in the necessity of the work they are undertaking, which is at the expense of others. Indigenous working classes suffer(ed) in poverty and were less inclined to believe in the beneficence of their superiors.

---

[18]Ibid.
[19]Ibid.
[20]Ibid.

# Chapter 3

# Indoctrination: 'Making minds'

*How can we detect fake news emanating from the top if we are conditioned in childhood to respect authority? How can we think critically about news when schooling imposes a system of inductive learning? If childhood conditioning is not effective, will rebels believe fake news emerging from the bottom simply because it opposes authority? Indoctrination has had a profound effect on our capacity to detect fake news. This chapter exposes the application of conditioning experiments on animals in the 20th century and how the state translated them to the conditioning of children in schools.*

'Reading, writing and reality: Today's students are growing up in a world where facts aren't what they once were', says Beau Yarbrough, a journalist writing for the *LA Daily News*. Forty-two states and DC have adopted Common Core Standards on fake news detection in schools. Meanwhile in Europe, the Organization for Economic Co-operation and Development (OECD)'s education director, Andreas Schleicher, says that children should be taught how to spot fake news. Until recently, young people could 'trust' the information in encyclopaedias, but now they turn to unreliable social media, says Schleicher. The new OECD standards on fake news detection will be incorporated into the international Pisa rankings. For Schleicher, fake news and cultural echo-chambers are interconnected.[1]

In order to detect fake news in the mainstream and alternative media, our critical faculties need to function. The first job of religion, the state and the corporation is to impair the individual's capacity for critical

---

[1]Beau Yarbrough, 'Fake news! How students are learning media literacy in the post-facts era', *LA Daily News*, 9 April 2017, http://www.dailynews.com/social-affairs/20170409/fake-news-how-students-are-learning-media-literacy-in-the-post-facts-era. Sean Coughlan, 'Schools should teach pupils how to spot 'fake news'', BBC News Online, 18 March 2017, http://www.bbc.co.uk/news/education-39272841.

thinking. As far as the state is concerned, the most effective method is through the bounding of choice: to give the individual several options, rather than letting them discover other options independently. Sunstein calls this 'choice architecture', school psychologists call it 'bounded choice'. School—not education or mentoring, but *school*—is designed to inflict psychological destruction on the child's ability to think independently, as this chapter will document. The aim is to prepare them for a life of obedience. In the West, violence was used by teachers until fairly recently. Today, however, the violence is much more difficult to detect and comes in the form of 'choice architecture'.

Once the critical faculties of the child and adolescent have been impaired, the adult is more easy to control. The adult might question the minutia of media data but will usually accept the underlying premise and tacit assumptions. If the underlying premise is false and the tacit assumption conflicts with reality, the adult might 'sense' that something is wrong with the world, but due to schooling and a lack of discussion among peers, is unable to articulate or rationalize that sense of unease.

Before looking into school as mind control, let's consider cases of teachers putting fake news–spotting on the curriculum.

## CHALLENGING THE CHALLENGERS

Teacher Scott Bedley writes: 'I've adapted my curriculum and teaching style to make sure my students know which sources to trust—and which to reject'. Bedley has seven techniques for teaching children to detect fake news:[2]

1) *Check for copyright.* The inference is that if the editor is selling the story it is more likely to be true. But this implies that money-motivated journalism and/or scholarship is reliable. Tacitly, this reinforces the widespread assumption that things working in favour of the market are good.

2) *Verify from multiple sources.* This is supposed to ensure the veracity of claims on the assumption that the more it is repeated, the more accu-

---

[2]Scott Bedley, 'I taught my 5th-graders how to spot fake news. Now they won't stop fact-checking me', Vox, 29 March 2017, http://www.vox.com/first-person /2017/3/29/15042 692/fake-news-education-election.

rate it is. This amounts to group-think. How many credible newspapers published articles as fact that Saddam possessed weapons of mass destruction, that the US is committed to the peace process in Israel-Palestine, that Russia is threatening America's national security? And on and on.

3) *Credible sources, such as History.com.* Interesting example. History.com is the website of the for-profit History Channel. Let's examine its page on Israel to see how reliable it is as a source:

It states correctly that the idea of a Jewish State (Zionism) was formalized by the Austrian Jew, Theodor Herzl, in 1896. That is true, but it leaves out a crucial statement written by Herzl: 'The Governments of all countries scourged by Anti-Semitism will serve their own interests in assisting us to obtain the sovereignty we want'. Zionists were more concerned with their own secular political movement (which later became a religious one) than with protecting Jews from anti-Semitism. Already, the History.com article paints Zionism (and thus Israel) as a champion of Jewish rights. The article mentions Britain's Balfour Declaration (1917), which promised a Jewish homeland in Arab-majority Palestine. It also mentions opposition to the move by 'Arab states'. It doesn't actually point out that Arabs lived in Palestine. The article omits the fact that the Nazis conducted secret deals with certain hard-line Zionists (the Haavara agreement 1933) with the aim of emptying Europe of Jews and filling Palestine. It omits the fact that Britain and America consciously aided the persecution of Jews by denying refugees asylum in Britain and the USA. It omits the British state's terror attacks (Operation Embarrass) on Jewish refugee boats in 1947. Most shockingly, it refers to the ethnic cleansing of 700,000 Arabs from Palestine by the Israeli Army (most of whom settled in nearby states, Lebanon and Jordan) as a 'departure' of Arabs.[3]

---

[3]History, 'On this day: 14 May 1948: State of Israel proclaimed', http://www.history .com/this-day-in-history/state-of-israel-proclaimed. Theodor Herzl, 'A Jewish State: An Attempt at a Modern Solution of the Jewish Question' (trans. Jacob de Haas), 1917 (1896), NY: Federation of American Zionists. On Haavara, see Edwin Black, 2001, *The Transfer Agreement: The Dramatic Story of the Pact Between the Third Reich and Jewish Palestine*, Carroll and Graf. On refugees, see Louise London, *Whitehall and the Jews, 1933–1948* (2003, Cambridge University Press). On the 'departure', see Ilan Pappé, *The Ethnic Cleansing of Palestine* (2008, Oneworld Books).

Returning to Bedley's seven methods:

4) *Date published.* This is recommended in order to update information. The danger of this approach is that 'facts' can change to suit political agendas. Take the Libyan Arab Spring. According to the BBC's live online timeline, the events went from peaceful protests to Libya's dictator Gaddafi murdering innocent people, to armed 'rebels' triumphantly standing up for democracy, to Gaddafi and his men threatening 'ethnic cleansing' against them and triggering a humanitarian intervention by NATO. The timeline was manipulated to suit a pre-existing political agenda, namely toppling Gaddafi, smashing up the country and opening it to foreign markets. Furthermore, the BBC Trust found bias in its own reporting.[4]

5) *The author of the given article should be an 'expert'.* Bedley says: '[A] university professor typically has increased credibility versus a hobbyist'. So, according to Bedley, the content is not relevant, more important is the prestige of the author. This is simply telling children to trust authority. This is an appeal to authority fallacy.

Notice that internet hobbyists become highly credible, according to the mainstream, when writing blogs that support the government's position. Mick West of Metabunk.org, for instance, is an admitted hobbyist with no specialist training in anything other than computer game design. Yet his years of online research into aeroplane contrails, undertaken as a hobby and posted on Contrailscience.com, led to him being taken seriously as a debunker of conspiracy theories and even published in a co-authored, peer-reviewed paper with qualified scientists. Likewise, a hobbyist named Eliot Higgins has gained credibility and widespread acclaim by analysing online images of atrocities allegedly committed by Russia and Russian-backed forces in Syria and Ukraine. His laser-like attention to alleged crimes of others and whitewashing of Anglo-American geopolitical atrocities has led

---

[4]For Libya details and chronology, see my *Britain's Secret Wars* (2016, Clairview Books). On the BBC, the Trust states: 'Some countries had little coverage, others could have been followed up more fully and there could have been fuller examination of the different voices which made up the opposition to various incumbent governments'. (BBC Trust, 'A BBC Trust report on the impartiality and accuracy of the BBC's coverage of the events known as the "Arab Spring"', June 2012, http://downloads.bbc.co.uk/bbctrust/assets/files/pdf/our_work/arabspring_-impartiality/arab_spring.pdf.

to the mainstream holding him in high regard, even though he admits to having no expertise in image-analysis.[5]

6) *Information should be 'matched' with the child's prior knowledge.* Matching can amount to 'confirmation bias' or the 'echo chamber effect'. This only reinforces one's beliefs, as listeners to Rush Limbaugh and Alex Jones know all too well.

7) *Children should use common sense and ask if something seems likely.* However, if crucial information is missing from the child's sources and world outlook, then information can seem fantastical; but in the context of more information it gains credibility. For example:

On the surface, the idea that the George W. Bush administration and the preceding Bill Clinton administration allowed Osama bin Laden to live and fund terrorism is absurd. However, when we hear the testimony of Michael Scheuer, the head of the CIA's bin Laden unit, stating on the record that Clinton had ten 'easy opportunities' to kill or capture bin Laden between 1998 and 1999 and gave the order not to kill or apprehend him, and when we read the report authored by Bush's colleagues about the need for what they call 'a catastrophic and catalyzing event' in order to justify war, global missile systems and expansion into Asia, it seems not only less absurd but logical that they would let bin Laden live and have a demon to chase.[6]

So what children are left with from Bedley's model is: if journalists make a living from their work it is more likely to be true than those who do it with passion or for a hobby; group-think is best; 'credible' information comes only from established sources; facts can change; knowledge must

---

[5]On how the mainstream built up Higgins, see for example: BBC, 'Syria crisis: How bloggers are playing part in weapons analysis', 17 September 2013, http://www.bbc.co.uk/news/av/world-middle-east-24120566/. Matthew Weaver, 'How Brown Moses exposed Syrian arms trafficking from his front room', *Guardian*, 21 March 2013, https://www.theguardian.com/world/2013/mar/21/frontroom-blogger-analyses-weapons-syria-frontline. Patrick Radden Keefe, 'The blogger who tracks Syrian rockets from his sofa', *Telegraph*, 29 March 2014, http://www.telegraph.co.uk/news/worldnews/middleeast/syria/10730163/The-blogger-who-tracks-Syrian-rockets-from-his-sofa.html.

[6]Scheuer interviewed by BBC in *The Conspiracy Files, Osama bin Laden: Dead or Alive?*, 27 February 2010. Thomas Donnelly, 'Rebuilding America's Defenses', Project for the New American Century, September 2000, Washington, DC, p. 51.

be reinforced; if something 'seems' unlikely it is unlikely; and content is less important than the credibility of the author.

The genius of Bedley's technique that it gets children to actually believe they've uncovered truth and that even Bedley could be giving them fake news. (He admits to testing them by asking them to detect fake news.) By constraining their critical thinking capacities with this 'bounded choice' of seven techniques, the children feel empowered as researchers while remaining in the mental prison set by Bedley. But the sad thing is that Bedley himself is probably unaware that he is shaping a prison because he has been indoctrinated by the education system to believe the lies of authority and rely on established sources. And so the cycle of mind control continues.

## SCHOOL AS SOCIAL CONTROL

Schooling, as opposed to learning, is little more than indoctrination. Education can be achieved and even surpassed with mentoring. Mixing with others and developing social skills happens in any number of contexts, so why confine children to schools?

Psychologists Garrison and Magoon write about '[t]he parallel that can be drawn between early Greece and contemporary America', noting that 'Greece after the Persian Wars ... caused the people to assume a more cosmopolitan attitude toward self and country'. Socrates/Plato and Aristotle 'refuted the "rugged individualism" of the Sophists because they felt such a position would not provide an acceptable basis for social, moral, or educational behavior'. Recall that 'morality' is whatever the elite determine it to be: from slavery to wars of conquest. The Socratic method used in contemporary 'democracies' 'is an inductive system because it requires the student to attempt definitions and explanations which eventually lead the student to the accepted position'.[7]

As noted above with the Bedley example, this is key to understanding how and why many people are vulnerable to being exploited by fake news. Bedley and others suggest that we should think critically about news by referring to 'established' sources. How, then, can a person think critically by consulting sources which present information inductively?

---

[7]Klaus C. Garrison and R.A. Magoon, *Educational Psychology* (1972, Charles E. Merrill).

Garrison and Magoon continue: 'In Plato's *Republic*, he envisions a society where men are assigned their appropriate levels by their intellectual competence'. By controlling the quantity and quality of knowledge, the elite determine an individual's intellectual competence. Headmaster Paul Kelley writes: 'How people learn in education systems is dominated by a very restricted approach from a neurological perspective: literally a medieval approach to learning, emphasizing the exposition of knowledge as a set of facts, subjects and formal rules'.[8]

The famous economist Adam Smith said: 'For a very small expense the public can facilitate, can encourage and can even impose upon almost the whole body of the people the necessity of acquiring those most essential parts of education'. Smith continued: 'children may be taught for a reward so moderate that even a common laborer may afford it ... [If] they were instructed in the elementary parts of geometry and mechanics, the literary education of this rank of people ... the inferior rank ... would perhaps be as complete as it can be'. Smith continued: 'The public can encourage the acquisition of those most essential parts of education by giving small premiums, and little badges of distinction, to the children of the common people who excel in them'. Smith's idea was eventually realized. 'The public can ... [oblige] every man to undergo an examination or probation in them [i.e., schools] before he can obtain the freedom in any corporation'.[9]

So, for Smith, 'education' was merely training for work. But not to work for oneself or community, but for the emerging industrialists.

Birmingham University's Richard Johnson notes that in England in 1839, the Education Department began 'moral and religious education to stem a rising crime rate, especially among the children of the urban poor ... [B]y blaming the poor for their poverty (and much else besides) the educationalist was *enabled to believe* that his was a humane, an adequate and an essentially Christian response to potentially removable evils' (emphasis in original). Johnson goes on to note that 'the school was to raise a new race of working people—respectful, cheerful, hard-working, loyal, pacific and religious', in other words: to inculcate from infancy the necessary characteristics of obedience to authority. Education specialist Andy Green argues that the 19th century school 'formed the responsible citizen,

---

[8]Ibid and Paul Kelley, *Making Minds* (2008, Routledge).
[9]Adam Smith, *Wealth of Nations* (Book 5, Chapter 1, Part 3).

the diligent worker, the willing taxpayer, the reliable juror, the conscientious parent, the dutiful wife, the patriotic soldier and the dependable or deferential voter'.[10]

Therefore, when governments gave fake news to soldiers about their 'civilizing' missions in colonies, or to women that it is their 'Christian duty' to remain in abusive marriages, the recipients of such news had already been well trained in school.

Elites feared that in poor, rural areas 'girls will be exposed on contact with rude, sensual and ignorant youths'. Their 'morals' (meaning obedience to patriarchs) might be corrupted. Other inspectors complained of the prevalence of 'long-haired idling youths, flaunting giggling girls'. The inspector had 'seen no other notice taken of the minister of religion than an impudent nod or a half impudent recognition', meaning that the young were not sufficiently subordinated to authority. Parents themselves said for their children: 'we wants a bit of reading, and writing, and summing, but *no'at* (nothing) else' (sic).[11]

So, by the time the child left school and all the violence (e.g., caning) that went with it, the child was taught inductive rather than deductive reasoning and only particular forms of critical thinking, such as that which can be deduced from selected textbooks as opposed to entire libraries of information. But perhaps more importantly, the factory-style school system, which prohibited communication during lessons and instilled values of obedience by fear, became a tool for preventing the working class from *sharing information.* Inspectors found that working people chatted among themselves about the failures of various institutions, including the church, economy and state. There was a real danger that if left to their own devices, working people might take control:

Weaving, for instance, was one of the many important professions of the period. One education inspector's report into Norwich weavers found: 'there was hardly a principle of religion, morals, society, trade, commerce, government, which I did not hear perverted by one or the other'. The weavers, he complained, concocted their own—and by definition incorrect—radical economic theories to explain their poverty. In contrast

---

[10]Richard Johnson, 'Educating the educators' in *Social Control in Nineteenth Century Britain*, A.P. Donajgrodzki (ed.), Croom Helm. Andy Green, *Education and State Formation* (1990, Palgrave), p. 80.

[11]Minutes of the Committee of Council on Education, 1844, Clowes and Sons, p. 261.

to the greats like Mill, Ricardo and Smith, these girls believed that the source of their poverty was 'scanty work and insufficient remuneration'. They had to be taught otherwise. The inspector went on to emphasize that 'unless some pains are taken ... to inform and fortify their minds with just principles', the girls as women 'will soon speculate upon the difficulties with which they find themselves surrounded' and be susceptible to 'pernicious dogmas', like Chartism and socialism.[12]

Today, elites in government and media are afraid of alternative media and are quick to label it fake news, because it enables non-elites to share information rapidly in a way that established forms of news, which stick to rigid principles, do not. Just as educators sought to get children into schools and stop them thinking too deeply about things and sharing their views, the big tech providers like Facebook and Google are now finding ways to lead news consumers back to established sources (as we shall see).

In the 19th century, the state should take over the role of the father, many of whom were at work, dead or absent. Inspector Sir James Kay-Shuttleworth wrote in 1844: 'The teacher of the peasant's child occupies, as it were, the father's place, in the performance of duties from which the father is separated by his daily toil, and unhappily at present by his want of knowledge and skill'. He concluded that 'the schoolmaster ought to be prepared in thought and feeling to do the peasant-father's duty'. Inspector Johnson realized that in order to make this policy a success, teachers should be culturally divorced from the children as not to be infected with their ideas and needs. Johnson described 'the school-teacher himself [as] the primary agent of "civilisation"'. Teachers themselves must be emancipated from the local community, made independent of the whims of the parent, more closely linked to local elites (and particularly the clergy), and provided with the financial means of a cultural superiority'.[13]

The psychological effects of schooling were noted at the time. Education specialist Florence Davenport-Hill noted in 1893 that '[t]he homebred child goes forth to earn his living with all his wits about him, while the child whose life has been spent in the school has had his dulled by want of use, and in like manner had his affections still more disastrously withered away'. She goes on to say, 'too often a deadness to all sympathy, or

---

[12]Minutes of the Committee of Council on Education, 1840–41, Clowes and Sons, p. 430.
[13]Johnson, op cit.

morose selfishness taking their place—while his knowledge of that world in which he must fight the battle of life is nil'. This resulted from the brutality of the school system (which led to children's anti-school revolts) but also from the fact that children, though physically herded into small classroom spaces, were emotionally and intellectual distanced from one another: talking in class, playing and learning by doing were forbidden.[14]

The situation was similar in the United States. Thomas J. Shuell (Buffalo University–NY) notes that 20th century schooling was 'based on a social philosophy and world outlook that is consistent with the Industrial Revolution', i.e., based on 'a factory model' which promoted the 'teacher as an authority'. Noreen M. Webb (University of California–LA) and Annemarie Sullivan Palincsar (University of Michigan–Ann Arbor) find that, '[i]n response to growing *laissez-faire* individualism in depression America [in the 1930s], an organized campaign was launched by a number of prominent businesses', including DuPont, General Motors and United Steel. 'Concurrently, organizations such as the American Legion and the New York State Economic Council determined that social science textbooks were too critical of the American way of life'. As a result, '[s]chools were called on to provide competitive situations that would mirror the competitive culture of North America and Western Europe'.[15]

## SCHOOL AS MIND CONTROL

This chapter in general is about standard education. Alternative schools (with the exception of a brief mention of Dewey) are not considered here because they influence comparatively few children.

In so-called regular schools, whatever method is used—peer pressure, gold stars, detention, caning—the common factor is the top-down desire to control the thoughts and more importantly behaviours of children. This attitude emerges more from the state and corporations than from individual teachers. With the best will in the world, teachers on the whole do not realize that they are trying to 'teach' (i.e., indoctrinate) in an environ-

---

[14]Florence Davenport Hill, 'The System of Boarding-out Pauper Children', *Economic Journal*, 1893, 3(9).

[15]In David C. Berliner and Robert C. Calfee (eds.), *Handbook of Educational Psychology* (1996, Routledge).

ment which has been carefully constructed to destroy the child's critical thinking capacities and limit them to critical thinking within extremely narrow bounds. Nor do they realize that the very environment of the classroom and the routines of school life make 'education' more of a conditioned response to authority and knowledge than a process of learning by discovery.

This kind of inductive learning translates to media and news because, as adults, we tend to merely absorb what is coming over the radio, TV or from print media rather than think critically about what we are told and compare it to other sources of information. Because most news channels are the same, comparing news coverage in a meaningful, non-superficial way is virtually impossible.

Winston Churchill was honest enough to say that '[s]chools have not necessarily much to do with education ... [T]hey are mainly institutions of control where certain basic habits must be inculcated in the young'. In school, children are conditioned to find 'truth' from one or more selected textbooks. Particularly in America, we find that a growing number of textbooks are sponsored by industry. With some exceptions, children are forced to sift through books with foregone answers in order to reach foregone conclusions.[16]

'School is prison', says psychologist Peter Gray: 'In both places you are stripped of your freedom and dignity. You are told exactly what you must do, and you are punished for failing to comply'. The late psychologist Carl Rogers pointed out that, '[w]hile being taught that freedom and responsibility are the glorious features of our democracy, students are experiencing powerlessness and have almost no opportunity to exercise choice or carry responsibility'. As the social controllers mentioned in the Introduction openly admit, this is an important feature of 'democracy': the public should not participate in the formation and implementation of policy, but rather vote every four or five years for one of several near-identical political parties.[17]

'When you take the free will out of education, that turns into schooling', said the late Roland Meighan of the University of Nottingham's School of

---

[16]Quoted in Clive Harber, *Schooling as Violence* (1999, RoutledgeFalmer).

[17]Peter Gray, ' "Why don't students like school?" Well, duhhhh', *Psychology Today*, 2 September 2009. Rogers quoted in Harber, op cit.

Education. The 'coercive and indoctrinational cultures of mass schooling are overlooked' in academic discussion. '[B]ased on the current model of the compulsory day-detention centre, the school itself is a bully institution'.[18]

In *Making Minds*, Monkseaton High School headmaster Paul Kelley says: '[p]risons, like schools, are a place to change behaviour through compulsion, routines and specially designed buildings'. The philosophy and business organizer Dr Charles Handy, who famously called institutions 'prisons of the soul', 'concluded that the nearest model of organisational style ... [of] schools was prisons'. This is because, in prisons, 'the inmates' routine is disrupted every 40 minutes, they change their place of work and supervisors constantly, they have no place to call their own and they are forbidden to communicate with each other'.[19]

With the emergence of Pavlovian conditioning in the 1920s and Skinnerian behaviourism in the 1950s, many educational institutions adopted cruel experiments on animals and children and made these experiments more subtle to fit into classroom scenarios.

In *Behavior Modification in Education* (1973), Donald L. MacMillan of the University of California's Education Department describes '[a] remarkable study' conducted by a student of Pavlov's work, N.I. Krasnogorski, who 'demonstrated the development of a neurosis in laboratory conditions' on 'a six-year-old boy ... give[n] a motor response to a metronome beat of 144 per minute ... [As] the difference was decreased, the subject showed emotional responses and disliked coming to the laboratory'. When the beat was 'increased to 132, the subject "broke down" and became disobedient, cried, became excited, and even went to sleep'. The experiment 'indicated that the concept of discrepancy between the child's capacity to behave and the demands of the environment is what counts for the development of many learning disorders'. Schools, as Kelley said, are environments deliberately constructed to achieve certain outcomes.[20]

In educational textbooks for teachers, it is freely admitted that much of today's applied child psychology is based on the results of callous laboratory tests. In a paper sponsored by the National Science Foundation, Uni-

---

[18]Quoted in Harber, op cit.
[19]Kelley, op cit. Handy quoted in Harber, op cit.
[20]Donald L. MacMillan, *Behavior Modification in Education* (1973, Macmillan).

versity of California–Los Angeles specialists Sandra Graham and Bernard Weiner write: 'the general laws of motivation based initially on animal research were successfully applied to predict the speed of human learning'.[21]

Cambridgeshire education specialist Martyn Long writes: 'Education is probably the largest single area of study of applied psychology'. One of the '[f]ive key perspectives in the psychology of education' is behavioural learning theory, 'based on observable behavior and developed by psychologists Pavlov, Watson and Skinner'. Each of these psychologists pioneered theories relating to conditioning and responses, usually by causing pain, distress and deprivation in animals and sometimes even children. 'Some early psychological theories of learning', Long continues, 'were derived largely from studying the responses of pigeons in cages and rats in mazes'.[22]

In *Educational Psychology* (2007), a textbook for teachers, Anita Woolfolk says: 'Research from animal and human studies shows that both experiences and direct teaching cause changes in the organization and structure of the brain'. So headmaster Kelley wasn't joking when he titled his book, *Making Minds*. In their book on education and psychology, Garrison and Magoon write that 'Pavlov found that when a stimulus such as a bell (conditioned stimulus ...) was sounded at the time food (unconditioned stimulus ...) [and] shown to a hungry dog, and this process was repeated several times, the dog came to salivate in response to the sound of the bell alone'. Snow and Jackson (Stanford) and Lyn Corno (Teachers College) remark on '[s]tudies in the Pavlovian tradition' concerning the nervous system in relation to memory. When applied to schools they note that 'anxious learners are helped by reducing threat, formality, and competition'; which is why schools are full of threats, formalities and competition. The effects of stimuli and every possible reaction of the child to the given stimuli has been conceived, contrived, applied and anticipated for use in schools.[23]

Classical conditioning induces physiological changes in the animal or person: altered heart-rate, higher blood-pressure, salivation, perspiration, dryness of the mouth, etc. Mentioning the work of Pavlov, Woolfolk writes: '[c]lassical conditioning has implications for teachers as well as

---

[21] Graham and Weiner in David C. Berliner and Robert C. Calfee (eds.), op cit.

[22] Martyn Long, *The Psychology of Education* (2000, Routledge).

[23] Anita Woolfolk, *Educational Psychology* (2007, Pearson). Garrison and Magoon, op cit. Snow, Jackson and Corno in David C. Berliner and Robert C. Calfee (eds.), op cit.

marketing managers'. It is easy to understand the desire to apply Pavlov to both. Marketers have products they want people to buy: schools have ideologies they want children to encode. In her section 'Guidelines: Applying Classical Conditioning', Woolfolk writes: '[a]ssociate positive, pleasant events with learning tasks'. The latter method incorporates so-called positive reinforcements (more below).[24]

## TORTURING ANIMALS & CHILDREN

This chapter ends with a discussion on the illusion of choice. It argues that when freed from the conditioning of school, adults have a 'choice' of which television stations to watch or which newspapers to read. This 'choice architecture' is deceptive because most news fits a pattern: that of being owned by private interests, generating revenue from advertising and having broadly the same commitments to shareholders and/or the state.

Turning to methods of conditioning, whether effective or desired:

The Rockefeller family funded Columbia University's Teachers College, whose trio—John Dewey, James E. Russell and E.L. Thorndike—pioneered applying psychology to education. Thorndike 'devised [a] "puzzle box," a cagelike container in which a cat could be placed and presented with a problem to solve' (Garrison and Magoon). Food could be obtained if the cat learned to manipulate a certain device (the 'law of effect'). '[W]hen a child is ready to act, to do so is satisfying and not to do so is annoying. Furthermore, when a child is not ready to act but is made to act, annoyance is caused'. Different levels of distress in children can thus be induced. Thorndike developed five 'supplementary laws': multiple response, mental set, partial activity, assimilation/analogy and associative shift. 'Though few teachers may have consciously based their classroom practice on [Thorndike's] law of effect, the myriad of educational tests that Thorndike and his colleagues at Teachers College ... designed to measure learning were enormously influential'.[25]

Harry Harlow worked at the University of Wisconsin–Madison's Primate Research Center. From the 1950s to the 1970s, the American taxpayer funded Harlow's experiments on infant rhesus monkeys. His re-

---

[24]Woolfolk, op cit.
[25]Beatty in David C. Berliner and Robert C. Calfee (eds.), op cit.

searchers' objective was to induce psychopathology in infants via maternal deprivation. Harlow and his team constructed barren environments in which the infants were raised; artificial 'monster mothers' would systematically abuse the infants; and real mothers were impregnated on a 'rape rack' and also deprived of environmental stimuli. In the latter instances, the mothers would abuse the infants to the point of death. In the case of the 'monster mothers', Harlow and his fellow sadists observed that the worse the abuse, the closer the infant clung to the mother.[26]

Harlow wrote: 'sufficiently severe and enduring isolation reduces these animals to a socio-emotional level in which the primary social responsiveness is fear'. Fear is the basis of conditioning: even the 'fear' that the positive reinforcement (e.g., candy) will be taken away. Professor Rose Laub Coser, who is not associated with Harlow's animal torture, found that the internalization of values begins at age six or seven, not long after the human child is snatched from the mother and placed into state-indoctrination prisons for seven hours a day. Because of economic factors, Coser discovered 'there are not many waking hours left in the day for parents to teach their children'. This creates a significant degree of maternal deprivation in human children, especially in relation to values.[27]

At a cost to 7,000 primates and a financial cost to American taxpayers of $58 million, others continued Harlow's work into the 1980s.[28]

The 1950s also saw the rise to prominence of B.F. Skinner. Greeno et al. note Skinner's stimulus-response association theory and that '[a] major influence of stimulus-response theory in education has been its support of a view: that of knowledge as an assembly of specific responses'. Thus children (at least in theories easy to disprove) are transformed into nothing more than 'an assembly' of conditioned responses. In contrast to Pavlov, Skinner developed a theory of operant conditioning by subjecting rats, pigeons and other animals (or 'complex organisms' in callous science terminology) to electric shocks and food deprivation. 'Although nowadays, especially with Skinner's death, dyed-in-the-wool classical behaviorists are hard to find, some of their attitudes are alive and well',

---

[26]Peter Singer, *Animal Liberation* (2015, Bodley Head). Quoted in Singer, op cit. Rose Laub Coser, 'The American Family: Changing Patterns of Social control' in Jack P. Gibbs (ed), *Social Control: Views from the Social Sciences* (1982, Sage).

[27]Ibid.

[28]Singer, op cit.

writes D.C. Phillips of Stanford.[29]

What does all this have to do with education, and thus our ability to think critically about what we are told, rather than accept information as a conditioned response?

For maturationists, '[t]he only difference between a pigeon learning to bowl ... and children learning how to solve math equations was a matter of degree, not of qualitative difference', writes Rita Watson of the Faculty of Education, University of British Columbia. Woolfolk jokes: 'Teachers cannot treat students like laboratory animals, delivering a mild shock to their feet until they give a right answer ... But teachers can make sure that unpleasant situations improve when student behavior improves'. According to Woolfolk, behaviour = reinforcer (consequence) = strengthened/repeated behaviour (effect). Positive reinforcement (e.g., praise, gold star) = strengthened behaviour, which can undermine teachers (attention, praise, reward). Negative reinforcement = shock, fear, embarrassment. In classrooms, '[n]egative reinforcement can also be used ... To do this you place students in mildly unpleasant situations, so they can "escape" when their behaviour improves'.[30]

The illusion of choice is key to social control. Both child and adult, psychologically wounded from mental abuse at school, continue living in the present socioeconomic order, accepting choices (between left- and right-wing governments, obeying the law or facing punishment, etc.) when in reality both options have been contrived by elites in advance. In *The Psychology of Education* (2000), Long writes: 'individuals who have been operantly conditioned have ... learned to *predict* what will happen in a given situation if they engage in certain behavior ... [Observational learning] depends on predictions and expectations about the consequences of behavior, rather than direct associations' (emphasis in original).[31]

# CONCLUSION

Indoctrination at school has complicated effects. For some children (like this author) it can instil a life-long contempt for and suspicion of author-

---

[29] Greeno and Phillips David C. Berliner and Robert C. Calfee (eds.), op cit.
[30] Woolfolk, op cit.
[31] Long, op cit.

ity, rendering top-down fake news useless. For others, however, it can turn them off education forever. To the majority of children, however, school appears to be a necessary and often enjoyable period of life, yet it encourages learning within fixed limits.

# Chapter 4

# Science and medicine: 'Fictionosis'

*The previous chapter included an analysis of 19th century English educa-*
*tion and 20th century American education. The turn of the last century*
*also saw a rise in quackery and fake science news, particularly in the*
*form of travelling medicine shows, where potion-makers and their shills*
*would pretend to have invented miracle cures. The Great Depression*
*made many desperate, ill Americans susceptible to these hucksters. In*
*more recent times, fake news has spread to the sciences, particularly in*
*the pharmaceutical industry, where even fake medical journals have been*
*funded and published.*

In the fake news epidemic, even the holy grail of science is not safe.

A few years ago, Obokata et al. worked at the RIKEN institute in
Japan. They claimed to have found the creation of stimulus acquisition of
pluripotency (STAP) cells. Their alleged breakthrough had the potential
to enable scientists to make stem cells for medical research. However, after
other researchers pointed to alleged plagiarism and data manipulation, a
panel ruled against the paper. Obokata, who led the study, denies any
falsification.[1]

Fraud in science writing is so common that a pair of Stanford researchers
(Prof. Jeff Hancock and David Markowitz) have devised ways to spot it.
They found that lying scientists tend to use more negative emotional
terms, fewer first-person pronouns and obfuscating language. Of the 253
science articles retracted between 1973 and 2013, most were in the biomed-
ical sciences. The average retracted fraud included 60 more jargon words
than unretracted ones. Hancock concludes: 'Science fraud is of increasing

---

[1]Monte Morin, 'Scientist accused of manipulating data in STAP stem cell study',
   *LA Times*, 1 April 2014, http://articles.latimes.com/2014/apr/01/science/la-sci-sn-
   japanese-lab-cites-misconduct-in-stap-cell-controversy-20140331.

concern in academia, and automatic tools for identifying fraud might be useful'.[2]

In the 1990s, Dr Masaru Emoto and his followers started screaming abuse at water droplets. Emoto then froze them and examined them under a microscope. The ice crystals were asymmetric and jagged. When Emoto said nice things to the water before freezing it, the ice crystals were smooth and symmetric. Stunned, Emoto and his followers repeated the experiment, adding over the years heavy metal music vs. pleasant classical, the names of dictators vs. famous pacifists, etc. The results were consistent: when positive intent is projected at water it is affected positively. When negativity is projected, it is affected negatively.[3]

Emoto's work purported to show the unconscious consequences of emotional affect on seemingly unconscious natural phenomena and organisms. Emoto and his followers saw enormous humanitarian potential in being nice to water: after all 70% of our bodies is water. New Agers and spiritualists were elated. Here was a scientist giving credibility to what they believed: that consciousness is not just a complex, but arbitrary, brain function. It permeates everything and will survive death.

Sadly, Emoto was a hoaxer. He released no procedural records concerning how he conducted the experiments, nor how to conduct repeats. He kept no lab records, worked for no established university and although he published a double-blind study, he failed to use conventional water-cooling techniques. (A little logic can easily disprove the alleged findings: Emoto claims that positive intent results in aesthetically pleasing water formations. But 'aesthetic pleasure' is entirely subjective.)[4]

But even scientists in the established and respectable fields fake results and evidence.

Around the time that Emoto was making a splash (no pun intended) with New Agers, a young science 'genius' named Dr Jan Hendrik Schön was dazzling researchers by publishing eight peer-reviewed papers a year

---

[2]Bjorn Carey, 'Stanford researchers uncover patterns in how scientists lie about their data', *Stanford News Service*, 16 November 2015, http://news.stanford.edu/2015/11/16/fraud-science-papers-111 615/.

[3]One of many: Masaru Emoto (trans. David A. Thayne), *The Hidden Messages in Water* (2004, Atria Books).

[4]Kenneth G. Libbrecht, 'The Hidden Messages in Water', *Snow Crystals* (Caltech University), www.its.caltech.edu/~atomic/snowcrystals/myths/myths.htm.

in major journals, including *Nature* and *Science*. Dr Schön worked as a physicist for Bell Labs and published in the fields of physics, nanotech and quantum mechanics. Schön found that organic crystals have such a significant conductive capacity that they can be used for superconductivity and laser applications. He then produced a molecular-level transistor and assembled organic dye molecules in an electrical current to behave as a transistor. In theory, this would have led to the use of organic instead of silicon-based electronics, reducing cost and expanding life-spans significantly.[5]

The science community was slow to smell a rat. Professor Lydia Sohn tried to raise red flags when she noticed that two alleged experiments carried out by Schön produced identical noise. Schön dismissed the criticism as a submission error on his part. When asked for evidence, he claimed that he kept no lab notes and had destroyed his digital records. When other scientists noted the same error in several Schön papers, the game was up. Lucent Technologies (which ran the Bell Labs) opened an investigation and found 16 out of 24 instances of scientific misconduct.[6]

This chapter looks at historical fraud in science, particularly the phenomenon of miracle cures and medicine shows. It then goes on to examine the invention of disease by the pharmaceutical industry, whose main aim is making money. The point is to demonstrate that fake news is not the exclusive purview of media and the internet.

## MEDICINE SHOWS

The 1800s were plagued with cholera, typhoid, typhus and yellow fever. Louis Pasteur introduced germ theory as late as 1861. Until then, mothers were doctors, giving their children homemade remedies. But soon 'the spirit of profit took hold'. Entrepreneurs bottled traditional remedies in an effort to appeal to people's sense of maternal comfort and tradition. In reality, the main ingredients were often alcohol and opium.[7]

---

[5]Geoff Brumfiel, 'Physicist found guilty of misconduct', *Nature News*, 26 September 2002, http://www.nature.com/news/2002/020 923/full/news020 923-9.html.

[6]Ibid.

[7]Peggy M. Baker, 'Patent Medicine: Cures and Quacks', Pilgrim Hall Museum, http://www.pilgrimhallmuseum.org/pdf/Patent_Medicine.pdf.

Colourful imagery was employed by medicine sellers. Trade cards included motherly images as well as drawings of vigorous young remedy-drinking men contrasted with the enfeebled and elderly. One before-and-after card showed a diseased young woman in pale colours before miraculously transforming into a bright, healthy debutant.

Before:

> Once bright and beautiful, a maiden well beloved, adorned the social circle where she moved, but in her veins there lurked the pois'nous taint of scrofula, and many a sad complaint that hid the beauty of her radiant face beneath unseemly blotches nothing could efface, but for Scovill's Sarsaparilla, hope had flown had Scovill's Blood and Liver Syrup been unknown.

After:

> Now every trade of scrofula has disappeared, her face, ever marred by blotches, which she feared would never go away, is fair once more and brighter, handsomer than ever before. For all diseases of the blood and liver, something from their fury to deliver, or for a pleasant tonic, all your blood to stir up, take Scovill's Sarsaparilla or Blood and Liver Syrup.[8]

The century saw a dramatic rise of a US phenomenon called patent medicine. The medicines were almost never patented and not real medicines. The Pilgrim Hall Museum reckons that privatization made medicine too expensive for the majority who therefore put their faith in travelling medicine shows. Medicine quacks used the private mass media after the Civil War, when Americans were extra hungry for information, to spread their fake news about miracle cures. These were based on 'unproved' recipes and 'unreliable' testimonials. The 'second revolution' in printing, with the advent of the printing press, led to improvements and the marketing of cheap wood pulp. This enabled the quacks to reach a mass audience.[9]

Dr Ayer of Massachusetts had advertising contracts with 1,900 newspapers and periodicals. Ayer was making 630,000 doses of remedies a year.

[8]Ibid.
[9]Ibid.

C.I. Hood Company appealed to historic patriotism in the native Massachusetts by featuring a drawing of a beautiful young woman, 'Priscilla', whom the trade card described as The Mayflower of Plymouth, in reference to the ship and town on which, and from where, the Pilgrim Fathers set sale for America to escape persecution in England and establish a colony for investors. The reverse included fake testimonies from people who allegedly took remedies since infancy and maintained their vigour into middle age.[10]

Ayer's Hair Vigor '[r]estores gray hair to its natural vitality and color ... The Vigor is not a dye; but daily applications for a week or two so stimulate the roots and color glands, that faded or gray, light or red hair, gradually changes to a rich brown color, or even black' (Baker's ellipsis). Dr E. Rowell's Invigorating Tonic and Family Medicine claimed to cure 'dyspepsia, indigestion, constipation, loss of appetite, biliousness, headache, jaundice, loss of memory, piles, eruptions of the skin, general debility, rheumatism, and all diseases rising from disordered liver, bowels or kidneys'. Brown's Iron Bitters read:

> highly recommended for all diseases requiring a certain and efficient TONIC; especially Indigestion, Dyspepsia, Intermittent Fevers, Want of Appetite, Loss of Strength, Lack of Energy, Malaria, etc. Enriches the blood, strengthens the muscles and gives new life to the nerves ... As Brown's Iron Bitters is specially adapted to diseases incident to female, we will send in a plain sealed envelope to any lady desiring it, a circular containing testimonials from ladies.[11]

## FAKE DIAGNOSES

Dr Larry Dossey writes that in the 1900s, medical companies sought 'to inflate a common, everyday condition to the level of pathology, which, if not attended to, could blight one's prospects for happiness and success'. And so by spreading fake news, that normal odors were signs of illness, the chemical-medical industry created a new market for personal hygiene, including breath fresheners and deodorants. This was the beginning of

---

[10]Ibid.
[11]Ibid.

what science writer Julie Deardoff calls 'fictionosis'.[12]

Ray Moynihan and David Henry perpetrated a hoax in the *British Medical Journal* 'to show how easy it is to talk up a disorder. Using authoritative sources, you can make it all sound very plausible', says co-author Henry. The authors claimed that a new laziness disease had been discovered, which they called motivational deficiency disorder. It can be fatal in some cases, they warned, because it destroys an individual's motivation to breathe. The neurological data were supposedly supplied by one Dr Leth Argos; a pun on lethargy.[13]

Moynihan and Henry performed a service in making authorities at the *BMJ* more skeptical and less susceptible to fake news in the sciences and medical professions.

The term 'disease mongering' was coined by Lynn Payer in her eponymous book, subtitled, *How Doctors, Drug Companies, and Insurers Are Making You Feel Sick*. She identifies ten methods: abnormalizing normal conditions; portraying potential consumers as sufferers; identifying common conditions to maximize target audiences; defining conditions as diseases; working with medical professionals to gain credibility; selecting issues; using the selective application of statistics; using end point references; implying that technology is risk-free; and devaluing real ailments.[14]

In the 1960s, Dr Keith Connors of Johns Hopkins University was paid by the drug company CIBA to trial a new drug, Ritalin. Connors set a precedent for trialing big pharma–sponsored drug studies on children via university-affiliated clinics. Connors watched this model get out of control to the point where he called misdiagnosis of Attention Deficit Hyperactivity Disorder (ADHD) 'a national disaster'.[15]

Journalist Alan Schwarz revealed the devastating fact that although only 5% of US children have so-called ADHD, 15% of all American children are diagnosed with it. This is due largely to big pharma pushing its products on doctors and families. When the data are stratified, we find

---

[12]Larry Dossey, 'Listerine's Long Shadow: Disease Mongering and the Selling of Sickness', *Explorations*, 2(5), September-October, 2006, pp. 379-85.

[13]Quoted in ibid.

[14]Ibid.

[15]Gareth Cook, 'Investigative journalist Alan Schwarz sounds the alarm', *Scientific American*, 11 October 2016, https://www.scientificamerican.com/article/big-pharma-s-manufactured-epidemic-the-misdiagnosis-of-adhd/.

that in the American south (i.e., the poor region), misdiagnoses are applied to 30% of all boys. Schwarz claims that big pharma paid 'all the top researchers' to publish studies claiming that ADHD drugs are safe, necessary and can solve the phony epidemic. The top representatives came from the University of California, Harvard and Johns Hopkins.[16]

Big pharma took the false data from their subsidized studies and constructed advertisements targeted at worried parents. The advert for Adderall XR, for instance, claimed that the drug will boost the child's grades to 'match' their intelligence. What's more, Schwarz writes: 'Every ADHD drug – Adderall XR, Concerta, Vyvanse, Metadate, you name it – has received a formal reprimand from the F.D.A. [Food and Drug Administration] for false and misleading advertising. Every one'. Yet, many remain on the market.[17]

# FAKE AUTHORS, FAKE JOURNALS

A decade ago, Elsie Langdon-Neuner published a paper about the phenomenon of ghost-writing in science journals. She notes several 'scandals revealed misleading content in some articles'. Medical ghost-writers are paid by companies to influence both policy-makers and doctors. Adverts might name the company behind the drug, but ghost-writers don't disclose their paymasters. Langdon-Neuner estimates that a minimum of 11% of journal publications are ghost-written. Usually ghost-writing only becomes apparent thanks to whistleblowers, court orders or public refusals to be named as author. Data stored in the File Properties of Word documents can also reveal the real author. At its worst, medical ghost-writing can create markets for new drugs, bypassing Food and Drug Administration rules. Langdon-Neuner discusses ghost-writers:

> Some ghost-writers have spoken out about instructions they have received on the slant and emphasis to be used in articles. Marilynn Larkin was given an outline, references and a list of drug-company-approved phrases. Ronni Sandroff was told what to play up and what to play down. Susanna Dogson was asked to slant a paper in favour of [a] drug company. Susanna Rees was told to replace the

[16]Ibid.
[17]Ibid.

names of drug company employees with those of the named authors
in the File Properties of MS Word manuscripts.[18]

Drug giant Pfizer owns an anti-depressant called Zoloft. Researchers
Healy and Cattell found, through court orders, academic papers which
had been written by drug companies with the author's name still to be
determined. Eighty-five such documents were discovered. Of these, 55
were written by Pfizer employees and 30 were either funded by Pfizer or
based on their own data, which were denied to outsiders. In total, just
two declared a conflict of interest. Each article reported positive results.[19]

In 1999, Merck introduced the painkiller, Vioxx. By 2004 it was withdrawn after alleged links to cardiovascular disorders. Before the withdrawal, Merck had hired ghost-writers despite having internal knowledge
that the drug may increase the risk of thrombus formation.[20]

But big pharma has gone even further: publishing fake peer-reviewed
journals. Elsevier's Australia office published six journals between the
years 2000 and 2005, sponsored by big pharma. They appeared to be
peer-reviewed medical journals but, what Elsevier didn't tell readers, is
that they were financed by drug companies and published results mostly
favourable to big pharma: *Australasian Journal of General Practice, Australasian Journal of Neurology, Australasian Journal of Cardiology, Australasian Journal of Clinical Pharmacy, Australasian Journal of Cardiovascular Medicine* and *Australasian Journal of Bone & Joint Medicine.*[21]

## FAKE TEXT & JOURNALS

In 2005, a group of MIT students invented an algorithm, SCIgen, to auto-
generate text (not particularly well, as it happens). In 2010, Cyril Labbé
of Joseph Fourier University, France, changed the algorithm to *detect* auto-
generated text. He discovered that at least thirty auto-generated texts

---

[18]Elise Langdon-Neuner, 'Medical ghost-writing', *Mens Sana Monographs*, 6(1), 2008, pp.
    251-73.
[19]Ibid.
[20]Ibid.
[21]Bob Grant, 'Elsevier published 6 fake journals', *The Scientist*, 7 May 2009,
    http://www.the-scientist.com/?articles.view/articleNo/27383/title/Elsevier-
    published-6-fake-journals/.

had been published between 2008 and 2013, including in major journals by *Springer* and the *Institute of Electrical and Electronic Engineers.*[22]

Anna Olga Szust is an Associate Professor at Adam Mickiewicz University, Poland. She has a solid reputation, having published book chapters, delivered conference papers and lectured. She had published no peer-reviewed papers, however, and had no experience as an editor. Despite this, she applied for an editorial job and immediately received fifty job offers. But Professor Szust is a fictional character. She was invented by University of Sussex psychologist Katarzyna Pisanski and three of her colleagues. Katarzyna perpetrated the hoax in an effort to draw attention to the growth of frivolous scientific journals. The word *oszust* in Polish means fraud. Her point was to show that so many fake, for-profit journals exist that they are willing to employ editors who have no experience.[23]

The journal industry has become a travelling medicine show, with hack editors offering pay-to-publish deals to desperate academics who want prestige.

Between 2011 and 2017, the number of shoddy online journals ballooned from 18 to well over a thousand. Between 2010 and 2014, articles published in these so-called predatory journals grew to nearly half a million from just 53,000. In 2014, Peter Vamplew of Federation University Australia submitted a paper to the predatory *International Journal of Advanced Computer Technology*. His paper was entitled, 'Get Me Off Your Fucking Mailing List'. The text of the paper consisted of the title repeated: for ten pages. It was immediately accepted by the journal for the small fee of $150.[24]

## CONCLUSION

Science is mostly about utility. If a product goes to market and is ineffective due to fake science, it will not survive. Fake science therefore can

---

[22]Bjorn Carey, 'Stanford researchers uncover patterns in how scientists lie about their data', *Stanford News Service*, 16 November 2015, http://news.stanford.edu/2015/11/16/fraud-science-papers-111615/.

[23]Alan Burdick, ' "Paging Dr. Fraud: The fake publishers that are ruining science', *New Yorker*, 22 March 2017, http://www.newyorker.com/tech/elements/paging-dr-fraud-the-fake-publishers-that-are-ruining-science.

[24]Ibid.

only work in concert with public relations in a market place, the most notorious examples are big pharma and quack alternative medicines; not that all mainstream or alternative medicines are fake, of course.

# Chapter 5

# Film and photography: 'Seeing isn't always believing'

*In the Introduction, I argue that not all fake news is entirely fake. Some contains 'grey propaganda', part truth and part lies. When it comes to the revolution in photography and film in the latter decades of the 19th century, fake news (including grey) received a boost. The very fact of technological novelty and newness makes consumers more susceptible to believing stories, particularly where real events occurred but were then recreated on celluloid and sold as documentary.*

Most people assume that the images informing their perception of modern history are accurate. In the latter part of the 19th century photos and eventually film authenticated world events in ways that illustrations apparently could never do. It would profoundly shake our faith in established history, and thus the authorities that perpetuate it, if we were to learn and accept that many classic images from history are faked, manipulated, or representations of real events. Yet many of them are.

John D. Tippett, the London representative for Universal Film Manufacturing Co. wrote about WWI photography: 'Anything you see in America of any consequence is fake ... Cameramen are forbidden to go anywhere near the points of interest'. However, Tippett also warned that 'the advertiser is very foolish to try to fool the American people in that manner with some old faked-up junk'. Not everyone listened.[1]

Photography changed the power of fake news. Where colonialists and travelling medicine show salesmen (most were men) had to rely on illustrations to disseminate their fake news, journalists and editors could now

---

[1] Raymond Fielding, *The American Newsreel: A Complete History*, 1911–1967 (2nd ed., 2011, McFarland and Co.).

'illustrate' their stories with films and photographs, i.e., seemingly real images. The story might have been true, but the image was fake in that it was a representation, often using actors, of real events. This muddied the definition of fake news. One of the first fake war photos was Roger Fenton's classic, 'The Valley of the Shadow of Death' (1855). Fenton shows cannonballs scattered over a road on the battlefield of Crimea. But a second photo emerged with no cannon balls on the road. Filmmaker Errol Morris reckons that Fenton's assistant cleared the balls from the road to enable them to continuing travelling, when a second photo was taken. But Susan Sontag reckons that the balls were put there for dramatic effect.[2]

In 1863, Alexander Gardner was photographing the Battle of Gettysburg. He captured a dead Confederate soldier on the battlefield. It later emerged that the photo was staged. Gardner found a corpse, moved it to another location, gave it a fake gun and twisted the body to get an aesthetically pleasing look. Today, photographic staging of 'real' events is universally condemned as unethical. But historian William A. Frassanito argues that when the medium was first developed (no pun intended), mores were different. Frassanito writes: 'When photography was invented, it was thought that it was going to replace art'.[3]

After President Lincoln's assassination in 1865, propagandists realized they hadn't enough 'heroic' images of Lincoln. Their solution was to create a composite image: an image made up of other images. It is not known by whom, but a print of the American statesman and theorist John C. Calhoun was altered to replace his head with Lincoln's. Newspapers on the table originally read, 'strict constitution', 'free trade' and 'the sovereignty of states'. This was changed to read 'constitution', 'union' and 'proclamation of freedom'. Readers seeing the Lincoln image would falsely believe its authenticity.[4]

---

[2]Errol Morris, *Believing is Seeing* (2011, Penguin).

[3]Michael E. Ruane, 'Alexander Gardner: The mysteries of the Civil War's photographic giant', *Washington Post*, 12 December 2011, https://www.washingtonpost.com/local/alexander-gardner-the-mysteries-of-the-civil-wars-photographic-giant/2011/12/12/gIQAptHhDP_story.html?utm_term=.ece8270afdab.

[4]*Chicago Tribune*, 'The Head was the Head of Lincoln but the Body was that of Calhoun', 10 April 1910, http://archives.chicagotribune.com/1910/04/10/page/55/article/the-head-was-the-head-of-lincoln-but-the-body-was-that-of-calhoun.

# FILM & FAKERY

British print media regularly reported on the war between Britain and Holland over territory in South Africa in the late-19th century. Photographs helped to sell more papers, adding stark visual realism to dramatize the events. The trouble is that the papers never told their audiences that such images were staged. According to producer Albert E. Smith, his US-based Vitagraph studios got some British soldiers to dress as Dutch Boers and act out a battle, which Smith and his team photographed as real. Vitagraph went on to fake newsreel films. But they were by no means the only ones.[5]

Film fakery and politics have been linked since the beginning of film. In fact fakery 'became as much the rule as the exception in the newsreel business', writes historian Raymond Fielding. 'Apparently there was not a single major film producer in the period 1894 to 1900 that did not fake news films as a matter of common practice'. Fielding's history of newsreels ('actualities') describes frequent fakery. 'For every genuine news film photographed under difficult and sometimes dangerous conditions, an equal amount of energy was spent by the same producers to fake outstanding news events of the day'. The practice of fakery was so common that Fielding identifies four characteristics:

1) *Theatrical.* In such cases, events were so dramatically re-enacted that they were 'not intended or likely to fool audiences'. Distributors, however, might sell them as real. 2) *Realistic re-staging.* Such films were purposefully made to deceive the viewer. 3) *Rough re-creations.* These films were made to deceive audiences by fictionalizing events for which detail and evidence was lacking. 4) *Outright lies.* These films were depictions of events that never happened, usually in the context of wider, verifiable events. 'The fourth kind of fake was the most common', writes Fielding. '[T]he most difficult to detect, the most difficult to expose, and the most hardy news-film footage activities alleged to have been associated with famous events'.[6]

The pioneering documentary-makers, the Lumière Brothers, hired one Francis Doublier who made a newsreel about the Dreyfus affair (1894–

---

[5]Fielding, op cit.
[6]Ibid.

1906). Captain Alfred Dreyfus was a man of Alsatian-Jewish descent, sentenced to life imprisonment for giving military secrets to the German Embassy in Paris. When new evidence proved his innocence, senior officers suppressed the new evidence and pardoned the real culprit. After five years in prison and following immense pressure from activists, he was acquitted following a retrial. The filmmaker Doublier was 'one of the first motion picture cameramen to fake a news film'. Doublier himself said: 'I worked up a little film-story which made me quite a bit of money. Piecing together a shot of some soldiers, one of a battleship, one of the Palais de Justice, and one of a tall grayhaired man, I called it "L'affaire Dreyfus." People actually believed that this was a filming of the famous case'.[7]

'Vitagraph', the Boer War fakers, 'continued to fake news films for many years', says Fielding. In 1911, Vitagraph made a film purporting to show atrocities committed by Italians against Turks. Italian-Americans were so incensed that Vitagraph was forced to withdraw the hoax and apologize to the Italian consulate. A trade paper from the time called for media censorship in the face of such 'an abominable lie'.[8]

Noted film historian Stephen Bottomore writes that the first known war footage occurred during the Greco-Turkish War (1897). '[T]his was also the earliest war to be faked on film', says Bottomore. 'But if filmmakers proved remarkably prescient in producing both actuality and reconstructed or fake films of this war, exhibitors were equally quick to make exaggerated, sometimes dishonest, claims for such films'. Bottomore also notes that '[t]he issues seen here in 1897 for the first time, notably those of truth, artifice and deception, were to dominate the representation of war in the visual media for years to come, and this war therefore may be seen as setting something of a pattern for all future coverage of warfare by the moving image'.[9]

German-trained and -armed Turkish soldiers continued the brutal occupation of the Greek island, Crete. Uprisings were crushed. Europe's major powers sent occupation forces to the island. When full-scale war broke

---

[7]Ibid.

[8]Ibid.

[9]Stephen Bottomore, *Filming, faking and propaganda: The origins of the war film, 1897–1902* (2007, doctoral thesis), Onderzoekinstituut voor Geschiedenis en Cultuur, Netherlands, https://dspace.library.uu.nl/bitstream/handle/1874/22 650/full.pdf.

out between Turkey and the inferior Greek army in 1897, the Europeans stepped in to allow Crete a degree of autonomy in their effort to block Turkish expansion. International media, including American newspapers, despatched correspondents. French director and animator Georges Méliès filmed horrific scenes of death and beheadings during the war. His short film *Sea Battle in Greece* depicts sailors loading and firing a cannon as the ship sways on the waves.[10]

But Méliès's footage was all fake. The ship was a painting and it swayed because it was built on a pivoted deck in Méliès's Montreuil studio. The 'beheadings' were a speciality of Méliès, who was very much interested in magic and conjuring. Bottomore writes: 'arguably, they were the first ever films to reconstruct a current news event'. Méliès's other footage from the war included *Mohammedan inhabitants of Crete massacring Christian Greeks*, *Turks attacking a house defended by Greeks*, *The Greek man-of-war "George" shelling the Fort of Previsa* and *Execution of a Greek Spy at Pharsala*. *Turks attacking a house defended by Greeks* 'is clearly staged', says Bottomore. The film is less than a minute in length and depicts Turks supposedly chasing Greeks out of a courtyard. The Greeks enter a house and lock it, after which the Turks plant explosives and are shot by other Greek soldiers who scale the wall.[11]

Early filmmakers and photographers also faked events in the Spanish American War. E.H. Amet constructed a set with miniature mountains and battleships for his depiction of the sinking of Admiral Pascual Cervera's fleet in Santiago Bay, Cuba. 'The Edison organization was especially known for its many re-creations', writes Fielding. These included the eruption of Mount Pelée and the Bombardment of the Taku Forts during Boxer Rebellion in China (1899–1901). A biographer of the famous inventor Thomas Edison writes: 'it is an open secret that for weeks during the Boer War regularly equipped British and Boer armies confronted each other on the peaceful hills of Orange, New Jersey'. Many 'Edison fakes', which Fielding puts into the fourth category (outright lies), were easy to identify due to 'the absurd histrionics of the actors and the impossible positioning of the camera in the very midst of hand-to-hand fighting'.[12]

---

[10] Ibid.

[11] Ibid.

[12] Frank Lewis Dyer and Thomas Commerford Martin, *Edison: His Life and Inventions* (1910, Harpers & Bros).

But war isn't the only subject faked by filmmakers eager for a scoop.

J. Stuart Blackton and Albert E. Smith of Vitagraph filmed the burning of the Windsor Hotel, New York, and the deaths of some forty-five people. Or so the public thought. Smith wrote in his journal: 'March 30, 1899: Filmed miniature of Windsor Hotel fire with little rubber figures jumping out of windows of cardboard model. Ignited gunpowder for fire and smokes. Used toy squirt guns for streams of water. Film very successful among Vitagraph customers'. Today, the fakery is obvious to the point of comedy.[13]

A known faker employed by Edison was William Kennedy Dickson. His work included *Eruption of Mt. Vesuvius, Battle of Mt. Ariat, The Battle of the Yalu* and *An Execution by Hanging*. Dickson's Biograph company was notorious for faking news footage of the San Francisco fire and earthquake (1906) under the direction of George E. Van Guysling. The team built a miniature of San Francisco in their New York studio. The fake fooled politicians, including Californian Senator James Phelan. Biograph's fake film even beat Harry Miles at the box office. The cruel irony is that Miles had filmed actual, less dramatic footage of the disaster.[14]

In 1915, *Literary Digest* ran a piece exposing the practices of news fakery. It describes farmers and villagers dressed as soldiers walking into exploding shells, gassings and trenches. The water columns representing explosions were filled with gunpowder and concealed under the stream. Explosions on the ground were enhanced by the use of mannequins.[15]

In the previous chapter, I document cases of medical forgeries. During and after the First World War, medical practice met film fakery. The Royal Victoria Hospital housed the army's D-Block asylum, where new techniques in trauma cures were tested on soldiers. In 2014, Philip Hoare produced a show for BBC Radio 4 exposing the fact that many before-and-after shellshock victims captured on film by the newsreel company Pathé News were actually acting.[16]

---

[13]Fielding, op cit.

[14]Ibid.

[15]Ibid.

[16]BBC, 'Watching the fake shell shock footage: Royal Victoria Hospital: Behind the scenes at the military hospital', http://www.bbc.co.uk/programmes/p01zxclb/p01zxc7v.

# 'DIGITAL NECROMANCY'

Before computer-generated imagery (CGI) was close to producing real-life images, film companies used body-doubles to finish movies in which lead actors died before completion. One of the most notorious (and hilarious) cases is that of B-movie independent director, Ed Wood. When Wood's lead Bela Lugosi died, Wood replaced him with a stand-in who held a cape over his face to hide the fact that he bared no resemblance to Lugosi.[17]

In 1979, the Lugosi family unsuccessfully sued Universal for using images of their deceased relative to promote Dracula movies; the role for which Lugosi is most famous. The California Supreme Court ruling opened the floodgates for future profiteers. They ruled that images of celebrities could be used as common-law trademarks. The rulings gave to corporations the legal power of 'postmortem right of publicity' (sic), in the words of State Senator Sheila Kuehl (Democrat for Santa Monica), herself a former TV star.[18]

In 1981, IBM (whose early punch-card machines were used by the Nazis to send millions of non-Aryans to their deaths) hired the actor Billy Scudder to play Charlie Chaplin, whom he closely resembled, to sell the company's new brand of personal computer. In one of the ads, 'Chaplin' climbs a ladder to reach some paperwork. As he tries to grab a sheet, the pile magically doubles. Chaplin rushes off with the ladder and replaces it with a trampoline. He springs to the top of the pile and sits on it, struggling to maintain his balance. The new IBM machine magically floats up to Chaplin as a visual demonstration of its memory capacity (i.e., no need for mountains of paperwork anymore). As Chaplin types into the computer, the pile gets smaller and he safely reaches the bottom.[19]

Audiences seemed to like Charlie Chaplin and IBM. Sales increased. PR companies were hired to come up with creative solutions to dead but highly marketable celebrities and find lookalikes. Chaplin lookalike Scudder was found by the ad agency, Lord, Geller, Federico, Einstein. A few years later, Young and Rubicam found a lookalike for Colonel Sanders

---

[17] Rob Craig, *Ed Wood, Mad Genius* (2009, McFarland).

[18] Patrick McGreevy, 'A bid to protect stars' images', *LA Times*, 23 July 2007, http:// articles.latimes.com/2007/jul/23/local/me-marilyn23.

[19] Denver D'Rozario, 'Dead Celebrity (Deleb) Use in Marketing: An Initial Theoretical Exposition', *Psychology and Marketing*, 33(7), pp. 486-504.

and used him to sell Kentucky Fried Chicken.[20]

In 1991, advertisers turned to digital manipulation. The extant Elton John sang about Diet Coke. In the same commercial, three extinct stars of the silver screen returned from the dead to hawk the product: Louis Armstrong, Humphrey Bogart and James Cagney. In the advert, footage from the movies of the three stars was digitally spliced into newly produced footage of a dance ball, at which Elton John sings about the wonders of Diet Coke. Bogart and Cagney make comments to their respective partners, while Louis Armstrong jams with Elton. At the time, Keith LaQua of the Artists Rights Foundation (sic) said: 'An Orwellian picture of what can happen is here, now'. The art of filmmaking is being exploited to sell products, says LaQua. 'Can you image buying a David Hockney and then cutting it up in pieces to auction it off to the highest bidder?', asked LaQua, in reference to the fact that selected portions of Bogart et al.'s films were included in the ad.[21]

*TIME* magazine calls this 'digital necromancy'.

Director Joe Dante (then speaking for the Directors Guild of America), said: 'For economic gain, the people who own the copyright to these films are doing what they want with them without regard to the original artist and that is not right'. Critics say that digital manipulation of films 'only promises to worsen as technology improves' (*LA Times*). Jesse Meyers of *Beverage Digest* said: 'They can resuscitate the dead ... I think that this new 'morphing' process they've used in the Michael Jackson music video ("Black or White") will mean even greater usage of old movies because it will get less and less expensive to use'.[22]

Corporations have databases on the marketability of dead stars. Steven Levitt of Marketing Evaluations says that the most likeable dead stars include, in America: Lucille Ball, Johnny Carson, Bob Hope and John Wayne. Likeability 'depends on what the person died with, how much

---

[20]Ibid.

[21]Dennis McDougal, 'Not quite the real thing: Old movie clips used in commercials leave a bad taste in filmmakers' mouths', *LA Times*, 16 December 1991, http://articles.latimes.com/1991-12-16/entertainment/ca-555_1_diet-coke-commercial. Irene Lacher, 'Image control for Fred Astaire', *Baltimore Sun*, 21 August 1997, http://articles.baltimoresun.com/1997-08-21/features/1997233108_1_astaire-robyn-devil-vacuum.

[22]Ibid.

baggage, and how long they have been dead'. Levitt says that the king of pop, Michael Jackson, became less marketable during his lifetime, due to allegations concerning child abuse and his bizarre public persona (such as naming his child Blanket before dangling him from a window). But since Jackson died in 2009, things have changed. '[P]eople tend to forgive and forget once the person is deceased ... We are almost certain Michael Jackson's likability ratings will get a whole lot better than they ever were when he was alive'.[23]

In 2001, *Forbes* began ranking the highest-earning dead celebrities. 'Delebs' are appealing to some consumers on account of the 'pleasure of imagination', i.e., that they are still alive. Another factor is 'nostalgia theory'. In 'celebrity contagion theory', fans are willing to buy products 'endorsed' by their deceased star in order to feel closer to them. According to the 'Savanna Principles', the human brain evolved to recognize only living humans because artwork could not realistically resurrect the deceased. Digital necromancy therefore appeals to this perceptual flaw. This is coupled with the 'uncanny valley' principle, which stems from 1970s' robotics theory. Humans anthropomorphize things in the natural and created world. At some point, the fake thing 'uncannily' resembles a living thing (particularly a human) and the brain's interest is peaked. We know the given celebrity is dead, but the digital likeness is too realistic for our instincts to ignore. By 2013, delebs were worth $2.25bn via annual licensing and royalty revenues.[24]

# 'A WEAPON OF THE FUTURE'

Like adverts, movies are made to make money, but they have at least the pretence of artistic integrity. Many filmmakers have used CGI to complete the scenes of actors who died during the production.

The earliest success story of using CGI footage of dead actors was Brandon Lee (son of Bruce, who also died during filming) in the movie, *The Crow* (1994). Lee was accidentally shot and killed onset with a loaded

---

[23] Anne-Marie Dorning, 'Hawking from the grave: a tribute or a disgrace', ABC News, 28 October 2009, http://abcnews.go.com/Entertainment/dead-people-tv-commercials/story?id=8934 866.

[24] D'Rozario, op cit.

prop gun. Director Alex Proyas filmed Lee's remaining scenes with a body-double. Dream Quest Images digitally imposed Lee's face on the head of the stand-in. A shot of Lee in his apartment was needed, but the scene had not been filmed. Dream Quest Images took an existing shot of Lee walking down an ally and superimposed it on an empty shot of Lee's apartment, deleting the background images of the ally.[25]

Parallel to these commercial developments, the Pentagon developed digital audio and video fakery. In 1999, William Arkin in the *Washington Post* authored an important article about the use of digital fakery: both visual and audio. US General Carl W. Steiner announced: 'we are going to overthrow the United States government'. Or so it sounds. In reality, Steiner had said something rather mundane, such as what he'd eaten for breakfast. US military voice morphing specialists fed Steiner's mundane statements into a computer and digitally altered it to say something entirely new with his voice: a phony plot to overthrow the government. At Los Alamos National Laboratory in New Mexico (home of the atomic bomb), a team of scientists led by George Papcun developed technology 'to clone speech patterns and develop an accurate facsimile ... in near real time'.[26]

Daniel T. Kuehl of the US Defense University's Information Operations department says, '[o]nce you can take any kind of information and reduce it to ones and zeros, you can do some pretty interesting things'— like deceive both foreign and domestic audiences by taking audio samples and making opponents appear to say incriminating things. Arkin writes: 'Digital morphing ... has come of age, available for use in psychological operations [PSYOPS]'. PSYOPS, says Arkin, 'is the nexus of fantasy and reality'. Keep that phrase in mind because nearly a decade later, the UK Ministry of Defence said the same thing about simulation. 'Being able to manufacture convincing audio or video', says the US military, 'might be the difference in a successful military operation or coup'. Kuehl says: 'We already know that seeing isn't necessarily believing ... [N]ow I guess hearing isn't either'.[27]

---

[25]Entertainment Tonite 1994. Uploaded by Warwolf 2008, 'The Crow - Behind the Special Effects', YouTube, 2009, https://www.youtube.com/watch?v=ROIuSx1KzgA.

[26]William M. Arkin, 'When seeing and hearing isn't believing', *Washington Post*, 1 February 1999, www.washingtonpost.com/wp-srv/national/dotmil/arkin020199.htm.

[27]Ibid.

When it comes to visuals, the Hollywood movie *Forrest Gump* (1994) pioneered the use of digitally altering old stock footage (e.g., of President Lyndon B. Johnson) and adding new footage (e.g., of actor Tom Hanks playing Forrest Gump) to make it look as though fictional characters were involved in real events. 'For Hollywood, it is special effects', says Arkin. 'For covert operations in the U.S. military and intelligence agencies, it is a weapon of the future'.[28]

By 1990, US military digital video manipulation was sophisticated enough for US PYSOPS units to consider using it in anti-Iraq propaganda. The units considered using 'computer-faked' video of Iraq's dictator (and former US-British ally) Saddam Hussein acting in 'unmanly' ways (such as crying) in order to damage his credibility. Others suggested staging footage of Saddam in sexually compromising situations. Videotapes of the footage would then be distributed throughout the region.[29]

Since the 1970s (as part of Project Pandora), the US has had the power to implant direct sounds (including voices) into people's heads at a distance, using electromagnetic waves as sound carriers. These are called voice-to-skull (V2K) technologies. One enterprising man, Woody Norris, has made a business of the technology, hoping to sell it to businesses to beam adverts into people's heads. Because of the targeted nature of the technology, no one else can hear the given sounds (effects, music, voices, etc.). In addition, the US military claims to have developed 3D holographic technology. As part of Gulf War PSYOPS, units considered beaming a 3D image of Allah, which would have to be invented as there are no images of Allah, combined with directions to Iraqis to surrender via V2K technology. Until the 2003 invasion, Iraq was not a particularly religious country by the standards of the region. The idea was therefore abandoned as unrealistic. Nevertheless, it demonstrates the kind of technology the US military possess and the length it is willing to go (albeit in the planning stages) to deceive.[30]

---

[28] Ibid.
[29] Ibid.
[30] Ibid.

# THE BIN LADEN FORGERIES

Osama bin Laden is or was a religious fanatic, unlike his relatives who are comparatively secular and connected financially to the Bush family via the Carlyle investment group. In the late-1970s, the CIA and Britain began funding, arming, training and organizing tens of thousands of Muslim extremists from all over the world to fight a holy war against the Soviets. The proxy battleground was Afghanistan. The operation was called Cyclone. The so-called freedom fighters ('mujahideen') were later called 'al-Qaeda' by the Bill Clinton administration, which according to Britain's late Foreign Secretary Robin Cook simply meant the 'computer file' of the thousands of terrorists organized by the UK and America in the late-1970s and throughout the 1980s.[31]

One such terrorist was Osama bin Laden. A construction expert, bin Laden built a series of caves in Afghanistan and Pakistan, where the terrorists hid from Soviet forces. After the Soviet withdrawal from Afghanistan in 1989, bin Laden wanted to fight his enemy Saddam Hussein, but the US refused to allow it. Bin Laden then reportedly turned against the US when the infidels built military bases on the holy soil of Saudi Arabia to protect the oil. Michael Scheuer, head of the CIA's bin Laden unit, told the BBC that between 1998 and 1999, they had 'ten ... easy opportunities' to kill or capture bin Laden. But on each occasion, President Clinton refused to authorize a kill or capture mission. A series of terrorist attacks linked with threadbare evidence to the non-existent organization 'al-Qaeda' were blamed on bin Laden's network, including the US embassy bombings in Kenya and Tanzania in 1998 and the attack on the *USS Cole* in Yemen in 2000.[32]

In 2001, bin Laden was blamed by the George W. Bush administration for the 9/11 attacks, despite the fact that bin Laden issued a statement at the time denying all responsibility. The 'war on terror' was re-launched (Reagan had declared one in the 1980s), Afghanistan was invaded, Iraq was framed for having alleged links with bin Laden, drones were used in Yemen and Pakistan to murder alleged terror suspects, and a never-ending war guaranteed the US access to crucial Middle Eastern and North African

---

[31] John K. Cooley, *Unholy Wars* (2002, Pluto Press).
[32] Scheuer interviewed in BBC, *The Conspiracy Files: Osama bin Laden - Dead or Alive?*, 10 February 2010.

resources into this century.[33]

In November 2001 rumours emerged in the mainstream press in Europe that bin Laden was not only receiving kidney treatment in the American military hospital in Dubai (*Le Figaro*), but that he might have died (BBC). A Pakistani journalist, Hamid Mir (later editor of Geo News), claims to have interviewed bin Laden in a cave somewhere. This appeared to prove that bin Laden was alive and well. Mir assured the BBC that bin Laden was still a keen horse rider and enjoyed eating meats and butter, disproving rumours that bin Laden had a kidney disease.[34]

But Mir's final photos of bin Laden, in my opinion, are photoshopped. Mir denies this, but the photos appear to show an airbrushed Mir where bin Laden's ally Zawahiri sits. The font of the timestamp on the two images of Mir and Zawahiri appears to be different. *Slate* also questions the authenticity of Mir's picture. 'The [photographic] negatives are the most persuasive piece of authentication, but they may merely indicate that this is an unusually sophisticated doctoring job'. Actually, they indicate an unsophisticated doctoring job (in my opinion).[35]

Quite apart from this, the CIA planned to make fake videos of Osama bin Laden drinking alcohol and bragging about sexual conquests with boys. CIA employees would play fellow al-Qaeda members in the videos, 'darker-skinned employees' interviewed by the *Washington Post* explain. The CIA Operations Division leaders, James Pavitt and Hugh Turner, reportedly rejected the idea. In the run-up to the Iraq invasion, the CIA's Iraq Operations Group plotted to make a fake video of Saddam having sex with a teenage boy. Another idea including getting 'Saddam' to cede power to his son, Uday. The CIA's Office of Technical Services have the capacity to hack into live TV broadcasts and insert spoof information. They planned to insert crawls—messages on the bottom screen—into Iraqi newscasts.[36]

---

[33] CNN, 'Bin Laden says he wasn't behind attacks', 17 September 2001, http://editi on.cnn.com/2001/US/09/16/inv.binladen.denial/index.html.

[34] David Ray Griffin, 2005, *Osama Bin Laden: Dead or Alive?*, Armchair Traveller. I cite Griffin because the sources can be found there. I am not endorsing his conclusions on the matter of bin Laden's supposed death.

[35] Tim Noah, 'Is the bin Laden interview authentic?', *Slate*, 13 November 2001, http://www.slate.com/articles/news_and_politics/chatterbox/2001/11/is_the _bin_laden_interview_authentic.html.

[36] Jeff Stein, 'CIA unit's wacky idea: Depict Saddam as gay', *Washington Post*, 25 May

Although the CIA allegedly had no luck selling these ideas to the top decision-makers, the Army's PSYOP units at Fort Bragg reportedly considered them, as they had the budget to conduct such operations.

In 2002, following rumours of his demise, an audio tape of Osama bin Laden emerged in which he (or an impostor, or a digital morph of his voice) makes reference to then-current events. In a study for France 2 television, Swiss researchers at the Dalle Molle Institute for Perceptual Artificial Intelligence ran hours of genuine bin Laden audio and compared it to the 2002 bin Laden audio. The software they used was developed for bank security. In 19 out of 20 tests, it correctly recognized bin Laden's voice. It then tested the 2002 audio and concluded with a 95% certainty that it was not bin Laden.[37]

In 2004, video of bin Laden emerged in which he threatened more terrorism. But controversy arose over the fact that bin Laden was sporting a black beard. Soon, a debate raged on the internet about whether it was in accordance with Islamic law to dye one's hair during battle. (The fact that the man in the video looked nothing like bin Laden should have been enough of a clue.) In a 2007 video released by al-Qaeda, bin Laden delivers his latest fatwa. But according to NBC News, a private computer security consultant called Dr Neal Krawetz says: 'Here is Bin Laden in the same clothing, same studio, same studio setup, and same desk THREE YEARS LATER' (emphasis in original). This time, bin Laden has a grey beard, leading some to suspect that the audio was real but the images had been altered by al-Qaeda to make bin Laden look healthier than he was. However, when Krawetz layers the videos over one another, the forgery becomes apparent. Because of pauses in the video, Krawetz reckons that al-Qaeda layered old video over new sound. But this is implausible because the voice and mouth movements are in synchronization, except for long instances of video freezing.[38]

---

2010, http://voices.washingtonpost.com/spy-talk/2010/05/cia_group_had_wacky_i deas_to_d.html.

[37] Brian Whitaker, 'Swiss scientists 95% sure that Bin Laden recording was fake', *Guardian*, 30 November 2002, https://www.theguardian.com/world/2002/nov/30/alqaida.terrorism.

[38] Robert Windrem and Victor Limjoco, 'Was bin Laden's latest video faked?', NBC News, 29 October 2007, http://www.nbcnews.com/id/21530470/ns/nbc_nightly_n ews_with_brian_williams/t/was-bin-ladens-last-video-faked/#.WPaH1GnyvIU.

# CONCLUSION

When utilized as part of a broader propaganda offensive, faked photos, audio and video can be very effective in convincing mass audiences due, in part, to our natural instinct to believe what we're seeing; something magicians understand and manipulate. It takes time for the technological novelty to wear off before many can spot that something is a clear fake.

# Part II: Fake news goes to war

# Introduction

The following chapters are an indictment of mainstream media and government lies concerning war and the justifications for war. They trace the roots of ongoing conflicts in Iraq, Libya and Syria in order to document not only how the West initiated the wars, but how Western governments keep them going, in part, with their fake news. It also shows how enemies use fake news for propaganda purposes.

## SECURITY SERVICES, THE MEDIA...

The security services and police have a long record of making the UK less secure. Historically, they have worked against socialists and left-wing political organizers, often allying with privately-owned right-wing media as well as infiltrating activist groups and unions. These abuses have been documented by Seamus Milne in *The Enemy Within* and Evans and Lewis in *Undercover*. Reaching the level of political intimidation, they also had a hand in stoking paranoia within the cabinet of Harold Wilson, as Ramsay and Dorril document in *Smear!*. We now know that MI6 and the CIA engaged in two media influence operations to take us into war with Iraq in 2002–03, Operations Rockingham and Mass Appeal.[1]

As a branch of the state, it's no surprise that the BBC is influenced by MI5 and MI6. The World Service is largely a Foreign Office operation.[2]

From 1937 to 1986, the BBC engaged in 'highly secretive political vetting', say Mark Hollingsworth and Richard Norton-Taylor. It was only after public pressure that the process was reformed. The vetting of employees was conducted via liaison officers working from Room 105 in Broadcasting House, London. Vetting affected 'all news and current affairs

---

[1] Milne (2014, Verso). Lewis and Evans (2014, Guardian Faber). Dorril and Ramsay (1992, HarperCollins).

[2] FCO, 'Official Development Assistance (ODA): BBC World Service', 24 February 2017, https://www.gov.uk/government/publications/official-development-assistance-oda-bbc-world-service.

journalists, film editors, directors and producers in every department'. Almost none of the journalists knew about the process. Tendencies toward far-left politics among individual reporters and editors were rooted out, giving the BBC the appearance of having a liberal bias without it actually having progressive or challenging content. The process was known internally as 'colleging' or 'the formalities'. MI5's C Branch received the names of outside applicants, which were passed on to F Branch's F7 division. F7 had records of millions of members of the public, including left-leaning journalists, lawyers, MPs, teachers and other potential threats to the establishment.[3]

When MI5 approved or rejected an applicant, its officers informed the BBC's Personnel Office of their decisions. But they never gave their reasons. If an applicant was deemed a security risk, they were blacklisted permanently. Only executive or editorial pressure from the BBC overturned a decision. Once the vetted applicant—internal or external—was successful, a file was kept on them. 'All BBC employees had a personnel file which included their basic personal details and work record. But there was also a second file', write Hollingsworth and Norton-Taylor. 'This included 'security information' collected by Special Branch and MI5, who have always kept political surveillance on 'subversives in the media''. Information included details such as subscriptions to socialist newspapers or sympathy with the Campaign for Nuclear Disarmament. By rooting out far-left sympathizers from the start, the organization had no need to directly control its content or output.[4]

Military Intelligence Six (MI6, also known as the Security and Intelligence Service) is Britain's foreign spy and influence agency. In 2001, ex-MI6 officer Richard Tomlinson claimed that on 40% of missions, spies posed as journalists.[5]

Turning to the British print media: Former editor of the *Mirror*, Roy Greenslade, said: 'Most tabloid newspapers – or even newspapers in general – are playthings of MI5'. Cecil King was a Bank of England director and chairman of Daily Mirror Newspapers, *Sunday Pictorial* and the International Publishing Corporation. Ex-MI5 agent Peter Wright claims

---

[3]Mark Hollingsworth and Richard Norton-Taylor, *Blacklist* (1988, Hogarth Press).
[4]Ibid.
[5]Richard Keeble, 'Hacks and spooks – Close encounters of a strange' in Jeffrey Klaehn, 2010, *The Political Economy of Media and Power*, Peter Lang, p. 101.

that King 'was a longstanding agent of ours ... [who] would publish anything MI5 might care to leak in his direction'. At least twenty journalists known to Wright 'were happy to be associated with us'. Agents of influence in the *Mirror* alone included: Hugh Cudlipp, editorial director (1952–74), who played a role in ousting Labour PM Harold Wilson; Cyril Morten, managing editor who worked for MI6 and hired an MI6 photographer; foreign correspondent, David Walker (MI6); and an agent unnamed by Wright handled by MI5's Section D4. During the 1970s–80s, three quarters of Fleet Streets industrial correspondents were agents of MI5 or Special Branch.[6]

Veteran journalist David Leigh quotes an MI5 journalist speaking about the 1960s–80s: 'We have somebody in every office in Fleet Street'. Leigh himself writes: 'they are very deliberately seeking to control us'. By the 1980s, at least 90 British journalists were on the CIA payroll via its front organization, the Bank of Credit and Commerce International. Professor of Journalism at the University of Lincoln, Richard Keeble, has written about MI5 and MI6 in the British media. Much of this subchapter is based on his research. Keeble writes that the famous MI6 agent-turned-novelist John le Carré (real name David Moore Cornwell) claims that when he worked for them between 1960 and 1964, the British secret services 'controlled large parts of the press – just as they may do today' (Keeble citing Dorril). Le Carré's allegations were confirmed by the BBC itself in a programme about the Cold War. Soviet documents alleging MI6–media connections were confirmed by experts (Dr Stephen Dorril and journalist Phillip Knightley).[7]

In *Flat Earth News*, journalist Nick Davies quotes CIA officers who claim that the Associated Press is practically run by them, just as Reuters is heavily influenced by MI6. Jeremy Paxman was the presenter of the BBC's current affairs programme, *Newsnight*. Paxman says that he wanted to join MI6, but claims he was rejected. In his book *Strange Places, Questionable People*, BBC World Affairs editor John Simpson reveals that in the 1980s, he was approached by a man from the Ministry of Defence who told him: MI5 'want you to be an agent of influence' (sic). Simpson received political photographs from an 'attractive woman

---

[6]Richard Keeble, *Ethics for Journalists* (2001, Routledge), pp. 274-78.
[7]Ibid.

from MI5'. After that, he claims to have rejected the agencies as a matter of professional integrity. Newscaster Sandy Gall was dined by the head of MI6, following the former's reporting from Afghanistan. 'I was flattered, of course, and anxious to pass on what I could in terms of first-hand knowledge'. *Telegraph* editor and former *Spectator* editor, Dominic Lawson, was exposed as an MI6 agent, a claim he denies.[8]

## ...AND THEIR INFLUENCE

Above, we document some of the extent of intelligence influence on the British mainstream media alone. But do these agencies spread fake news, and if so what kind?

One of the earliest examples of MI5 and MI6 influence over media and politics was the Zinoviev Letter 1924. As a result of the Chartist movement in the mid-1800s, mass popular activism won working men from the lower classes the right to vote. This came in the form of the Third Reform Act 1884. Trade unions organized politically and formed the first genuine party of, for and by working people: the Labour Party. The Tories failed to win an outright majority in the General Election 1923. As part of a Liberal coalition, Labour came to power for the first time in 1924, led by Prime Minister Ramsay MacDonald. The rise of the oppressed classes worried the establishment, including Winston Churchill who saw domestic political socialism as a Bolshevik conspiracy. A letter was forged by MI6, intercepted by MI5 and published in the right-wing *Daily Mail*. It purported to be a communication between Bolshevik sympathizers and members of the Labour Party. An MI6 officer and close friend of Churchill named Desmond Morton is believed by Parliament to be responsible for the forgery, as is an MI5 officer, Maj. Joseph Ball. The Comintern was the internal organization of Lenin's Communist Party. It was led by Grigori Zinoviev. The forgery was supposed to have been written by Zinoviev and sent to the Central Committee of the British Communist Party.[9]

---

[8]Nick Davies, *Flat Earth News* (2008, Vintage). Paxman details in Keeble, *Ethics*, op cit. John Simpson (1999, Pan Macmillan), p. 356. Gall in Keeble, 'Hacks and spooks', op cit.

[9]Richard Norton-Taylor, 'Zinoviev letter was dirty trick by MI6', *Guardian*, 4 February 1999, https://www.theguardian.com/politics/1999/feb/04/uk.politicalnews6.

The hoax letter says: 'A settlement of relations between the two countries [UK and Russia] will assist in the revolutionising of the international and British proletariat, ... [and] make it possible for us to extend and develop the propaganda and ideas of Leninism in England and the colonies'. The letter says that 'British workmen' have 'inclinations to compromise' and that rapprochement will eventually lead to domestic '[a]rmed warfare'. It was leaked by the services to the Conservative party and then to the media. Obviously, this went a long way towards discrediting socialism in the UK and thus the nascent Labour Party, which survived for only nine months in government. It was as late as 1999 under the so-called New Labour Party (which formally abandoned its socialist principles) that an official inquiry into the forgery was launched.[10]

Media analysts James Curran and Jean Seaton write about the power of the British press barons of the 19th and 20th centuries. The forgery was carefully timed to help Labour lose the next election. The *Daily Mail*'s fake news headline from 1924 read: 'Civil War plot by Socialists' Masters'. The *Daily Mirror*'s headline read, 'Vote British, not Bolshie'. The letter 'was given massive, largely uncritical publicity by all the press barons' papers, and was shamelessly exploited to define the choice before the electorate as a simple one between moderates and Marxists, British civilization or alien domination'.[11]

## LOOKING TOUGH, DENYING TRUTH

Before examining the three wars—Iraq, Libya, Syria—it is worth noting that sometimes armies and individuals use fake news to make themselves look stronger. The manipulation of film and photography is no longer the privilege of specialists. For more than a decade now, anyone wealthy enough to afford semi-decent photo manipulation products can manipulate images in a realistic way and upload them to websites. Photo analysts have little trouble exposing the manipulation of world leaders' photos. Here are some cases:

---

[10]Louise Jury, 'Official Zinoviev letter was forged', *Independent*, 4 February 1999, www.independent.co.uk/news/official-zinoviev-letter-was-forged-1068600.html.

[11]Curran and Seaton, *Power without Responsibility* (1997, Routledge), p. 52.

When one of Iran's four Shabab-3 missiles failed during its 2008 launch, the Revolutionary Guard added a photoshopped fourth missile to the launch, which Western media initially published without question. This made Iran look tougher militarily than it really is. This fitted the Western narrative that Iran is a threat. In 2012, Iran released a photo of what it claimed was a new vertical take-off drone called Koker-1. It turned out to be an edited photo of a Japanese drone from Chiba University. The chances are that Iran had no such drone. In 2013, Iran faked a photo of its Qaher-313 Stealth Fighter. The illustrators simply added an image of the plane over a stock photo of a snow-covered mountain.[12]

When it was rumoured that North Korea's Dear Leader (a.k.a. dictator) Kim Jong-Il had suffered a stroke in 2008, the regime released a badly photoshopped image of Kim standing in front of a unit of soldiers. The background barriers cease to run parallel behind Kim. In 2013, North Korea published photos of hovercraft storming a beach. The photo was published in the context of alleged nuclear weapons testing and tensions with the South over the latter's US-backed war games. But most of the hovercrafts are very poorly photoshopped.[13]

The so-called Middle East peace talks in 2010 were convened by the US and Egypt, which moderated more stalling on behalf of Israel. Egyptian state media (which gets indirect Pentagon funding) photoshopped an image of the negotiators of each country to put the Egyptian dictator (and one-time US-British ally) Hosni Mubarak in front of the delegates, when in fact he was walking behind.[14]

---

[12]Mike Nizza and Patrick J. Lyons, 'In an Iranian image, a missile too many', The Lede (New York Times blog), 10 July 2008, https://thelede.blogs.nytimes .com/2008/07/10/in-an-iranian-image-a-missile-too-many/. Alexander Abad-Santos, 'The Secret to Iranian Drone Technology? Just Add Photoshop', The Atlantic, 28 November 2012, https://www.theatlantic.com/international/archive/2012/11/iran-drone-photoshopped/321 070/. Adam Sherwin, 'Iran's new stealth fighter jet caught out by bloggers in 'faked' Photoshop image blunder', Independent, 13 February 2013, http://www.independent.co.uk/news/world/middle-east/irans-new-stealth-fighter-jet-caught-out-by-bloggers-in-faked-photoshop-image-blunder-8493 530.html.

[13]Telegraph, 'Was Kim Jong-il photo manipulated?', 6 November 2008, http://www.tele graph.co.uk/news/worldnews/asia/northkorea/3393 688/Was-Kim-Jong-il-photo-ma-nipulated.html. Alan Taylor, 'Is this North Korean hovercraft landing photo faked?', The Atlantic, 26 March 2013, https://www.theatlantic.com/photo/2013/03/is-this-north-korean-hovercraft-landing-photo-faked/100 480/.

[14]Jack Shenker and Haroon Siddique, 'Hosni Mubarak left red faced over doctored

Media can also fake images in order to make leaders seem kind. A 2015 photo purports to show a caring Indian PM, Narendra Modi, looking down from an aircraft to flooded Chennai. But the photo is obviously fake because the porthole through he's looking doesn't fit the image of the city below. The photoshopped layer protrudes from the circumference of the porthole and its perimeter looks sharper than the circumference of the porthole.[15]

(On a personal note, my first article for AxisofLogic.com back in 2011 was published by the editors complete with an obviously fake image of a US drone firing multiple Hellfire missiles, when in fact that original photo shows the drone firing a single missile.)

## WERE THEY REALLY FAKE?

There are also cases of one party claiming fakery and another claiming authenticity.

There is no doubt that British forces tortured Iraqis during the occupation (2003–08). Some alleged abuses were published by the only newspaper with an openly anti-war editor (Piers Morgan), the *Daily Mirror*. Nobody has ever proved that the photos were fake, but the Ministry of Defence claimed they were and people believed the MoD. The photos were withdrawn as hoaxes, and the editor Piers Morgan fired. It was unclear as to who alleged that the pictures were hoaxes, but one can guess. Britain's Royal Military Police had investigated the authenticity of the pictures and took it upon themselves to determine that they were fake:[16]

---

red carpet photo', *Guardian*, 16 September 2010, https://www.theguardian.com/world/2010/sep/16/mubarak-doctored-red-carpet-picture.

[15]BBC, 'Chennai floods: Edited Modi photo sparks online mockery', 4 December 2015, http://www.bbc.co.uk/news/world-asia-india-34991 822.

[16]The now-defunct *News of the World* obtained footage of eight British soldiers torturing Iraqi children with punches, kicks and batons. (Jo Revill and Ned Temko, 'British troops videoed 'beating Iraqis'', *Guardian*, 12 February 2006, https://www.theguardian.com/uk/2006/feb/12/military.iraq.)

More generally, Britain's most senior military lawyer, Lt. Col. Nicholas Mercer, told the *Independent*: 'Seeing prisoners in stress positions and hooded was serious ... [Politicians] knew there were allegations not only of hooding and stress positions but also mistreatment itself within the first month of the war'. (Jonathan Owen, 'Lieutenant-Colonel Nicholas Mercer says it is 'beyond question' that British soldiers

The UK's then-Armed Forces Minister, Adam Ingram, acting as a spokesman to the media, agreed with the Royal Military Police that the pictures were hoaxes. Piers Morgan said: 'We have listened to what Mr. Ingram has said today, but he has still not produced incontrovertible evidence that the pictures are faked', nor have any independent experts. Just because the military of the occupying power says evidence is fake, it doesn't mean it is, especially given: 1) their vested interests in dismissing claims of abuse; 2) the overwhelming evidence of other abuses committed by the MoD; the emergence of Fusilier Gary Bartlam's 15–22 photographs of Brits abusing Iraqis, which the MoD never denied were authentic, and in fact used for convictions; 3) and the fact that no independent source determined whether or not the *Mirror*'s pictures were fake.[17]

What would have happened under normal circumstances is that the MoD would have taken the *Mirror* to court on a charge of libel, alleging that the pictures are fake. As part of the court case, independent experts would have then presented the evidence to a judge to determine the verdict on the allegation of fakery. Had the judge determined that the pictures are fake, the *Mirror* would have withdrawn them, apologized and probably paid compensation. Had the judge determined the pictures authentic, the *Mirror* would have been allowed to go ahead with the publication and the charge of fakery would have been dropped.

Nothing was ever determined in court. That the Royal Military Police claimed without evidence that the pictures were fake, that the *Mirror* ditched Morgan and replaced him with a new editor who instantly agreed with the RMP's allegation of fakery, is highly unusual. It is more likely to be a case of a vehemently pro-New Labour newspaper (*Mirror*) having a non-conformist on its editorial board (Morgan) who exposed the truth and the newspaper buckled under government pressure to withdraw evidence of war crimes which had emerged so early on in the near-unanimously unpopular 'war'.

---

tortured Iraqis', 8 January 2016, http://www.independent.co.uk/news/uk/home-news/lieutenant-colonel-nicholas-mercer-says-it-is-beyond-question-that-british-sol-diers-tortured-iraqis-a6803 281.html.) One such case of 'mistreatment' was that of hotelier Baha Mousa, who was beaten up so badly by British soldiers that he died.

[17]BBC, 'Piers Morgan's statement in full', 13 May 2004, http://news.bbc.co.uk/1/hi/uk_politics/3712 469.stm. BBC, 'Profiles: Iraq abuse soldiers', 25 February 2005, http://news.bbc.co.uk/1/hi/uk/4294 765.stm.

A subsequent RMP investigation, not an independent one, included 'evidence' from a forensic expert (who was drafted by the RMP) who claimed that the urine patterns (a British soldier allegedly pissing on an Iraqi) did not look authentic. In 2004, Private Stuart Mackenzie was charged with 'obtaining property by deception' (not fakery). But in 2005, the charge was dropped due to lack of evidence. Even more bizarre, Mackenzie's regiment was the one linked to the murder of Baha Mousa. Mackenzie later served as a witness for the prosecution in the Mousa case.[18]

---

[18] *Independent*, 'The fakes that finished an editor, and the truth that won't go away', 15 May 2004, http://www.independent.co.uk/news/media/the-fakes-that-finished-an-editor-and-the-truth-that-wont-go-away-563576.html. Janina Struk, *Private Pictures: Soldiers' Inside View of War* (2011, I.B. Tauris), p. 125.

# Chapter 6

# Iraq: 'Psyops on steroids'

*The invasion of Iraq in 2003 is the biggest war crime of the 21st century to date. The lies leading up to the invasion concerning non-existent weapons of mass destruction and false links between Iraq's dictator Saddam Hussein and the terrorist Osama bin Laden have been extensively covered by other authors. After sketching a background to the invasion, this chapter documents cases of fake 'al-Qaeda in Iraq' videos made by a UK-based PR firm, false claims by the US military that bin Laden's operative Zarqawi was a major presence in Iraq and the use of hi-tech video (including green screen) by Islamic State propagandists.*

The BBC has been notoriously mendacious in its coverage of Iraq, giving less than 5% of its airtime to persons and groups who opposed both wars against Iraq in 1991 and 2003. This is despite the fact that a large majority of Britons were against the 2003 invasion. The BBC simply did not reflect the views of the majority of Britons on the issue of invasion. The BBC famously fired a reporter, Andrew Gilligan (resigned, technically), for daring to cite a source (probably the late Dr David Kelly) who confirmed what we already knew: that the intelligence leading to the mass slaughter of Iraqis was false.[1]

## ISIS & ANDREW NEIL

Fourteen years later, BBC presenter Andrew Neil continued the lies when he interviewed Labour Party leader, and staunch anti-war activist, Jeremy

---

[1]Piers Robinson, Peter Goddard and Katy Parry, 'U.K. media and media management during the 2003 invasion of Iraq', *American Behavioral Scientists*, 2009, 52(5), 678-88. Danny Hayes and Matt Guardino, 'Whose views made the news? Media coverage and the march to war in Iraq', 2010, *Political Communication*, 27, pp. 59-87.

Corbyn. British media in general spun Corbyn's historical peace-making efforts (mainly his meetings with leaders of organizations which have engaged in terrorism) as threatening British security interests. Corbyn never committed to stop bombing Iraq in the alleged war against ISIS; but that was the implication. Shortly before the General Election 2017, Manchester was attacked by an alleged ISIS affiliate (Salman Abedi, whose father Ramadan, it turns out, worked for MI6 against Gaddafi in Libya). The terror event stopped Labour's surge in the public opinion polls, in part because the media had already created a narrative that Corbyn is weak on 'security'.[2]

Citing intelligence experts, Corbyn implied, but did not state directly, what we all know: that a brutal foreign policy creates a backlash and leads to domestic terrorism. In an effort to undermine Corbyn's position and exonerate the British state from any guilt in the Manchester bombing, presenter Andrew Neil told a monumental lie which Corbyn never challenged. Neil actually said: 'I'm struggling to find the role of foreign policy. See, Islamic State was founded well before the invasion of Iraq'.[3]

*What?* Could there be a more glaring example of fake news?

I filed a Freedom of Information request with the BBC in an effort to identify Neil's source for the absurd claim that ISIS existed prior to the invasion of Iraq. The BBC replied to my Freedom of Information Act request as follows: 'The information you have requested is excluded from the Act because it is held for the purposes of 'journalism, art or literature'. The BBC is therefore not obliged to provide this information to you'. As this was the case, I emailed Andrew Neil asking what his source was for this claim. He never replied.[4]

Neil, like all presenters, gets his information from researchers who hand him copy to read on air. Neil continued on with the second lie. In an extraordinary twist, he actually went on to quote a fake edition of ISIS's magazine, *Dabiq*. This is important because 1) the anti-war movement believes we should not bomb other countries for reasons of basic morality. 2) Even if we divorce the issue from morality and concentrate on self-

[2]See John Pilger, 'What did the Prime Minister know?' in T.J. Coles (ed.), *Voices for Peace*, (2017, Clairview Books).

[3]Blighty TV2, 'Jeremy Corbyn – The Andrew Neil Interviews GE2017 (26May17)', YouTube, 26 May 2017, https://www.youtube.com/watch?v=KkbmKUiCP2k.

[4]FOIA, 26 June 2017, RF120170809.

interest, the anti-war movement believes that bombing other countries provokes terrorism at home. 3) The leader of Britain's main opposition party also believes this and had a chance to come to power, partly on this platform. 4) This narrative suits neither the government nor the media, whose overall agenda is to perpetuate war. 5) Therefore, the government and media want to shift part of the responsibility away from themselves and their war-mongering and put it onto Islam. 6) By quoting the words of ISIS—that they hate us because we are non-Muslim—the government and media not only spread fake news, but more dangerously, undermine the efforts of the anti-war movement, obfuscate the real reasons for terrorism and do so by lying.

The facts are as follows:

In July 2014, the Islamic State of Iraq and the Levant started publishing a propaganda magazine call *Dabiq*. In April 2016, the *New York Times* reported that the US Cyber Command was disrupting ISIS and ISIL operations: 'The goal of the new campaign is to disrupt the ability of the Islamic State to spread its message, attract new adherents, circulate orders from commanders and carry out day-to-day functions, like paying its fighters'.[5]

Two months after the Pentagon announced its cyber war on ISIS, ISIS issued a statement that Issue 15 of *Dabiq* is a forgery and is *not* authored by them: 'Brothers and sisters, We noticed that dubious attempts were made to spread a fake *Dabiq* magazine issue (claimed to be 'Issue 15', with two varying covers) ... We would like to clarify that Al-Hayat Media Center has not yet released any new *Dabiq* issues. We advise you not to download this fake magazine for your own safety'.[6]

Issue 15 made some extremely far-fetched claims. Chief among them is that Western foreign policy has nothing to do with ISIS attacks in Europe. In an article entitled, 'Why We Hate You and Why We Fight You', the forged Issue 15 states: 'even if you were to stop bombing us, imprisoning us, torturing us, vilifying us, and usurping our lands, we would continue

---

[5]David E. Sanger, 'U.S. cyberattacks target ISIS is a new line of combat', NYT, 24 April 2016, https://www.nytimes.com/2016/04/25/us/politics/us-directs-cyberweapons-at-isis-for-first-time.html.

[6]Davide Mastracci, 'Someone is spreading fake copies of the Islamic State's magazine', *Vice*, 15 June 2016, https://news.vice.com/article/someone-is-spreading-fake-copies-of-the-islamic-states-magazine.

to hate you because our primary reason for hating you will not cease to exist until you embrace Islam'. This is music to the ears of war-mongers. They were right all along: we, civilized Western liberals would continue to be attacked even if we withdraw from the Middle East.[7]

Omitting the ISIS statement confirming that Issue 15 and thus the above quote is a hoax, far-right alternative media in USA, notably Breitbart News (which many have labelled fake news), reported Issue 15 as authentic with a smug we-told-you-so tone to their reporting. British media picked it up, too. The right-wing *Daily Mail* reported it as authentic at the time. After the terror attack in Manchester in 2017, the left-wing *Mirror* reported it, too.[8]

The ex-Israeli military officer Rita Katz has a history of fabricating information. She wrote a book called *Terrorist Hunter*, which purported to be an undercover exposé of jihadis preaching hate in US mosques. The fact is that many of the quotes actually came from preachers preaching in their own countries. All of the context concerning foreign occupation and the Jewish State of Israel attacking Muslims was omitted by Katz. Katz later founded the US-based private organization with links to the Pentagon, Search for International Terrorist Entities (SITE), which has an impressive ability to find terrorist videos and statements supposedly posted on the dark web. Even Katz with her dubious record confirmed that the cyber attacks against ISIS were being conducted by the US. 'As governments and vigilantes around the world continue targeting IS online, apps circulated outside of Google Play or iOS stores provide new opportunities to plant disguised malware into the mix, and thus infiltrate the community. And indeed, as seen in [the June 1 (2016)] warning by IS of fake apps, such entities appear to be doing just that'.[9]

---

[7] *Dabiq*, 'Break the Cross', Issue 15, https://clarionproject.org/factsheets-files/islamic-state-magazine-dabiq-fifteen-breaking-the-cross.pdf.

[8] Sarah Dean, "Jesus was a slave of Allah", *Daily Mail*, 2 August 2017, http://www.dailymail.co.uk/news/article-3719701/Sick-ISIS-magazine-tries-justify-barbaric-killings-Western-liberals-atheists.html. Jon Dean and Sophie Evans, 'ISIS reveal 6 reasons why they despite Westerners...', *Mirror*, 26 May 2017, http://www.mirror.co.uk/news/world-news/why-isis-hate-you-reasons-8533563. Dr. Thomas D. Williams, 'Islamic State: 'Why we hate you and why we fight you'', Breitbart, 2 August 2016, http://www.breitbart.com/national-security/2016/08/02/islamic-state-muslims-command-terror/.

[9] Rita Katz, 'ISIS's mobile app developers are in crisis mode', *Vice*, 3 June 2016, mother-

Returning to BBC presenter Andrew Neil:

After the Manchester attack in 2017, candidate Corbyn looked weak on security. During their interview, Neil told his second lie when he quoted from the fake *Dabiq* Issue 15 in order to 'prove' that ISIS's actions have nothing to do with British foreign policy and can be solely explained by their hatred of non-Muslims. 'Only last year [2016], they [ISIS] said this', Neil claimed, before going on to quote ISIS: 'Some might argue that your foreign policies are what drive our hatred. But this particular reason for hating you is secondary. Even if you were to stop bombing us, we would continue to hate you. Our primary reason for hating you will not cease to exist until you embrace Islam'.[10]

1) The quote did not come from ISIS, as noted. 2) ISIS already denounced the edition of the magazine as a forgery. 3) The US Pentagon confirmed that it had been launching disruptive cyber attacks on ISIS before the fake issue appeared. 4) The Pentagon-linked Rita Katz (more below) confirmed that the issue is likely a forgery by foreign intelligence agencies. 5) Instead of checking it out, the mainstream and alternative media reported on Issue 15 as if it was real. 6) Not a single mainstream source issued a retraction. 7) The quote only resurfaced after the Manchester attack, i.e., the mainstream were quoting it again one year later for political reasons. 8) Crucially, Neil did not identify the source of his ISIS quote. I found it by typing key phrases into an internet search engine.

## BACKGROUND

Iraq is the shame of the West. The Anglo-American blockade, which lasted from 1990–2003, killed over million Iraqis. The British House of Commons admits that at least 200,000 died and the former US Secretary of State Madeleine Albright acknowledged that half a million Iraqi children had died from lack of medicines and sanitation by the year 2000. The US-British invasion in 2003 had wiped out another 700,000 lives by 2016, according to the most conservative estimates. Others put the toll at over 1 million. About 3 million Iraqis are long-term disabled because of the war. Most of them can't get sufficient healthcare because the sanctions

---

board.vice.com/en_us/article/qkj34q/isis-mobile-app-developers-are-in-crisis-mode.
[10]Blighty, op cit.

collapsed the medical system and the bombing in 2003 weakened what was left of the medical infrastructure. This is coupled with the fact that many doctors fled Iraq to live in the West with the onset of war.[11]

Long before the Islamic State of Iraq and Syria (ISIS) became a powerful force, Iraqis were in a severe state of trauma. Apart from the relatively stable semi-autonomous Kurdistan region, Sunni loyalists were resisting the occupiers as were some Shia; other Shia were collaborating with the invaders against the Sunnis; Kurdish forces were also brought in to fight the Sunnis; some Sunnis joined forces to fight 'al-Qaeda', which allegedly had a presence in Iraq as a result of the invasion (and not before as Bush and Blair claimed); and US-British forces continued military operations against the resistance on all sides.[12]

Ordinary Iraqis suffered. By the time ISIS came to prominence in 2014: The UN says that over 2 million left the country and 2 million were internally displaced. Oxfam and Save the Children estimated that one in three Iraqis (about 8 million people) had no access to clean water. The US Office of the Special Inspector General for Iraq Reconstruction says that life expectancy had dropped to 58 years and infant mortality rose to 130 deaths per 1,000 births. Psychology studies note that levels of mental illness were extraordinarily high, given that many Iraqis had never known peace. They had known only the Iran-Iraq war, the Gulf War 1991, the sanctions, the internal brutality of Britain's one-time ally Saddam Hussein and the invasion and civil war of 2003.[13]

The Maliki government was as ruthless as ISIS, but in the flourishing democracy of a newly liberated Iraq, the Western media kept the reality hidden from the public. By the time ISIS rose from the ashes of Iraq, Amnesty says that over 1,000 Iraqis were on death row: many of them journalists, students and union organizers. Human Rights Watch says that journalists were regularly tortured and killed for not reporting the government's views. The same human rights groups say that thousands of Iraqi prisoners (many of them Shia) were raped with sharp objects and tortured with drills and electricity by the US-UK-trained Iraqi security forces. The Red Cross says that tens of thousands of women lost their

---

[11]See my *Britain's Secret Wars* (2016, Clairview Books).

[12]Ibid.

[13]For details and sources, see my 'Remembering Iraq' series March 2013, http://axis oflogic.com/artman/publish/Article_65 480.shtml.

livelihoods when their husbands were rounded up by British and American forces and arbitrarily placed into prisons.[14]

ISIS copied their abusers. The majority of ISIS foot soldiers are young Iraqis who grew up knowing nothing but massive amounts of war and poverty inflicted by the West, persecution by Shia leaders and betrayal at the hands of collaborators. Is it really any wonder that ISIS emerged from the ashes of Iraq, adopting the same kind of abusive tactics as their abusers?

## LESSER-KNOWN FAKE NEWS

The lies and fake news spun and reported in the run-up to the invasion of Iraq in 2003 have been well documented by journalists, scholars and even government reports. In brief: the George W. Bush administration told three lies about the dictator of Iraq, Saddam Hussein: 1) he had an ongoing weapons of mass destruction programme, consisting of nuclear, chemical and biological elements; 2) he was allied with al-Qaeda, whom the administration had blamed for the 9/11 attacks; and 3) he was an imminent threat to the US and the world at large.

By the end of 2002, the UN International Atomic Energy Agency and the UN chemical and biological inspection agencies (UNSCOM and UN-MOVIC) confirmed that there were no such weapons programmes and that the nuclear element was a total fabrication as Iraq had no nuclear weapons capabilities. US diplomats (notably John Bolton) obstructed efforts of other independent chemical inspectors—the Organization for the Prohibition of Chemical Weapons—to independently verify the Bush administration's claims.[15]

Despite secret advice from the Attorney General Lord Goldsmith (subsequently leaked) that any act of war against Iraq would be unlawful aggression (because UN Security Council Resolution 1441 did not authorize the use of force), the Blair government joined America in attacking Iraq.[16]

---

[14]Ibid.

[15]UNMOVIC, 'Unresolved disarmament issues: Iraq's proscribed weapons programmes', 6 March 2003, http://www.un.org/depts/unmovic/documents/UNMOVIC %20UDI%20Working%20Document%206%20March%2003.pdf.

[16]Goldsmith memo, http://news.bbc.co.uk/1/shared/bsp/hi/pdfs/28_04_05_attor-

Much less well known is the role of public relations firms hired by the Pentagon and other government agencies to sell their ludicrous lies to gullible, corrupt and/or sympathetic journalists. Terrorist organizations, including the CIA, have a history of employing PR firms. In the 1980s, the CIA hired the Rendon Group to boost the profile of Panama's future President, Guillermo Endara, whom they helped install. In 1990, Hill & Knowlton was hired by the government of Kuwait to spread false atrocity propaganda, that Iraqi soldiers were removing Kuwaiti babies from incubators. In the early-1990s, the Rendon Group was hired again by the Bush I administration. It came up with the name 'Iraqi National Congress' (INC), which the US formed as a proxy opposition party to Saddam Hussein. Founder John Rendon told the US Air Force academy in 1995: 'I am an information warrior and a perception manager'. In the late-1990s, the separatist, terror militia, Kosovo Liberation Army (which was receiving training from Britain and America to help break up Serbia), hired the PR company Ruder Finn to portray the war in Serbia as an ethnic cleansing of Kosovars.[17]

In October 2001—just one month after 9/11 (for which Iraq was partly blamed) and one-and-a-half years before the invasion—the Bush administration paid the Rendon Group to plant fake stories in the press about Iraq's weapons of mass destruction. Reports from UN inspectors were suppressed. A Kurdish enemy of Saddam called Adnan Ihsan Saeed al-Haideri pretended to be an engineer who had worked on burying tonnes of biological, chemical and nuclear components for the Saddam regime. A CIA polygraph 'proved' that he was telling the truth. One of Iraq's opposition leaders in exile Ahmed Chalabi (another US puppet) and INC spokesman Zaab Sethna started giving the story to journalists sympathetic to the INC. One was former Rendon Group and INC employee, the late Paul Moran, the other was *New York Times* propagandist, Judith Miller, whose article on the piece quotes unnamed US officials as verifying the fake polygraph results.[18]

From the outset, the Rendon Group was no ordinary PR firm. Its

---

ney_general.pdf.

[17] Jane Mayer, 'The manipulator', *New Yorker*, 7 June 2004, https://www.newyorker.com/magazine/2004/06/07/the-manipulator.

[18] James Bamford, 'The Man Who Sold the War', *Rolling Stone*, 18 November 2005, https://www.commondreams.org/headlines05/1118-10.htm.

founder lived in close geographic proximity to members of the Bush II administration. It had a long history of working in deep politics. After 9/11, Pentagon documents revealed that it was given its own Information War Room, where supercomputers monitored newswires before they reached the mainstream media outlets. The system was called Livewire. Pentagon documents obtained by journalist James Bamford say that journalists should be 'punished' for not reporting information favourable to the mounting attack on Iraq. A senior officer admitted to the mainstream media that the overall objective was to 'formalize government deception, dishonesty and misinformation'. Air Force Col. Sam Gardner (Rt.) said in 2005: 'It was not just bad intelligence – it was an orchestrated effort ... It began before the war, was a major effort during the war and continues as post-conflict distortions'.[19]

# FAKE NEWS AFTER THE INVASION

The first lie told by Bush and Blair during the war was that civilians were being avoided by the bombers. In reality, the US used an air war doctrine called Shock and Awe. The Shock and Awe strategy devised several years earlier states: 'The intent here is to impose a regime of Shock and Awe through delivery of instant, nearly incomprehensible levels of massive destruction directed at influencing society writ large, meaning its leadership and public, rather than targeting directly against military or strategic objectives even with relatively few numbers or systems'.[20]

A concomitant lie spread by the media, possibly because of deep shame rather than government pressure (but who really knows?), was the denial of the civilian toll. An epidemiological study co-authored by researchers from Johns Hopkins University and published in *The Lancet* medical journal estimated that at least 98,000 civilians had perished in the first year of the occupation. As Anbar province was excluded from the analysis, the death toll was probably much higher, said the authors. As the war took its bloody course, the same methodology was applied and it was estimated that by 2007 nearly 600,000 Iraqis had died. A couple of years later, a different polling agency (Opinion Research Business) put the toll

---

[19]Ibid.
[20]See my *Fire and Fury* (2017, Clairview Books).

at 1.03 million deaths. The current scholarly estimate is that 700,000 Iraqis died from 2003 to 2016. With regards to the first two *Lancet* studies, the few British media to report the studies denigrated the authors and their methodologies, even though the same media reported that 3.6 million Congolese had died in the 'civil war'; a figure estimated by the same authors of the two Iraq studies, using the same methodologies.[21]

The next lie told by the BBC was that Basra had fallen. Basra is Iraq's second city. It is a Shia-majority town with a port on the Persian Gulf. While America took Baghdad, Britain was assigned to conquer Basra. In order to make it look easy and bloodless, the BBC falsely reported that the city had fallen to British troops long before it had. Then-BBC world affairs reporter, Rageh Omaar, who covered the US invasion of Baghdad in 2003 said: 'Basra was reported as having fallen *seventeen times* before it actually fell. And yet within 24 hour news, when you're reporting it for seventh time in that chain of 17 times when the city has fallen falsely, the fact that it's been wrong the previous seven times just doesn't matter' (his emphasis).[22]

The British PR firm Bell Pottinger started working for the Pentagon on Iraq propaganda operations shortly after the invasion, selling Iraq's first election to the West as a democratic triumph in a once-oppressed nation. The reality was the opposite. In a long article written years after the invasion, the *New York Times* fessed up about their colleagues' role in broadcasting a false image of Iraq as a liberated regional bastion of progress:

> harsh realities were elided, or flatly contradicted, during the official presentations for the analysts, records show. The itinerary, scripted to the minute, featured brief visits to a model school, a few refurbished government buildings, a center for women's rights, a mass grave [to emphasize Saddam's evil—TC] and even the gardens of Babylon.
>
> Mostly the analysts attended briefings. These sessions, records show, spooled out an alternative narrative, depicting an Iraq bursting with political and economic energy, its security forces blossoming. On the crucial question of troop levels, the briefings echoed the White House line: No reinforcements were needed. The "growing

---

[21]See Cromwell and Edwards, *Newspeak in the 21st Century* (2009, Pluto Press).
[22]Interviewed by John Pilger, *The War You Don't See* (2010, ITV).

and sophisticated threat" described by [Paul Bremer, head of the Coalition Provisional Authority] was instead depicted as degraded, isolated and on the run.[23]

The Pentagon and private contractors fed false information to mainstream television news: 'Federal agencies, for example, have paid columnists to write favorably about the administration. They have distributed to local TV stations hundreds of fake news segments with fawning accounts of administration accomplishments'. The article notes that '[t]he Pentagon itself has made covert payments to Iraqi newspapers to publish coalition propaganda'.[24]

Seventy-five ex-military officers were hired by networks in an effort to give a false impression about Iraq: the reasons for invading, military successes, the avoidance of civilian casualties and the blame for various disasters on enemies, like Zarqawi. There was a strong element of self-interest. ABC's Gen. William L. Nash (Rt.) said, '[i]t is very hard for me to criticize the United States Army ... It is my life'. But more importantly, after leaving armed service, many had gone into the mercenary or private-security industry. The *New York Times* points out that the more times the given analyst appeared on a major network, the more they were paid and, crucially, the more free advertising they got for their private companies.[25]

Lt. Col. Timur J. Eads (Rt.) was a relations officer at the military contractor, Blackbird Technologies. He also worked as an analyst for Fox News. William Cowan (retired Marine) was chief executive of WVC3 Group, which won 'rebuilding' contracts in Anbar Province (Iraq). Cowan was also a Fox News analyst. Lt. Gen. Thomas McInerney (Rt.) worked for the communications network, Nortel Government Solutions, as well for Fox News. Fox analyst Capt. Charles T. Nash (Rt.) acted as a consultant for Emerging Technologies International, which specialized in getting small military firms big contracts. Gen. James Marks (Rt.) worked for McNeil Technologies as a senior executive as well as for CNN. Another analyst, Dr Jeffrey McCausland, worked for the lobbyists Buchanan Ingersoll and Rooney, which represented military contractors. Gen. Joseph

---

[23]David Barstow, 'Behind TV Analysts, Pentagon's Hidden Hand', *NYT*, 20 April 2008, http://www.nytimes.com/2008/04/20/us/20generals.html.

[24]Ibid.

[25]Ibid.

W. Ralston (Rt.) was chair of the Cohen Group (founded by ex-Secretary of Defence William Cohen) and an analyst with CBS. Barry R. McCaffrey and Wayne A. Downing were advisors to the government's Committee for the Liberation of Iraq as well as major analysts at NBC.[26]

'I felt we'd been hosed', said Kenneth Allard of NBC, who had previously taught information warfare at the National Defense University. These analysts were engaging in 'psyops on steroids'. Summarizing the use of military-linked analysts, Brent T. Krueger, a White House press aide, said: 'You could see they were taking verbatim what the secretary was saying', referring to propaganda invented by Secretary of Defense Donald Rumsfeld. '[O]r what the technical specialists were saying. And they were saying it over and over and over ... [Often w]e were able to click on every single station and every one of our folks were up there delivering our message. You'd look at them and say, "This is working"'.[27]

The Pentagon paid Omnitec Solutions to monitor the appearance of paid analysts, even in small circulation newspapers, like *The Daily Inter Lake* (Montana. Circulation: 20,000). Following media coverage concerning several visits to Iraq in 2005, an Omnitec report concluded, to give one example, that coverage 'was extremely positive'. Had it been negative, the Pentagon could have fine-tuned their message based on these algorithms and analyses. Rumsfeld himself came up with some strategies in memos obtained by the *NYT*: 'Link Iraq to Iran. Iran is the concern. If we fail in Iraq or Afghanistan, it will help Iran'. Another said: 'Focus on the Global War on Terror – not simply Iraq. The wider war – the long war'.[28]

The Bureau of Investigative Journalism discovered that, 'between 2006 and 2008 more than 40 companies were being paid for services such as TV and radio placement, video production, billboards, advertising and opinion polls'. The Bureau goes on to note that '[t]hese included US companies like Lincoln Group, Leonie Industries and SOS International as well as Iraq-based firms such as Cradle of New Civilization Media, Babylon Media and Iraqi Dream'.[29]

---

[26]Ibid.
[27]Ibid.
[28]Ibid.
[29]Crofton Black and Abigail Fielding-Smith, 'Fake News and False Flags', Bureau of Investigative Journalism, 2 October 2016, http://labs.thebureauinvestigates.com/fake-news-and-false-flags/.

# 'AL-QAEDA' IN IRAQ

The presence of al-Qaeda in Iraq was largely a lie; at the very least a gross exaggeration. It was told by the Bush administration and repeated by the media in order to justify the ongoing occupation, as the Rumsfeld memo demonstrates.

Before the invasion there was a small presence of jihadists who had fought in Afghanistan in the 1980s. They were based in the Kurdish region of Iraq. As Saddam opposed Kurdish autonomy, he may have tolerated their presence as part of an anti-Kurdish tactic. But there is no evidence that Saddam had connections with al-Qaeda.

After the US-British invasion in 2003, Sunni jihadists from Britain's ally Saudi Arabia poured across the border to fight with Iraq's Sunnis who were resisting the occupation. Because most of Saddam's loyalists in the Baath Party were Sunni, the US and Britain faced armed opposition primarily from Sunni Iraqis. They therefore worked with some Shia groups, including the Supreme Council for Shia Iraq, in anti-Sunni counterinsurgency operations, which included the use of death squads (the 'Salvador Option') and torture. Power was given to Shia politicians and the wave of alleged suicide bombings that swept the country for five years into the occupation was blamed on al-Qaeda.[30]

Al-Qaeda in Iraq was supposedly led by a Jordanian called al-Zarqawi, who supposedly corresponded with Osama bin Laden and pledged his allegiance to Iraq. However, a report discovered by Thomas E. Ricks of the *Washington Post* revealed that Zarqawi was largely a phantom menace, whose profile was inflated by US intelligence. Instead of blaming the invaders and occupiers for the carnage in Iraq, and especially their divide and rule strategy to keep Sunnis out of the government, all civilian deaths could now be blamed on Zarqawi as part of his evil plot to turn Iraqis against Iraqis and come to power in a caliphate once the infidels on all sides had slaughtered each other.[31]

---

[30] *Britain's Secret Wars*, op cit.

[31] Thomas E. Ricks, 'Military plays up role of Zarqawi', *Washington Post*, 10 April, 2006, http://www.washingtonpost.com/wp-dyn/content/article/2006/04/09/AR2006040900 890.html.

'The U.S. military is conducting a propaganda campaign to magnify the role of the leader of al-Qaeda in Iraq [Zarqawi], according to internal military documents and officers familiar with the program', says Ricks. 'The documents explicitly list the "U.S. Home Audience" as one of the targets of a broader propaganda campaign'. Col. Derek Harvey is quoted as saying: 'Our own focus on Zarqawi has enlarged his caricature, if you will – made him more important than he really is'. One document obtained by Ricks says: 'Through aggressive Strategic Communications, Abu Musab al-Zarqawi now represents: Terrorism in Iraq/Foreign Fighters in Iraq/Suffering of Iraqi People (Infrastructure Attacks)/Denial of Iraqi Aspirations'.[32]

Sure enough, Zarqawi became the new bin Laden and suddenly every atrocity in Iraq could be blamed on him. The CIA or related agencies forged a letter, supposedly between bin Laden and Zarqawi. The US claimed to have 'intercepted' the letter, which 'admits' Zarqawi's intention to cause further divisions between Sunni and Shia Iraqis. The letter was supposedly written by Zarqawi (i.e., US military intelligence) and sent to Osama bin Laden (a former CIA asset). It was supposedly obtained by the US Government in Iraq and translated by the Coalition Provisional Authority. Zarqawi (US intel) claims to be at war with infidels, including the 'Zionized' US occupiers and the indigenous Shia. Al-Qaeda, says Zarqawi, 'must ... strive to establish a foothold in this land', meaning Iraq: then one of the more secular countries in the Middle East.[33]

A unified opposition to US-British occupation by Sunni and Shia would have made a prolonged occupation impossible. Referring to America's practises in Latin America, US special forces brought what they called the Salvador Option to Iraq. They worked with Shia death squads in a divide and rule war against Sunnis, many of whom were still allied to the toppled Saddam regime. A few years into the occupation, following a spate of alleged suicide and car bombings, which killed both Sunni and Shia, so-called moderate Sunnis worked with the US and the Shia in opposition to the al-Qaeda presence, which, by 2008, had been defeated. (Al-Qaeda then regrouped as Islamic State).[34]

---

[32]Ibid.

[33]US Department of State, 'Zarqawi Letter', February 2004, https://2001-2009 .state.gov/p/nea/rls/31 694.htm.

[34]*Britain's Secret Wars*, op cit.

Rather than admit their well-documented tactic, which contributed to the massive civilian toll, the US and British militaries and thus governments, who repeat much of what their military sources tell them, claimed that the 'civil war' was in large part due to 'al-Qaeda in Iraq' sowing seeds of chaos. The 'proof' was the Zarqawi letter. But it was a forgery. As the documents obtained by Ricks reveal, the divide and rule strategy was an American one and blamed on Zarqawi. 'Al-Qaeda' mostly came from neighbouring two countries: Saudi Arabia, whose state indoctrinates children from infancy with a fascistic form of Islam (Wahhabism); and Pakistan, whose secret service (the ISI) has connections with both al-Qaeda in Pakistan and British intelligence.[35]

'Zarqawi' says in the letter to bin Laden: 'The solution that we see, and God the Exalted knows better, is for us to drag the Shi'a into the battle because this is the only way to prolong the fighting between us and the infidels'. Like the fake Issue 15 of ISIS's *Dabiq* magazine, al-Qaeda denied the authenticity of the Zarqawi letter. Even the BBC acknowledged: 'It is not possible to verify either the letter or the subsequent denial'.[36]

After the Pentagon decided to make Zarqawi the pantomime villain of Iraq, fake al-Qaeda videos shot by Pentagon contractors started appearing online.

From 2006 to December 2011, the Pentagon paid Britain's Bell Pottinger PR company (mentioned above) $500m to make fake al-Qaeda video segments from the Baghdad Camp Victory base under the command of the US Information Operations Task Force and the Joint Psychological Operations Task Force. (Financial records start from May 2007. There is no suggestion here that the company engaged in illegal activity.) The company hired 300 staff for these operations alone. Documents unearthed by the Bureau of Investigative Journalism verify the claims. Video editor Martin Wells, who worked for the company, blew the whistle.[37]

According to Wells, these so-called information operations consisted of making fake TV commercials 'portraying al Qaeda in a negative light'. Others included filming news items as if they were made by 'Arabic TV'

---

[35]Ricks, op cit. and BBC News Online, 'Al-Qaeda disowns 'fake letter'", 13 October 2005, http://news.bbc.co.uk/1/hi/world/middle_east/4339 912.stm.
[36]Ibid.
[37]Black and Fielding-Smith, op cit.

(whatever that means). Finally, low-definition videos of al Qaeda bombings were also staged and sent out to TV stations around the world. Turning to black ops, Wells also confirmed that special units would make mock
al-Qaeda videos for him to edit. The files would be burnt on CDs and
planted on targets during raids on Iraqi houses. Wells would encode the
CDs, linking them to a Google Analytics account to provide lists of IP
addresses. Thanks to the internet, uploads of the fake videos could be
watched anywhere in the world and traced to the homes of viewers. These
included Iraqis who might be sympathetic with 'al-Qaeda'.[38]

(Reviewing my book *Britain's Secret Wars*, Ian Sinclair implied that
I am a conspiracy theorist because I document the fact that 'al-Qaeda
in Iraq' was largely—but not completely—a Western intelligence fabrication. I also speculate, citing some available evidence, that many 'suicide'
attacks in Iraq could have been Western special forces remotely detonat-
ing car bombs. The Bureau's revelations about fake 'al-Qaeda' videos
only adds more evidence to my claims. Will Sinclair amend his review,
which SourceWatch quotes to discredit me?)[39]

# ISIS DOES GREEN-SCREEN

Major powers have created ISIS and continue to use the organization for
their own ends. Britain and America have trained jihadis to fight in Syria
from Jordanian bases. Some of these fanatics took their Western training
and joined ISIS. The Chechen fighter, Tarkhan Batirashvili (a.k.a. Abu
Omar al-Shishani), was trained by the US in Georgia and then went on to
fight in ISIS. Canadian agents have been caught trafficking foreign fighters
to Iraq and Syria. The Saudi state uses ISIS for ideological purposes;
to spread their extreme version of Islam (Wahhabism) across the Middle
East. To a lesser extent, Qatari leaders use ISIS for similar purposes. The
Turkish state uses ISIS strategically; as a weapon against Kurds in Iraq
and Syria. Turkey provides ISIS with logistical and targeting support and

---

[38]Ibid.

[39]Ian Sinclair, 'TJ Coles, Britain's Secret Wars – how and why the United Kingdom
sponsors conflict around the world', *Peace News*, October-November 2016, Issue
2598-2599,     https://peacenews.info/node/8510/tj-coles-britain%E2%80%99s-secret-
wars-%E2%80%93-how-and-why-united-kingdom-sponsors-conflict-around-world.

helps fund it by buying oil on the black market. For a while, Britain and America used ISIS in Syria as a weapon against the Assad government.[40]

ISIS's predecessor al-Qaeda was an amorphous movement of jihadis broadly opposed to US foreign policy. Consequently, al-Qaeda's use of social media as a propaganda and recruiting tool was limited. Given that most people in the Middle East are too poor to have regular internet and smart phone access, al-Qaeda's outreach was limited. ISIS's outreach is also limited regionally for the same reason. However, most of their members are foreign, stretching from Saudi Arabia to Chechnya. Therefore, ISIS's multilingual propaganda is aimed at a world audience of Muslims, many of whom feel disrespected in their home countries and join ISIS in part for prestige. Many Iraqis who join ISIS, however, do so for cash, the way they did ten years earlier when joining al-Qaeda in Iraq.[41]

Beheadings and other outrages are a crucial element of ISIS's propaganda.

Every year, Western armed forces use missiles to murder alleged terrorists and militants. These often result in civilian deaths, as the armed forces and politicians who vote for war freely acknowledge. Deaths and injuries from Western Hellfire and other missiles fired from Predator and other drones and aircraft include blowing people into tiny pieces and decapitating, dismembering, amputating and disembowelling innocent men, women and children. Governments go to great lengths to prevent these horrific images (accessible online) from reaching domestic audiences. The last time such an image was shown to the public was in 2003, when 12-year-old Ali Abbas was featured on the front pages with his arms amputated and his chest lacerated by US bombs. This is the one and only time the British public got a glimpse of the reality of bombing since the Blitz. Other atrocity images were either attacks on British soldiers (as in coverage of the Falklands War 1982) or images of selected enemies attacking propagandized targets (like Assad's alleged chemical attacks in Syria in 2013).[42]

For shielded Westerners, beheadings are particularly offensive. Sam Harris in *The End of Faith* notes that Westerners feel more comfortable

---

[40] *Britain's Secret Wars*, op cit.

[41] Ibid.

[42] For details about Abbas's torture, see the website of retired trauma surgeon, Dr David Halpin, http://dhalpin.infoaction.org.uk.

when bombs are dropped because the use of machinery distances one's sense of moral culpability.[43] Right next door to Iraq in Saudi Arabia, the state beheads, crucifies and amputates for such crimes as apostasy and homosexuality. But they, the Saudis, are allies. On the other side, Free Syrian Army fighters have beheaded Christians. But again they are allies. On the other side of the world, Colombia and Mexican gangs cut people up with chainsaws, but many are allied to politicians and paramilitary forces who receive support from the West; so it's fine.

In Iraq, beheadings became a propaganda weapon in 2004, when the Zarqawi network (which as we learned above was largely an intelligence fabrication) started beheading hostages. This offended Western audiences who were largely shielded from the similar effects of America's Shock and Awe bombing. The beheadings made certain Iraqis look barbaric and reinforced the civilized 'us' versus medieval 'them' dialectic.

In 2001, a young man called Nick Berg was riding a bus to a University Camp in West Chester, Oklahoma. On that bus, a man who later turned out to be an alleged terrorist linked to al-Qaeda, Zacarias Moussaoui, borrowed Berg's laptop. Berg travelled to Iraq after the invasion in 2003 on business matters to help install a radio tower. In March 2004 in an effort to return home, Berg was detained in Mosul and turned over to US officials, as confirmed (and later denied) by the US consul. A month later, he was supposedly released and travelled to Baghdad. A month later, he was murdered and left on a roadside.[44]

A few days later, video emerged on the website of the extremist group, Muntada al-Ansar. The video depicts five masked jihadis, one of whom is supposedly Zarqawi. Analysts cited by journalist Nick Davies ask why Zarqawi is wearing a mask. They also point to the fact that the alleged Zarqawi (who was said to be Jordanian) does not have a Jordanian accent in the video.

In 2004, journalist Ritt Goldstein interviewed doctors John Simpson of the Royal Australasian College of Surgeons and Jon Nordby, Fellow of the American Board of Medicolegal Death Investigators. Both thought it 'highly probable that Berg had died some time prior to his decapitation.

[43]Sam Harris, *The End of Faith* (2004, Free Press).

[44]CNN, 'Berg's encounter with 'terrorist' revealed', 13 May 2004, http://www.cnn.com/2004/US/Northeast/05/13/berg.encounter/.

A factor in this was an apparent lack of the "massive" arterial bleeding such an act initiates'. Referring to Berg's total lack of reaction to being pulled in preparation for the decapitation, Simpson said: 'The way that they pulled him over, they could have used a dummy at that point'. That was 'al-Qaeda'.[45]

ISIS uses beheadings to similar effect.

In August 2014, Britain's *Telegraph* newspaper reported that 'a study of the four-minute 40-second clip' of US journalist James Foley's apparent beheading by IS members was 'carried out by an international forensic science company which has worked for police forces across Britain'. Experts from the team 'suggested camera trickery and slick post-production techniques appear to have been used', according to the article. 'A forensic analyst told *The Times* that no blood can be seen, even though the knife is drawn across the neck area at least six times ... One expert commissioned to examine the footage was reported as saying: "I think it has been staged. My feeling is that the execution may have happened after the camera was stopped"'.[46]

The UK Metropolitan Police cautioned that it would be 'illegal' to watch the video, i.e., to verify the evidence of that alleged beheading. The Met issued the following statement: 'The MPS Counter Terrorism Command (SO15) is investigating the contents of the video that was posted online in relation to the alleged murder of James Foley. We would like to remind the public that viewing, downloading or disseminating extremist material within the UK may constitute an offence under Terrorism legislation'.[47]

In film and television, producers will include a backdrop in order to convince viewers that action is taking place at a particular location, when in fact it is taking place in a studio. News also uses backdrops for illustrative purposes. For instance, if a correspondent or interviewee is in

[45]Ritt Goldstein, 'Berg beheading: No way, say medical experts', *Asia Times*, 22 May, 2004, http://www.atimes.com/atimes/Middle_East/FE22Ak03.html.

[46]Bill Gardner, 'Foley murder video 'May have been staged'', *Telegraph*, 25 August, 2014, http://www.telegraph.co.uk/journalists/bill-gardner/11054 488/Foley-murder-video-may-have-been-staged.html.

[47]PIPR.co.uk, 'Foley Beheading Fake, Say Experts: Verifying Evidence a Crime, Say Police', 3 September 2014, http://www.pipr.co.uk/all/foley-beheading-fake-say-experts-verifying-evidence-a-crime-say-police/.

London, Big Ben might be seen in the background of the interview. In reality, they have been filmed in a studio with a green or blue screen behind them. In post-production or sometimes live feeding, the given image (e.g., of Big Ben) will be inserted into the green or blue. To the viewer, the green or blue background is invisible and the digitally-inserted backdrop is visible.[48]

Veryan Khan is editorial director of the Terrorism Research and Analysis Consortium in the US. Khan says: 'The Islamic State has been revolutionary in using the green screen technique'. One reason, says Khan, is that IS knows that the entire region is under surveillance from drones and real-time satellites and that any mass atrocity, such as large-scale beheadings and drownings, will be seen and possibly pre-empted. Ergo, the group commits atrocities in studios and selects digital locations when broadcasting the finished product. 'The Islamic State's manipulation of their high-production videos has become commonplace'.[49]

In 2015, ISIS marched 21 Coptic Christians along Sirte beach in Libya, made them kneel before the camera and beheaded them. The video was made like a Hollywood movie. Dressed head to toe in black, the executioners towered above their victims, each dressed in orange, Guantanamo-style jumpsuits. The ISIS cameramen (presumably they were men) had cranes for overhead shots and dollies for right-to-left camera movements. There were titles and sound effects. The Christians prayed silently in close-up. After the ISIS commander (speaking with a North American tinge) delivered his anti-Western speech, the victims were laid head to sand and decapitated. The video, complete with music soundtrack, concludes with an image of 'crusader' blood washing into the sea. Khan says the blood is CGI.[50]

Hollywood film director, Professor Mary Lambert, was hired by Fox to analyse the footage. She agrees with Khan: that ISIS is faking footage. Specifically referring to the alleged beheadings of Coptic Christians on

---

[48] For example, Jeff Foster, *The Green Screen: Real-World Production Techniques* (2014, CRC Press).

[49] Malia Zimmerman, "ISIS' army of 7-footers? Experts say video of Copt beheadings manipulated', Fox News, 21 February 2015, http://www.foxnews.com/world/2015/02/21/isis-army-7-footers-experts-say-video-copt-beheadings-manipulated.html.

[50] Quoted in ibid.

Sirte beach, Libya. 'The close-ups of Jihadists on the beach are most likely green screen', says Lambert. She also reckons that there are no 'more than six men on the beach'. They are stretched with a computer to look seven feet tall compared to their much shorter Christian counterparts and the ISIS fighters are rotoscoped: they are removed from the video, digitally altered (including doubled to make them look more numerous) and inserted back into the video.[51]

Khan also reckons that the final beheading in the beach video is fake. There is no suggestion that the victim is fake or that the victim is still alive, but rather that the death was visualized in ways that make it sensational for the so-called propaganda of the deed. Khan says: 'Not only did it lack the correct blood pulsation for decapitation, but seems to have had the blood 'faked' with cornstarch'.[52]

In 2015, ISIS beheaded two Japanese hostages, Kenji Goto Jogo and Haruna Yukawa. The murders were videoed and broadcast on social media. Fox's Catherine Herridge said that 'the tape itself is drawing new scrutiny from outside analysts who believe it was altered and perhaps filmed in a studio where the background could be changed using ... a green screen'. Herridge goes on to note that '[t]hese analysts point to apparent discrepancies, such as the jumpsuit of one of the hostages flutters in the breeze but no wind is actually heard on the soundtrack'. Herridge concludes that 'ISIS has a very deep media production arm and control of a dozen [or] half-a-dozen TV stations in Iraq and Syria ... The US intelligence community believes all of these videos ... were all shot near the stronghold Raqqa, in Syria'.[53]

But Metabunk.org (run by an ex-computer game developer, Mick West) reckons it is an authentic video. Metabunk is the kind of website complicating the distinction between truth and lies in the internet age. Using re-enactments, West says the shadows in the video are not anomalous. Added to which, the ISIS video is shot from two angles, minimizing the chance that green-screen was used. West also uses his design skills to build a computer model recreating the beheadings in order to demonstrate the

---

[51] Ibid.

[52] Ibid.

[53] Fox News uploaded to YouTube by DAHBOO777, 'BOOM! Expert on Fox Admits ISIS Video is Fake, Using Green Screen and Teleprompter', YouTube, 23 January 2015, https://www.youtube.com/watch?v=_M5BSCMVhRQ.

authenticity of the image concerning where light falls in the frame.[54]

In 2015, a hacker group called CyberBerkut released a video purporting to show non-Muslims filming a beheading in a studio. The film is in long-shot, so details are not clear. It may or may not be attempting to replicate Foley and his murder. The filmmakers (lighting crew, cameramen (they all look like men) and director) are clearly Western. There is no sound and the video lasts for a few minutes. It is filmed in front of a green screen. The implication is that the Foley or related beheading videos are staged by Western intelligence agencies using actors.[55]

Metabunk's analysis shows that the CyberBerkut-'released' video is not Foley's real or alleged execution because 1) the lighting is different, 2) the actions don't quite match, 3) the green-screen is too dark to be conventional green-screen, and 4) the executioner is too tall. Whether or not the video 'reveals' the alleged faking of the Foley video is secondary to the fact that the 'leak' supposedly came from Russian hackers. Ergo, it is likely that if the video did come from Russia, it is Russia's propaganda efforts to make it look as though the US is faking ISIS beheading videos. This is complicated by the fact that we now know that Bell Pottinger did indeed fake al-Qaeda videos for the Pentagon, which paid handsomely. Is it then so far-fetched that some PR firm or in-house psyops unit is faking ISIS videos? We know from the Issue 15 *Dabiq* incident (above) that certain agencies are faking ISIS publications.[56]

## CONCLUSION

Only in the USA was the fake news about Iraq in 2002/03 effective in persuading the public; most Americans backed the invasion, initially. But the fake news—and selective morality—about ISIS has been more effective, with a plurality of Britons supporting drone strikes against ISIS, having previously opposed war. The supposed unique barbarity of ISIS

---

[54]Mick West, 'Debunked: The latest ISIS video of two Japanese men is a fake, shadows wrong [Perspective]', Metabunk.org, 22 January 2015, https://www.metabunk.org/debunked-the-latest-isis-video-of-two-japanese-men-is-a-fake-shadows-wrong-perspective.t5614/.

[55]Ibid.

[56]Ibid.

was a stronger motive for supporting war among voters in 2014 than the 'security' interests in taking out Saddam in 2003.

# Chapter 7

# Libya: 'The British people are very humane'

*This chapter is based on an article first published in 2012 by Axis of Logic. I was nominated for the Martha Gellhorn Prize in 2013 for a series in which the article was included. It was written a year after the illegal US-British-French bombing of Libya in 2011. The war was based on one lie after another. Using open sources, many of which are government documents and publications by business-funded think tanks, this chapter exposes the fake mainstream-government news from February 2011 to October 2011.*

As I document in *Britain's Secret Wars* (2016, Clairview Books):

In October 2010, Britain organized a large number of armed, Islamic terrorists as a proxy to overthrow their former and ephemeral ally, Muammar Gaddafi; the dictator of Libya. Gaddafi sat on the biggest oil reserves in Africa. The British and American publics knew nothing about the secret organization of anti-Gaddafi forces because the entire media machine, with the sole exception of two articles in the *Daily Mail*, kept it hidden. The *Daily Mail* articles were published after the fact. One of them was actually written about a separate subject, namely the botched British SAS evacuation mission, which turned out to be cover for making contact with anti-Gaddafi terrorists.[1]

When protests erupted across the Middle East and North Africa, dictators—including Gaddafi—used force to quell them. But what the media were late reporting was that not all the demonstrators were peaceful. By March 2011, it was clear that many were armed. Many dictators, including Assad of Syria and Gaddafi, were using force to protect themselves from armed insurrection portrayed in the Western media as entirely peaceful.[2]

---

[1] *Britain's Secret Wars*, op cit.
[2] Ibid.

Mainstream media spread the Cameron government's fake news about Libya. In reality: Britain helped murder 30,000 people, deprive tens of thousands of their homes, contribute to what became a refugee crisis, trigger a real (as opposed to rhetorical) ethnic cleansing (of black Libyans by allied terrorists) and cause injury to tens of thousands of people. The British House of Commons Foreign Affairs Committee report (2016) concludes:

> [Cameron's decision to bomb] was not informed by accurate intelligence. In particular, the Government failed to identify that the threat to civilians was overstated and that the rebels included a significant Islamist element. By the summer of 2011, the limited intervention to protect civilians had drifted into an opportunist policy of regime change. That policy was not underpinned by a strategy to support and shape post-Gaddafi Libya. The result was political and economic collapse, inter-militia and inter-tribal warfare, humanitarian and migrant crises, widespread human rights violations, the spread of Gaddafi regime weapons across the region and the growth of ISIL in North Africa.[3]

When he was an MP, Michael Fallon voted for the invasion of Iraq and later, as Defence Secretary, confirmed that Saddam Hussein did not have WMD, that the Blair government had deceived him. However, that WMD pretext was irrelevant because Fallon then went on to say he'd have voted for invading Iraq anyway because Saddam was a dictator. Turning to Libya, BBC presenter Andrew Marr then quoted the Foreign Affairs Committee above report, but, typical of the BBC, omitted the crucial line about false intelligence and then-PM Cameron's culpability. Unlike his honesty (and utter immorality) over Iraq, Fallon went on to repeat the lie about averting a 'humanitarian catastrophe in Benghazi, where an entire city was going to be wiped out'. The lie was unchallenged by Marr. (Notice also how the phrase 'ethnic cleansing' used widely at the time changed in the following years to 'humanitarian crisis', etc.)[4]

---

[3]House of Commons Foreign Affairs Committee, 'Libya: Examination of intervention and collapse and the UK's future policy options', Third Report of Session 2016–17, HC 119, 6 September 2016.

[4]BBC uploaded by I Am Incorrigible, 'GE2017: Emily Thornberry v Michael Fallon (and the Syrian ambush)', YouTube, 14 May 2017, https://www.youtube.com/watch?v=1ccEKqGNKrI.

Turning to 2011, let's look at some of the lies told at the time by the mainstream media and how establishment sources quietly acknowledged that the opposite was true:

## LIE #1

The anti-Gaddafi demonstrations in February, 2011, were peaceful. (This paints a picture of 'good' demonstrators versus 'evil' Gaddafi.)

## FACT

Many of the demonstrators, who were primarily based in Benghazi, were part of the MI6-sponsored armed coup. (In fact, one of the jihadis, Ramadan Abedi, has historic links to MI6 when he battled Gaddafi in the 1990s. His son, Salman, allegedly blew up the Manchester Arena in May 2017, shortly before the General Election, killing 22 people, including 9 children.)[5]

Press reports revealed that MI6 agents had been training Gaddafi's opposition since late 2010. Added to which, the Elite UK Forces website acknowledged that Britain was supplying the anti-Gaddafi rebels with weapons in the early phases of the uprising. America's AFRICOM Commander, General Carter Ham, noted on 4 March that 'the government of Libya continued its more than two-week campaign of attacking demonstrators *and rebel groups*' (emphasis added). This was not clarified in media reports.[6]

The Statoil–, Talisman Energy–, Shell–sponsored International Crisis Group (ICG) noted that the opposing Transitional National Council 'was headquartered in the eastern city of Benghazi, a traditional base of anti-regime activity that provided army defectors a relatively secure area of operations'. The ICG quoted one Libyan as saying that 'a big misconception is that the Libyan uprising was organised in the east; in fact, the online protest calls originated from Libyans abroad, in Switzerland and the United Kingdom'.[7]

---

[5] John Pilger, 'What did the Prime Minister know?' in T.J. Coles (ed.) *Voices for Peace* (2017, Clairview Books).

[6] Carter Ham, AFRICOM, 5 March 2011, https://web.archive.org/web/20121001231 440/ http://www.africom.mil/getArticle.asp?art=6134&lang=0.

[7] International Crisis Group, 'Popular Protest in North Africa and the Middle East

Hillary Clinton's State Department reported a year before the coup that its Middle East Partnership Initiative, which is part of the Broader Middle East and North Africa Initiative, trained Gaddafi's opponents in the use of the internet. One of the ten Libyan dissidents who received training commented: 'This conference has opened my mind to all of the tools available, which I will use to promote various projects and engage different audiences'.[8]

This way, revolution seems indigenous, not a covert method of external regime change. (LIE #8, below, reveals that America's newfound 'reluctance' to engage in international affairs is part of its contemporary propaganda strategy targeted at the war-weary American public.)

The British naval commodore Steven Jermy said that the Libyan Army and Police Force 'were forced from Benghazi by 18 February [2011]' by the rebels. Imagine if Iranian intelligence had been arming and training the Occupy London demonstrators in 2010 with instructions to overthrow the unelected Cameron–Clegg regime, and had driven the Metropolitan Police force out of London, all the while establishing an alternative government. Most Britons would expect the Army to be brought in to quell the insurrection. Yet, when the British secret services do exactly the same in Libya, the Gaddafi regime is expected to sit back quietly and wait to be overthrown.[9]

## LIE #2

Gaddafi's air force bombed civilians. (This is a reflexive appeal to the emotions of Western media audiences, designed to get them to support military intervention.)

---

(V): Making Sense of Libya', Crisis Group Middle East/North Africa Report N°107, 6 June 2011, Brussels: ICG, https://web.archive.org/web/20110711043903/https://www.crisisgroup.org/~/media/Files/Middle%20East%20North%20Africa/North%20Africa/107%20-%20Popular%20Protest%20in%20North%20Africa%20and%20the%20Middle%20East%20V%20-%20Making%20Sense%20of%20Libya.pdf.

[8]Middle East Partnership Initiative (US State Department), 'MEPI Highlights North African Activists Use New Media Technology to Engage Citizens', https://web.archive.org/web/20110202081357/https://mepi.state.gov/mh_05032010a.html.

[9]House of Commons Defence Committee, 'Operations in Libya', Ninth Report of Session 2010–12, Volume II, 8 February 2012, Stationary Office.

## FACT

The oil company–sponsored ICG reported that 'there are grounds for questioning the more sensational reports that the regime was using its air force to slaughter demonstrators'. On 8 March 2011, the US Ambassador to NATO—and 'liberal interventionist'—Ivo Daalder informed the press that, 'to date, the overall air activity has not been the deciding factor in the ongoing unrest'.[10]

In a pro–No Fly Zone paper published weeks before the NATO bombing, Britain's Royal United Services Institute acknowledged 'Libya's obsolete air defence systems and its depleted air force' and 'an unprofessional military, shorn of many of its units'. At the commencement of the NATO bombing, the House of Commons Library acknowledged that 'the Libyan air force ... consist[s] mainly of ageing Soviet-era MiG and Sukhoi fast jet aircraft, a small number of Mirage F1s and 35 attack helicopters'. The report concluded that 'Many of those aircraft are thought to be non-operational or currently in store'.[11]

## LIE #3

Libyans asked for intervention. (By omitting all of the vested business and energy interests that the Western powers have in Libya, the media portrayed the bombing as a selfless act, driven by the request of helpless civilians to be saved from imminent slaughter. In the minds of the Western publics, this absolved their governments of guilt and provided a legal-moral veneer to the bombing.)

## FACT

The media reports quoting Libyans calling for military intervention came mainly from Benghazi—the very place where the Western-backed Transitional National Council were orchestrating an armed uprising. Septem-

---

[10]ICG, 'Popular Protest...', op cit. Julian Borger, 'Nato weighs Libya no-fly zone options', *Guardian*, 8 March 2011.

[11]Shashank Joshi, 'Arguments for a No Fly Zone over Libya', Royal United Service Institute, Claire Taylor and Ben Smith, 'Establishment of a Military No-Fly Zone over Libya', House of Commons Defence Library, Standard note SN/IA/5909, 21 March, 2011.

ber-October 2010 (i.e., before the NATO bombing) Gallup polls found that 50% of Libyans in Tripoli were 'satisfied' with 'Freedom in your life', compared to 29% who were not. Benghazi was more evenly split, but even there little indicates that most people sought regime change (thus armed intervention): 34% of Benghazis were 'satisfied', compared to 33% who were not. On the basis of the polls, it would appear that the Western powers decided to continue basing the opponents in Benghazi because that is where Libyans were less satisfied with Gaddafi.[12]

The factual reports of a few newspapers were swamped by the relentless coverage of pro-war networks and newspapers. Although they were in the minority, sources as diverse as Al-Arabiya, *Eurasia Review*, and the *Guardian* reported that the majority of Libyans did *not* want Western intervention, and contrary reports failed to acknowledge that the pro-interventionist calls were coming largely from Benghazi (almost certainly from the Western proxy militias).[13]

In her Chatham House speech attended by anti-Gaddafi rebels and Libyan British Business Council (LBBC) delegates, Channel Four's Lindsey Hilsum, for instance, admitted to reporting primarily from Benghazi. This exemplifies the incestuous nature of the establishment and the media.[14]

## LIE #4

Gaddafi was about to commit an 'ethnic cleansing' or 'genocide' in Benghazi. (In other words, Gaddafi was going to crush the Western-backed uprising, so the Western powers had to convince their domestic publics to support armed intervention in order to save their proxies. In doing so,

---

[12] Julie Ray, 'Ahead of Protests, Many Libyans Discontent With Freedom, Jobs', Gallup, 25 February 2011.

[13] *Guardian*, 'Libya is united in popular revolution – please don't intervene', 1 March 2011. *Eurasia Review*, 'Libyans Want The World To Keep Out', 9 March 2011. Al-Arabiya, 'Libya rebels form council, oppose foreign intervention', 27 February 2011.

[14] Alistair Burt (member of the LBBC), Sir Richard Dalton (member of the LBBC), Lindsey Hilsum, Ashur Al-Shamis, and Claire Spencer, 'Libya: Prospects and Challenges', Chatham House, 8 June 2011. Hilsum: 'I spent about six weeks in Benghazi. I got to Tubruq on 23 February – that was just under a week after the uprising – athen [sic] spent that time in Benghazi, Ajdabiya and along that shifting frontline around Brega and Ra's Lanuf'.

they had to pretend that the armed rebels were not only civilians, but civilians who represented the majority of opinion in Libya. Using the Iran example above, imagine that Iran sat on the UN Security Council and imagine that if the British Army was on its way to London to quell the insurrection Iran accused the Cameron–Clegg regime of planning an 'ethnic cleansing'. In doing so, it passed a UN Resolution calling for a No Fly Zone over Britain to prevent the British Army from quelling the armed rebellion.)

## FACT

As noted, the ICG reported that 'there are grounds for questioning the more sensational reports that the regime was using its air force', adding: 'let alone engaging in anything remotely warranting use of the term "genocide"'. The *Chicago Tribune*'s Steve Chapman noted in *Foreign Policy*:

> Obama implied that, absent our intervention, Gadhafi might have killed nearly 700,000 people, putting it in a class with the 1994 genocide in Rwanda. White House adviser Dennis Ross was only slightly less alarmist when he reportedly cited "the real or imminent possibility that up to a 100,000 people could be massacred." But these are outlandish scenarios that go beyond any reasonable interpretation of Gadhafi's words. He said, "We will have no mercy on them" – but by "them," he plainly was referring to armed rebels ("traitors") who stand and fight, not all the city's inhabitants. "We have left the way open to them," he said. "Escape. Let those who escape go forever."

Chapman continued:

> [Gaddafi] pledged that "whoever hands over his weapons, stays at home without any weapons, whatever he did previously, he will be pardoned, protected["]. ... I emailed the White House press office several times asking for concrete evidence of the danger, based on any information the administration may have. But a spokesman declined to comment. That's a surprising omission, given that a looming holocaust was the centerpiece of the president's case for war.[15]

---

[15]Steve Chapman, 'Did Obama avert a bloodbath in Libya? Panicking over a dubious threat', *Foreign Policy* (also *Chicago Tribune*), 3 April 2011.

It is interesting that Gaddafi 'left the way open' to the rebels: when Anglo-American troops bombed Fallujah, Iraq, in 2004 with some form of nuclear weapon, leaving thousands of children severely deformed to this day with virtually no medical care, they sealed it off (in violation of the Geneva Conventions), preventing women and children from leaving.[16]

Returning to Gaddafi's phantom 'ethnic cleansing', even University of Texas academic, Alan J. Kuperman, who openly supports aggression against Iran, in which 'there is no doubt some people will die', had to admit that:

> Gadhafi directed this threat only at rebels to persuade them to flee. Despite ubiquitous cellphone cameras, there are no images of genocidal violence, a claim that smacks of rebel propaganda. ...
>
> Indeed, Libya's rebels started the war [read: Euro-American allied powers 'started the war' via their proxies—TC] knowing that they could not win on their own, and that their attacks would provoke harm against civilians.[17]

In contrast, Amnesty, Human Rights Watch and the UN reported that the Western-backed rebels committed *actual* ethnic cleansing against Sub-Saharan Africans in Libya, driving out the entire 30,000 residents of Tawargha, killing women and children, burning down their homes and barring them from returning (documented below).[18]

## LIE #5

Gaddafi employed mercenaries. (Like the allegations concerning Gaddafi using his air force, and the reports about an impending 'ethnic cleansing',

---

[16]Courageously, Oxfam stayed in the city: Oxfam, 'Rising to the Humanitarian Challenge in Iraq', July 2007, Briefing Paper, Oxfam. On the use of nuclear weapons, the US-UK governments have not admitted this, but there were higher levels of radiation found in Fallujah than in Hiroshima: Chris Busby et al., 'Cancer, Infant Mortality and Birth Sex-Ratio in Fallujah, Iraq 2005–2009', *International Journal of Environmental Research and Public Health*, 6 July 2010 and Patrick Cockburn, 'Toxic Legacy of US Assault on Fallujah 'Worse Than Hiroshima'', *Independent*, 24 July 2010.

[17]RT, 'CrossTalk on Iran: Strike 3 – US out!', YouTube, 22 September 2010, https://www.youtube.com/watch?v=WCPaKTb0MIQ. Alan J. Kuperman, '5 things the U.S. should consider in Libya', *USA Today*, 22 March, 2011.

[18]For the shocking details and sources, see my 'One year on. Why we attacked Libya', Axis of Logic, 28 March 2012.

these media rumours were designed to further demonize the Colonel, and by association garner support for the use of force.)

## FACT

The UN Human Rights Commission reported that:

> an organised group of Sudanese fighters were brought in by the Qadhafi government specifically to fight the thuwar [anti-Gaddafi rebels]. The Commission has not found that these fighters were promised or paid material compensation substantially in excess of that promised or paid to local Qadhafi forces, a requirement for these individuals or groups to fall within the definition of a "mercenary" under the United Nations Convention against Mercenaries or under Organization of African Unity (OAU) Convention on Mercenarism. The Commission also determined that there were fighters within the Qadhafi forces who, though of foreign descent, were born in Libya or resident there. They would also fall outside the definition of mercenaries.[19]

It is also worth remembering that when Britain and America employ mercenaries, the media describe them as 'private security contractors'.

In March 2011, Amnesty reported no evidence of the use of mercenaries by Gaddafi. In 2012, Amnesty reported on the presence of 'suspected foreign "mercenaries" – most of whom were in fact migrant workers'.[20]

By accusing black Libyans of being mercenaries for the sole purpose of demonizing Gaddafi in support of the bombing, Western media were complicit in the UK-backed ethnic cleansing, demonizing thereby dehumanizing black Libyans in the eyes of Westerners, as well as contributing to the racist positions of the anti-Gaddafi rebels. Amnesty reported: 'Sub-Saharan Africans and black Libyans remain particularly vulnerable to arbitrary arrest on account of their skin colour and the belief that al-Gaddafi forces used African mercenaries'.[21]

---

[19] Human Rights Council (UN), 'Report of the International Commission of Inquiry on Libya', 8 March 2012, A/HRC/19/68 Advance Unedited Version, http://www.ohchr.org/Documents/HRBodies/HRCouncil/RegularSession/Session19/A.HRC.19.68.pdf.

[20] Amnesty International, 'Q&A', 21 March 2011.

[21] Amnesty International, 'Militias threaten hopes for New Libya', Index: MDE 19/002/2012, February 2012. Amnesty International, 'Detention Abuses Staining the New Libya', Index: MDE 19/036/2011, October 2011.

What was not reported is the fact that the Olive Group, a UK mercenary firm, was contracted to protect the Western businesspeople who have
descended upon Libya. One of the most fervent pro-war politicians was
the British MP, Malcolm Rifkind (former Defence Sec.), who, as noted
below, tacitly acknowledged that protecting civilians was not the UK's
concern. Rifkind is also the Executive Chairman of ArmorGroup, another
mercenary firm, which, along with Aegis, occupied Iraq (with 20,000 mercenaries) in order to guard the Department for International Development
personnel who were privatizing Iraq's businesses and resources.[22]

## LIE #6

The Arab League was first to call for armed 'intervention'. (A racist
propaganda technique that made it appear to non-Arab Westerners that
the very dictators whom the Western powers have backed for decades
suddenly expressed concern for Libyan civilians, and that they were the
real drivers of the war, asking the Western powers to help their 'fellow
Arabs'. Just like Lie #3, the technique was designed to give Western allied
powers a veneer of 'moral legitimacy' and to dissuade Western publics
from thinking that the invasion was a war of imperialism.)

## FACT

Christian Tuner, Middle East and North Africa Director of the UK Foreign
Office, confirmed that '12 March [2011] is the key moment at which the
Arab League was calling for that no-fly zone to be implemented and, in
terms of the diplomatic co-ordination [between Allied nations] ... that was
what led to a strong call for action which the League was supporting'.[23]

   Indeed, if one checks the chronology of reporting, British PM David
Cameron's speechwriters announced that Britain was considering imposing a No Fly Zone as early as 28 February 2011, not long after Hillary
Clinton's speechwriters and the rebels announced that they would not
negotiate with Gaddafi.[24]

---

[22]Tuner, 'Operations in Libya', op cit., p. EV 15.

[23]Tuner, 'Operations in Libya', op cit., p. EV 15.

[24]Alex Stevenson, 'UK military prepares for Libyan no-fly zone', Politics.co.uk, 28 February 2011, politics.co.uk, http://www.politics.co.uk/news/2011/2/28/uk-military-pre-

## LIE #7

The anti-Gaddafi militias, represented by the Transitional National Council (NTC), were popular and represented the majority of opinion in Libya. (This thickens the veneer of 'moral legitimacy'.)

## FACT

The oil company-funded International Crisis Group noted that:

> the NTC has had to struggle with internal divisions, a credibility deficit and questions surrounding its effectiveness ...
>
> Formation of a new cabinet was supposed to curb militia-on-militia violence as well as defiance of the National Army; it has done nothing of the kind. Instead, violence in the capital if anything has escalated, with armed clashes occurring almost nightly ...
>
> Many Libyans felt that a disproportionate number of committee members were from eastern regions which were the first to escape regime control ... [R]esponding to criticism, the NTC announced that it would "systematise representation" on the basis of population and area size, though this initiative seems never to have fully materialised.[25]

A Chatham paper, commenting on a debate attended by rebels and Western businesspeople, conceded that 'participants disagreed over the degree of support for the TNC in the streets of Benghazi'.[26]

Under the Orwellian appellation Stabilisation Response Team (read: occupation force), the UK sent a coterie of taxpayer-funded propagandists to support the TNC, which indicates the extent of the TNC's popularity among Libyans. The report reads:

> Continuing to develop communications and ensuring transparent decision-making can help contribute to maintaining and deepening understanding and acceptance of the NTC. ... Strong communications

pares-for-libyan-no-fly-zone.

[25]International Crisis Group, 'Holding Libya Together: Security Challenges After Qadhafi', Middle East/North Africa Report No. 115, 14 December, 2011, https://web. archive.org/web/*/https://www.crisisgroup.org/~/media/Files/Middle%20East%20N orth%20Africa/North%20Africa/115%20Holding%20Libya%20Together%20–%20Sec urity%20Challenges%20after%20Qadhafi.pdf.

[26]Chatham House, 'Libya's Future: Towards Transition', May 2011.

are critical to maintaining popular support for the NTC and to explain what is already being done. Delivering concrete action, and being seen to do so, is also important in meeting already high expectations of the Libyan people and in sustaining their support.[27]

The document goes on to offer suggestions on how to deceive the Libyan public.

## LIE #8

The Obama regime were reluctant to 'intervene'. (This technique is designed to portray the US as a 'reluctant interventionist' in order to deny the fact that its primary foreign policy objective is accessing resources and imposing favourable climates for business, as well as Presidential posturing on the side of a war-weary public.)

## FACT

In 1997, the Pentagon committed the United States to achieving Full Spectrum Dominance of land, sea, air, space and information by the year 2020, 'to close the ever-widening gap between diminishing resources and increasing military commitments'. With the largest known oil reserves in Africa, Libya, along with Nigeria, Iraq, Iran and the Caspian, is key to Full Spectrum Dominance. Indeed, numerous establishment reports—e.g., from Anthony Cordesman, the European Council on Foreign Relations— noted the presence of dozens of international, mainly US, energy companies in Libya dating back to 2004, after Gaddafi agreed and then failed to economically liberalize the country.[28]

Oxford specialist, Professor M.J. Williams, testified to the British Parliamentary Committee:

---

[27]International Stabilisation Response Team, 'Libya', 20 May-30 June 2011, https://www .gov.uk/government/uploads/system/uploads/attachment_data/file/67 470/libya-isr t-June2011.pdf.

[28]US Space Command, 'Vision for 2020', February 1997. Anthony H. Cordesman, 'Libya: Three possible outcomes and the role of governance, money, gas, and oil', Center for Strategic and International Studies, 22 March 2011 and Daniel Korski, 'What Europe needs to do on Libya', European Council on Foreign Relations, 25 February 2011.

On the surface it looked as if the US was largely not engaged in the operation, the reality is quite different. The plan was to pursue a "covert intervention" strategy rather than an overt one. The US was involved in all planning and deliberations regarding the campaign for the duration of the operation. This reflects a new US approach to international affairs, one that will remain the de facto course under the Obama Administration and may reflect a wider change due to mounting domestic pressure from the US electorate to save money by [sic] cutting back on foreign adventures. ... The reality is that this war, just like the wars in Iraq, Afghanistan and Kosovo, was largely an American operation.[29]

UK Armed Forces Minister, Nick Harvey, wrote:

The majority of effective strike power has been provided by the aircraft carrier Charles de Gaulle, the United States Marine Corps Harriers (until withdrawn for political reasons by President Obama—too visible involvement for the American public to stomach) and, quietly and with no fanfare, by United States naval and air force aircraft (3,475 sorties—approximately 1/3rd of the total).[30]

# LIE #9

NATO's role in Libya was humanitarian intervention.

# FACT

NATO's self-appointed mission is energy 'security' (a.k.a. theft). In 2007, NATO's then-Secretary-General, Jaap de Hoop Scheffer, informed a NATO meeting that:

it was the oil companies which already quite some time ago approached NATO – not exclusively NATO, also the European Union – to see how these international organizations could be helpful ...

I can tell you that the present strategic concept of NATO, of dating back, as you know, to 1999, is already talking about the free

---

[29] House of Commons Defence Committee, 'Operations in Libya', Ninth Report of Session 2010–12, Volume II, 8 February 2012, London: Stationary Office.
[30] Ibid.

flow of energy ... Let's be glad that the gas is flowing again [referring to Kosovo].[31]

Kosovo makes for an interesting comparison. British House of Commons Library papers published at the commencement of NATO's bombing in 1999 acknowledged that, like Gaddafi in more recent years, Serbia's Milošević was not carrying out an ethnic cleansing of Kosovar Albanians, that 2,000 people on both sides had been killed in the civil war—not ethnic cleansing—from 1998–99, and that the Finnish forensic team could find no evidence to prove who committed the Račak massacre.[32]

Added to which, the mercenary construction company Kellogg, Brown & Root was the first to arrive in Kosovo in 1998 to construct Camp Bondsteel—the world's biggest US military base—right on the Former Yugoslavia's main energy pipeline junction.[33]

Returning to NATO's role in energy 'security', its website explained, shortly after the bombing:

> NATO looks to protect critical energy infrastructures, transit areas and lines, while cooperating with partners and other organisations involved with energy security ...
>
> NATO leaders recognize that the disruption of the flow of vital resources could affect Alliance security interests ...
>
> Some 65 per cent of the oil and natural gas consumed in Western Europe passes through the Mediterranean each year, with major pipelines connecting Libya to Italy and Morocco to Spain. Since October 2001 NATO ships have been patrolling in the Eastern Mediterranean.[34]

## LIE #10

NATO's mandate was to protect civilians.

---

[31] Jaap de Hoop Scheffer, 'Transatlantic leadership for a new era: Speech by NATO Secretary General Jaap de Hoop Scheffer at the Security and Defence Agenda', NATO, 26 January 2009, http://www.nato.int/docu/speech/2009/s090 126a.html.

[32] Tim Youngs, M. Oakes and P. Bowers, 'Kosovo: NATO and Military Action', House of Commons Library, Research Paper 99/34, 24 March 1999.

[33] Dan Briody, *The Halliburton Agenda: The Politics of Oil and Money* (2004, Wiley).

[34] NATO, 'NATO's role in energy security', undated (2012), https://web.archive.org/web/20120916200 314/http://www.nato.int/cps/en/SID-15CDB895-2387E351/n atolive/topics_49 208.htm?selectedLocale=en.

## FACT

NATO had no UN mandate. Added to which, under the Geneva Conventions, 'civilians', or non-combatants, is a loose term. That means that the UK-armed and -trained rebels were classified as 'civilians' by the allied powers. When the media and the Security Council discussed protecting 'civilians', they were not referring to the unarmed men, women and children of Libya who were not participating in hostilities. Rather, they were referring to the armed, Western-backed rebels. This point was not explained to the public in the media's version of events. This gave the false impression that allied powers wanted to protect the unarmed men, women and children of Libya, when in fact they wanted to provide air support to the rebels.[35]

An unreported House of Commons Library paper explained that Resolution 1973 'offers protection to a wide category of people in Libya, *even if they are or have been fighting.* In humanitarian law', the authors added, 'A "civilian" is "any person not a combatant"; but the definition of combatant is narrow and does not cover rebel forces', unless they abide by the Geneva Conventions (carrying arms openly, wearing uniforms, etc. Emphasis added).[36]

The allied powers took it upon themselves to designate the Libyan Islamic Fighting Group and other proxies, civilians (non-combatants).

## LIE #11

There were no alternatives to the use of force.

## FACT

That UK Special Forces were training and arming the opposition as early as October 2010 proves that the allied powers had no interest in peace: they wanted to overthrow Gaddafi, impose a Western-friendly regime, and do so under a humanitarian pretext. The US had no intention of finding a peaceful solution either:[37]

---

[35] Ben Smith and Arabella Thorp, 'Interpretation of Security Council Resolution 1973 on Libya', House of Commons Library, SN/IA/5916, 6 April, 2011.

[36] Ibid.

[37] *Britain's Secret Wars*, op cit.

On March 7, United Press International reported that US General David Petraeus was caught asking Defense Secretary Robert Gates if he was 'Flying a little bigger plane than normal – you gonna launch some attacks on Libya or something?', to which Gates replied, 'Yeah, exactly'.[38]

A day later, following previous peace efforts made by Venezuela's late President, Hugo Chávez (rejected outright by the US-backed rebels as 'a trap'), ABC News Australia reported that 'Gaddafi this morning offered to meet rebel leaders in a "people's conference" and step down with certain guarantees'. Again rejected.[39]

This important story was not reported at all in Britain or America. We will never know what the 'certain guarantees' were, but we can assume that Gaddafi wanted to step down in a way that would allow him to save face (and his life).[40]

The oil company–sponsored International Crisis Group reported that '[t]he complaint that Qaddafi cannot be trusted is one that can be levelled at any number of leaders on one side or another of a civil war'. Given that the British secret services were working with the opposition in the 1990s, then with Gaddafi from 2000 onwards, then with the rebels again, and that the US is formally committed to Full Spectrum Dominance, the real question is: could Gaddafi trust the West?[41]

'To insist that he [Gaddafi] both leave the country *and* face trial in the International Criminal Court is virtually to ensure that he will stay in Libya to the bitter end and go down fighting', the ICG reported (emphasis in original). That was precisely the idea. A Chatham House paper published in June acknowledged that the goal was to 'maintain the status quo' in order to 'deplete the regime's resources'.[42]

The ICG commented that:

> the longer Libya's military conflict persists, the more it risks under-mining the anti-Qaddafi camp's avowed objectives. Yet, to date, the

---

[38] Roger L. Wollenberg, 'Petraeus, Gates joke about Libya strike', United Press International, 7 March 2011.

[39] Associated Press, 'Chávez proposes 'committee of peace' to mediate between west and Gaddafi', *Guardian*, 3 March, 2011.

[40] ABC, 'Rebels say Libya peace talks offer a trap', 8 March 2011.

[41] ICG, 'Popular Protest...', op cit.

[42] Alistair Burt MP, Sir Richard Dalton, Lindsey Hilsum, Ashur Al-Shamis, and Claire Spencer, 'Libya: Prospects and Challenges', Chatham House, 8 June 2011 and ibid.

latter's leadership and their NATO supporters appear to be uninterested in resolving the conflict through negotiation. To insist, as they have done, on Qaddafi's departure as a precondition for any political initiative is to prolong the military conflict and deepen the crisis. Instead, the priority should be to secure an immediate ceasefire and negotiations on a transition to a post-Qaddafi political order.[43]

Knowing his days were otherwise numbered, Gaddafi continued to offer to negotiate and honour the ceasefire demanded by UNSCR 1970, which the rebels rejected. On 19 March, the UK's Ambassador to the Security Council, Mark Lyall Grant, referred to Gaddafi's compliance as 'a grotesque offer of amnesty'.[44]

In Western intellectual culture, dropping bombs on children is exercising a 'responsibility to protect' civilians, whereas abiding by Security Council Resolutions is 'a grotesque offer of amnesty'.[45]

## LIE #12

Gaddafi violated the ceasefire demanded by UNSCR 1970.

## FACT

In February 2011, the Security Council adopted Resolution 1970, which forbade foreigners from arming Libyan factions or supplying proxy finances. Britain immediately violated the Resolution by failing to withdraw the covert special forces already in Libya, by funnelling money to the rebels through Kuwait and by meeting with them to provide training and arms (which the Elite UK Forces acknowledged).[46]

Despite an effort by Gaddafi to negotiate, it was clear that both America and the rebels would not accept a peaceful settlement: 'The United States is not negotiating with Gaddafi', said Secretary of State, Hillary Clinton, on 27 February, mirroring what the rebels said on the same day: 'there is

---

[43]ICG, op cit.

[44]Mark Lyall Grant, Statement to the Security Council on UNSCR 1973, 17 March 2011.

[45]Ibid.

[46]UNSCR 2011, www.un.org/en/ga/search/view_doc.asp?symbol=S/RES/1970(2011).
For UK Elite Forces, see *Britain's Secret Wars*, op cit.

no room for negotiation'.[47]

UNSCR 1970 '*Demands* an immediate end to the violence', a demand
which the rebels ignored. Gaddafi, on the other hand, was expected to
abide by the Resolution as UK-armed and -trained proxies were tearing
the country to pieces. 'What will happen if Gaddafi not only announces
a ceasefire, but is forced to respect it, *as is likely* in the next few days?',
asked Malcolm Rifkind MP on 21 March (emphasis added). 'Does that
mean it is all over? I do not think that that would be an appropriate
interpretation of the resolution', proving that Britain had no interest in
peace, and that the goal was regime change.[48]

The allied powers had a problem, however: if Gaddafi was allowed to
step down early, how could the allied powers continue justifying bombing the country to smithereens? The goal was to wreck the country so
that the IMF and World Bank could loan Libya's new puppet regime 'reconstruction' money and to enable Euro-American businesses to establish
themselves in the country. Short of using nuclear, weather or seismic
weapons, this takes time.

The Libyan Foreign Minister, Moussa Koussa, announced that Libya
would abide by the ceasefire, but the rebels would not. A day before the
NATO bombing began, the Associated Press reported that '[a] Libyan
rebel spokesman has dismissed the cease-fire announcement, claiming
Moammar Gadhafi's forces are still attacking key cities in the east and
the west', providing no evidence.[49]

When asked for evidence by BBC's *Today* radio programme that
Gaddafi had violated the ceasefire, Britain's Foreign Secretary, William
Hague, provided none, replying: 'I think we will know a ceasefire when we
see it'. Natascha Engel MP informed Parliament: 'those words did not fill
me with complete confidence that we know what we are doing'. Agence
France-Presse reported that the rebels 'said they were coordinating with

---

[47] *Al-Arabiya*, 'Rebel Libyan army in east ready to help Tripoli, Offers 'any kind of assistance' to Libya uprising', 27 February 2011, and Mohammed Abbas, 'Libya rebels
form council, oppose foreign intervention', *The Windsor Star*, 27 February 2011.

[48] UNSCR 1970, op cit. House of Commons, 21 March 2011, Column 724, https://publicat
ions.parliament.uk/pa/cm201 011/cmhansrd/cm110 321/debtext/110 321-0002.htm.

[49] *Mirror*, 'Libya declares ceasefire after UN no-fly zone resolution', 18 March 2011,
http://www.mirror.co.uk/news/uk-news/libya-declares-ceasefire-after-un-176 954 and
Associated Press, 'Libyan rebels dismiss cease-fire declaration', March 18 2011.

Western nations on targets for air strikes against Qadhafi's forces, as a coalition of countries geared up to launch attacks'. In other words, while the allied powers prepared to bomb, Gaddafi was expected to cease firing.[50]

## LIE #13

United Nations Security Council Resolution 1973 authorized the use of force. (Perhaps the biggest lie of all.)

## FACT

'Acting under Chapter VII of the Charter of the United Nations', the US-UK-France-drafted Resolution 1973, '*Authorizes* Member States that have notified the Secretary-General, acting nationally or through regional organizations or arrangements, and acting in cooperation with the Secretary-General, to take all necessary measures, notwithstanding paragraph 9 of resolution 1970 (2011), to protect civilians'.[51]

Paragraph 9 of Resolution 1970 prohibited arming any faction in Libya and prohibited the deployment of ground forces. As noted, the UK had violated the Resolution since its inception and continued to do so.[52]

Returning to UNSCR 1973, which explicitly 'Act[ed] under Chapter VII of the [UN] Charter', Chapter VII does not authorize the use of force in sovereign nations' internal affairs. Had Libya invaded its neighbour Sudan, for instance, Chapter VII could have been invoked in order to maintain international peace. In fact, had he the power, Gaddafi could have invoked Chapter VII against the UK for invading Libya in October 2010 with MI6 assets and training rebels for revolution. Chapter VII of the UN Charter states:

---

[50]Hague and Engel in British Parliament, 'United Nations Security Council Resolution 1973', 21 March 2011 and Agence France-Presse, 'Libya accuses rebels of breaching truce', 19 March 2011.

[51]Charter of the United Nations 1945, https://treaties.un.org/doc/publication/ctc/unchar ter.pdf and UNSCR 1973, http://www.un.org/en/ga/search/view_doc.asp?symb ol=S/RES/1973(2011).

[52]UNSCR 1970, op cit.

**Article 39**

The Security Council shall determine the existence of any threat to the peace, breach of the peace, or act of aggression and shall make recommendations, or decide what measures shall be taken *in accordance with Articles 41 and 42*, to maintain or restore international peace and security.

...

**Article 41**

The Security Council may decide what measures *not involving the use of armed force* are to be employed to give effect to its decisions, and it may call upon the Members of the United Nations to apply such measures. These may include complete or partial interruption of economic relations and of rail, sea, air, postal, telegraphic, radio, and other means of communication, and the severance of diplomatic relations.

**Article 42**

Should the Security Council consider that measures provided for in Article 41 would be inadequate or have proved to be inadequate, it may take such action by air, sea, or land forces as may be necessary *to maintain or restore international peace and security.* (Emphases added).[53]

The British government appears to be aware that it committed aggression—the supreme international war crime—against Libya. A Tory-Liberal-Labour committee report concerning Operation Ellamy, the UK's role in NATO's Operation Unified Protector (i.e., the bombing), states:

> We commend the Government for publishing a summary of the Attorney General's legal advice and respect the decision not to publish the advice in full but are disappointed that the Prime Minister felt unable to share the advice with us on a private and confidential basis.[54]

Why, other than concealing an admission of the supreme international war crime, would the government publish only parts of the Attorney General's statement, and withhold the rest from an in-house committee?

---

[53]UNSCR 1973, op cit.

[54]House of Commons, *Operations in Libya* (Vol. II), op cit.

Added to which, NATO is not mentioned in UNSCR 1973, which makes NATO's use of force, and Britain's role therein, a war crime. Commodore Jermy testified that 'the use of NATO air power to support offensive operations by rebel forces against those of Gaddafi falls outside UNSCR 1973's authority, and thus do not appear to comply with international law'.[55]

Former UN Legal Advisor, Patrick M. Lavender, testified: 'The use of North Atlantic Treaty Organization (NATO) to implement United Nations' Resolution 1973 (2011), adopted by the Security Council at its 6498th meeting, is *ultra vires*' (beyond legal power). The Ambassador to the Security Council, Mark Lyall Grant, affirmed that 'The authorisation in the resolutions is for member states and organisations as appropriate; it does not mention NATO'.[56]

## LIE #14

NATO engaged in unprecedented 'precision air strikes' and made unprecedented efforts to avoid civilian casualties and civilian infrastructure.

## FACT

NATO bombed schools, hospitals, universities, water pipes and other infrastructure.

During the Parliamentary vote on the motion of whether or not to attack Libya, which, in keeping with the British concept of democracy, happened two days *after* the bombing had started, Madeleine Moon (Labour MP) noted: 'We must be up front and acknowledge that civilians will die'.[57]

Likewise, Diane Abbott (Labour) stated: 'There will be civilian casualties—there always are in such deployments', adding: 'The British people are very humane'—an example of the doublethink which so perplexed Moon. Both Abbott and Moon voted for the bombing. Other

---

[55] Ibid.
[56] Ibid.
[57] Moon, House of Commons, 21 March 2011, Column 756, https://publications.parliam ent.uk/pa/cm201011/cmhansrd/cm110321/debtext/110321-0002.htm.

MPs spoke of 'post-war reconstruction'. If the bombing was so precise, why would the country need 'reconstruction'?[58]

UK ambassador to NATO, Mariot Leslie, informed the post-war Parliamentary Committee that 'you cannot say with honesty and certainty "I know for a fact that I have not killed a civilian"'. Strange, then, that the 'unbiased' media would claim the opposite. '[Britain has] a higher respect for life than Gaddafi', claimed then-Defence Secretary Liam Fox, before he was disgraced for betraying national secrets. Presumably that is why: Fox's government armed Gaddafi until just weeks before the insurrection; the SAS trained Gaddafi's forces in the previous years; and Mariot Leslie informed the Select Committee that '[w]e will never know whether some civilians have been accidentally killed by NATO because we have nobody on the ground to do the post-strike assessments'.[59]

We care so much about human life that we don't investigate the deaths we cause. Major General Capewell acknowledged that 'it's difficult to determine who is a soldier and who is not'.[60]

## CONCLUSION

The fake news reports about Libya—including the broad justifications for the war—were not effective, as few Britons supported the war. However, in portraying Gaddafi as a demon as opposed to focusing on the obvious, future humanitarian costs of war, the propaganda machine did perhaps hobble potential anti-war protest, which compared to 2003 was non-existent.

---

[58] Abbott, House of Commons, 21 March 2011, Column 790, https://publications.parliament.uk/pa/cm201011/cmhansrd/cm110321/debtext/110321-0003.htm.
[59] *Operations in Libya* (Vol. II), op cit.
[60] Ibid.

# Chapter 8

# Syria: 'A dead body can't tell you anything'

*This chapter is about how the US, Britain and France launched an illegal, secret proxy war on Syria in 2011. The war has escalated to the point where said countries are providing weapons and training to anti-Assad terrorists as well as bombing Syria under the pretext of stopping the spread of ISIS. The chapter documents cases of fake news, particularly where alleged uses of chemical weapons are concerned.*

Statespeople and philosophers often say that truth is the first casualty of war. In April 2017, the BBC made a rare departure from its mendacity and interviewed the former UK Ambassador to Syria, Peter Ford. Remarkably for a diplomat, Ford did the right thing and told the truth about the US-British-French proxy war in Syria. Just days before, President Trump launched a missile attack on Syria, claiming that the government of Bashar al-Assad had used chemical weapons to murder Syrian civilians. The only trouble with this is that 1) the US had no legal right to bomb a sovereign nation without UN authorization, 2) Syria is overrun with jihadists trained and organized by the US, France and Britain, some of whom have access to chemical weapons, and 3) because there was no independent investigation into the attack it was impossible to identify the culprits.

## FORD & THE 'FAKE FLAG'

Ford used a term almost never uttered on the BBC but denotes a common tactic of warfare: false-flag. A false-flag operation involves force $x$ committing an atrocity, such as a terror bombing of civilians, and blaming it on force $y$. The ethos is codified in Sun's *The Art of War*, that deception is the essence of war. In a remarkable *Timewatch* documentary broadcast on BBC 2 in the early 1990s, the state-funded propaganda station departed from its usual lies and revealed that between 1945 and circa 1990, right-wing terrorists in nearly every European state targeted civilians in bombings, shootings, car crashes and political assassinations in order to blame it on socialists, left-leaning governments and progressive political movements. This was Operation Gladio. These were false-flags. Many of the groups, the documentary acknowledged, were trained and organized by Britain's MI6 and America's CIA.[1]

In 2002, PM Tony Blair and US President Bush II plotted a false-flag against Saddam Hussein. They planned to use an aircraft painted in UN colours to attack targets in Iraq and use Saddam's counterattack as a pretext for war, under the claim that Saddam had downed a UN plane. During the Bush II administration, Vice President Dick Cheney (some say he was the real power behind Bush) plotted with the Joint Chiefs of Staff (the organization consisting of the highest ranking members of the US armed forces) to start a war with Iran. In one of the many rejected false-flag plots, planners asked, 'Why don't we build, in our shipyard, four or five "Iranian" boats that look like Iranian [patrol] boats, put Navy Seals on them with a lot of arms and the next time one of our boats go through the Strait of Hormuz, start a shoot-up?' These are the words of journalist Seymour Hersh, who discovered the plot and paraphrased its content. Hersh concludes: 'It was rejected because you can't have Americans killing Americans'.[2]

Ironically for the BBC, their guest, former Ambassador Ford, gave a master class in how to deconstruct and expose fake news. He did it on the very news channel unquestioningly supporting what could very well be fake news spread by the intelligence agencies. Trump said: 'My fellow Americans, ... Syrian dictator Bashar al-Assad launched a horrible chemical weapons attack on innocent civilians'. As usual, the BBC broke its own alleged impartiality guidelines and parroted the views of the government. The BBC presenter said to Ambassador Ford: 'It's a statement of fact'. Ford responded: 'The statement is a misstatement of non-fact. We don't

[1]BBC Timewatch: Gladio, uploaded by Ichigi, YouTube, 21 September 2011, https://www.youtube.com/watch?v=yXavNe81XdQ. See also Daniele Ganser, NATO's Secret Armies (2005, Frank Cass). Richard Cottrell, Gladio, Nato's Dagger at the Heart of Europe (2015, Progressive Press).
[2]Quoted in David Swanson, Daybreak (2009, Steven Stories Press), pp. 35-36.

know [what happened in Syria]. What's needed is an investigation because there are two possibilities for what happened. One is the American version, that Assad dropped chemicals on this locality. The other version is than an ordinary bomb was dropped and it hit a munitions dump where the jihadists were storing chemical weapons. We don't know'. But Ford didn't stop there. He dared to say what all military planners know and what researchers are dismissed as 'conspiracy theorists' for saying: that the jihadists might have staged a false-flag, or fake flag, as Ford called it.[3]

Like Iraq in 2003, 'it's possible' that the intelligence agencies and government 'are wrong in this instance as well, that they're just looking for a pretext to attack Syria'. Ford also pointed out something that the BBC and other war-mongering institutions almost entirely overlook: that by bombing a country which possesses chemical weapons, the US and Britain are increasing the possibility that the Assad government will use chemical weapons as a deterrent against further bombing. In addition, says Ford, Assad and his Russian ally Vladimir Putin 'will give less cooperation in the fight against ISIS'.[4]

The BBC presenter then claimed that UK Defence Secretary Michael Fallon 'is convinced by the evidence' that Assad used chemical weapons. This was a lie. There was no evidence. None. Further, how does the presenter or indeed anyone know what a statesman does or doesn't believe as opposed to what they claim? 'I don't leave my brains at the door when I examine a situation', Ford replied. 'Analytically, I try to be objective and based on previous experience, including Iraq, we can see that we cannot take at face value what the so-called intelligence experts tell us, not when they have an agenda'.[5]

Ford continues: 'Trump has just given the *jihadis* a thousand reasons to stage fake flag operations, seeing how successful and easy it is with a gullible media to provoke the West into intemperate reactions. They will very likely stage an operation similar to what they did—and this was documented by the United Nations in August last year [2016]; they mounted a chlorine gas attack on civilians and they tried to make it look

---

[3]BBC News, ' "Trump has just given jihadis a thousand reasons to stage fake flag operations" BBC News', YouTube, 7 April 2017, https://www.youtube.com/watch?v=_L Ksn4ZutxQ.

[4]Ibid.

[5]Ibid.

like it was a regime operation. Mark my words', Ford continued: 'you're hearing it here, and it will happen and it will get all the war-mongers telling us that Assad is defying us and we must go in more heavily into Syria. This will be [a] fake flag'. When the BBC presenter tried to trick Ford by restating the false, tacit assumption that Assad dropped the chemicals, asking how Assad will react knowing that Trump is willing to bomb, Ford replied: 'But he [Assad] probably didn't do it in the first place. He can't change his behaviour if he didn't do it in the first place'.[6]

Neither Ford nor the BBC mentioned international law: that without a UN resolution, the US has no legal right to use force in Syria.[7]

## WHAT'S BEHIND THE MESS IN THE MIDDLE EAST?

When it comes to Syria, the BBC takes first prize in the fake news sweepstakes. In the first place, the BBC has not reported the real US-British-French motives for smashing up Syria. Second, it has not reported the sheer brutality of the Free Syrian Army and related Islamic terrorist groups. Third, it has not reported the extent of support given to these groups by the Western militaries. Fourth, it has used biased sources for information, including the Western government–funded White Helmets and the UK-based Syrian Observatory for Human Rights. Fifth, it has manipulated video and sound in order to demonize the admittedly brutal regime of Bashar al-Assad, particularly where the alleged use of chemical weapons is concerned.[8]

---

[6]Ibid.

[7]None of the UNSCRs on this website authorize use of force: Security Council Report, 'UN documents for Syria', http://www.securitycouncilreport.org/un-docum ents/syria/.

[8]Try to find any BBC reporting on the use of US-British-French proxies as early as November 2011 as the Elite UK Forces website acknowledges and, according to former French foreign secretary Roland Dumas, even earlier; as early as 2010 (all documented in my *Britain's Secret Wars*, 2016, Clairview Books). On the brutality of the FSA, see for instance Human Rights Watch, *"He didn't have to die"*, 2015,      https://www.hrw.org/sites/default/files/reports/syria0315_ForUpload.pdf. On Western backing for the allegedly neutral White Helmets, see Foreign and Commonwealth Office (UK), 'Providing non-humanitarian assistance in Syria', 1 December  2015,   https://www.gov.uk/government/publications/factsheet-the-uks-

Motives: The US—meaning the business community—has a project to transform the Middle East and North Africa into a neoliberal economic bloc conducive to US interests, especially for oil and gas-field acquisition, infrastructure modernization such as roads and pipelines, the privatization of education and water supplies, the introduction of money markets (like derivatives) and the formation of a consumer-class. This is a century-long project which began in circa 2001. George W. Bush called it the 'new Middle East'. Numerous think tanks and establishment institutions including the US State Department, USAID, Carnegie Endowment for International Peace, the National Endowment for Democracy and the US Congress call it the Broader Middle East and North Africa Initiative. When Israel bombed Lebanon in 2006, US National Security Advisor, Condoleezza Rice, called it 'the birth-pangs of a new Middle East'.[9]

The problem is that several of the secular despots propped up with US and British arms and often training, refused to go along with the privatization reforms. These dictators are named in several US and British documents, including Parliamentary and Congressional sources. They were: Muammar Gaddafi of Libya (who made only 'cosmetic' changes to the economy in the words of oil journals), Bashar al-Assad (who was 'thought to be a reformer', in the words of the British House of Commons Library) and Egypt's Hosni Mubarak and Tunisia's Zine El Abidine Ben Ali (who will be 'be kicked out of office if democratic change moves forward', in the words of the director of the US State Department's Middle East Program).[10]

The situation was delicate. A US military report from 2005 said that because the US had lost such standing in the Middle East because of its support for Israel and torture of Iraq since 1991, outside intervention to foster 'regime change' was not tenable. The paper suggested 'manufacturing democracy' from within. A RAND Corporation study from

---

non-humanitarian-aid-response-to-the-syria-crisis–2/providing-non-humanitarian-assistance-in-syria.

Manipulated video is examined in this chapter.

[9] For example, Marina Ottaway et al., 'The New Middle East', 2008, Carnegie Endowment for International Peace. CQ Transcripts wire, 'Secretary Rice holds a news conference', *Washington Post*, 21 July 2006, http://www.washingtonpost.com/wp-dyn/content/article/2006/07/21/AR2006072100 889.html.

[10] Details and sources (see footnotes) in my 'Britain's Secret Proxy War in Syria', Axis of Logic, 8 February 2012, http://axisoflogic.com/artman/publish/Article_64301.shtml.

2010 plotted working with pro-democracy groups in Egypt, specifically *Kifaya* (Enough!), which opposed the regime of Mubarak. The US wanted Mubarak in Egypt gone, but the Army to remain in power. In countries fully allied to US interests—Bahrain, Kuwait, Oman, Saudi Arabia and Yemen—Anglo-American training for dictators would increase so that pro-democracy uprisings would be crushed.[11]

In Syria and Libya the plan was to work with radical jihadists, many of them linked with al-Qaeda and the nascent ISIS, to depose the secular regimes of Assad and Gaddafi. A 2010 UK Ministry of Defence trends document discusses working with 'proxies', including terrorists. These proxies will 'prove difficult to control over time', says the document. The UK then approached France's former Foreign Minister, Roland Dumas, to work on a 'rebel invasion' of Syria, as he put it. Indicating the breadth of its reach abroad, it later emerged that MI6 had a plan to work with 100,000 terrorists (or 'rebels') to invade Syria. In October 2010, MI6 was organizing terrorists in Libya at a 'farm' under the command of an agent known only as 'Tom'. The 'farm' was a command centre where the anti-Gaddafi terrorists liaised with the British SAS. At the end of 2011, it emerged on the semi-official Elite UK Forces website that British, French and US special forces were training the anti-Assad terrorists in Syria from bases in allied Turkey.[12]

The Arab Spring was not only anticipated, it was fomented and hijacked. The US Strategic Studies Institute noted that there is not only enough hatred of Western-backed rulers in the region as to easily trigger a revolution, but that one was inevitable and could even erupt by the end of 2010, as indeed it did in Egypt. The US State Department meanwhile bragged of how it trained young Arabs in how to use social media to overthrow their governments. Knowing that the very armies backed by the US and Britain would use murderous force to crush the rebellions was a cruel trick played by the US policymakers who sought to use indigenous dissatisfaction with domestic rulers as a proxy for their own regional ambitions.[13]

---

[11]See my *Britain's Secret Wars* (2016, Clairview Books).
[12]Ibid.
[13]Ibid.

The gamble paid off. The oil-producing Gulf states were secure and protest was crushed with overwhelming force, particularly in Saudi Arabia where British-trained snipers prepared to shoot any dissidents. In Yemen, the protests proved too strong and despite murderous actions by the US-British-backed Saleh government, the crowd forced the president to stand down. The political vacuum was filled by the Shia Houthis, whom the Saudis tried to crush in the war beginning 2015. In doing so, they wrecked much of Yemen and opened the country to Euro-American investments. The US-allied regimes of Morocco and Algeria were safe from being overthrown. Ben Ali and Mubarak stood down, the Egyptian Army deposed the briefly-elected, anti-US Muslim Brotherhood leader, Mohamed Morsi, and imposed a pro-US dictator, General Sisi. The Arab Springs in Libya and Syria were hijacked by armed terrorists trained and organized by the US, Britain and France. Assad and Gaddafi's use of violence to prevent their countries from being overtaken by Muslim fanatics was used by the West as an excuse to launch a military assault. Libya was decimated by NATO. Assad clung to power in Syria and the proxy war (or 'civil war' as the media call it) dragged on for years, killing 300,000 people and displacing 11 million.[14]

# COVERING SYRIA

A UN inquiry into the mass murder of anti-government civilians in al-Houla town, Syria, in 2012 suspects that the Syrian Army and related militia were responsible, but draws no firm conclusions: 'With regard to the deliberate killing of civilians, the commission was unable to determine the identity of the perpetrators. Nevertheless, it considered that forces loyal to the Government were likely to have been responsible for many of the deaths'. As the tactics of the Assad regime are brutal enough, why did the BBC feel the need to tug the heart-strings of its online readers by including a photo actually taken in Iraq in 2003 and falsely attribute it to the Syria massacre?[15]

---

[14] Ibid.
[15] UN High Commissioner for Human Rights, 'Statement of Mr. Pinheiro, Chair of the Commission of Inquiry on the Syrian Arab Republic', UNHCHR, June 2012, http://www.ohchr.org/Documents/HRBodies/HRCouncil/CoISyria/Statement%2027June20

BBC News Online reported the Houla massacre. Although the report did include statements from the Assad government denying responsibility, as well as witnesses claiming that the anti-Assad terrorists were responsible, the majority of statements came from US spokespeople (Secretary of State Hillary Clinton), the French (who have a colonial interest in Syria, which the BBC omitted), head of the UN Ban Ki-moon and UN monitors, all of whom pointed to Assad as the culprit. But the accompanying photograph uploaded by the BBC was taken in Iraq in 2003. The photographer, Marco di Lauro, sold the picture to Getty Images. It depicts an Iraqi boy jumping over 'a line of hundreds of bodies, in a school where they have been transported from a mass grave, to be identified'. The bodies were discovered in a mass desert grave near al-Musayyib. Di Lauro reckons they are Shia murdered during the uprising in 1991, which Britain and the US sponsored and then ordered their then-ally Saddam to crush.[16]

The BBC lied about the image. It was a naive lie. The image is one of the most famous of the invasion of Iraq in 2003. The original BBC caption read: 'This image – which cannot be independently verified – is believed to show the bodies of children in Houla [Syria] awaiting burial'. Even if it was an honest mistake (which is highly unlikely), why was a respected institution like the BBC using an image 'which cannot be independently verified', other than for the purpose of anti-Assad propaganda?[17]

'[S]omebody is using my images as a propaganda against the Syrian government to prove the massacre', said di Lauro. 'I was surprised to see my image, which was captured in Iraq in 2003, used by the BBC in their recent article around the Syria massacre in Houla. It was reported that the image was captured and sent in by an activist; however this is not the case'. After the lie was exposed, the BBC removed the image and claimed that it had made a blunder. But if it really was an honest mistake, shouldn't there have been an inquiry into which editor and journalist allowed the image to be posted? An inquiry into who gave them the idea that it was an 'activist' in Syria? Shouldn't there have been questions raised about where the photo was found and why no attempt was made to identify the

---

12.pdf.

[16]BBC News, 'Houla massacre picture mistake', 29 May 2012, http://www.bbc.co.uk/blogs/theeditors/2012/05/houla_massacre_picture_mistake.html.

[17]Bronx Documentary Center, Altered Images, http://www.alteredimagesbdc.org/bbc-news/.

photographer, which would have been very easy in this case?[18]
(Di Lauro's photo was also used without accreditation in an article for
Axis of Logic in 2013 by this author. The lack of context implies that
Britain and America were directly responsible for the deaths depicted in
the photo, when in fact it was likely to be their former ally, Saddam
Hussein, who had the bodies buried in the mass graves. This shows that
sometimes journalists have no control over images selected by their edi-
tors.)[19]

# ON CHEMICAL WEAPONS

It is true that Assad's regime is brutal. We know this because the British
and American governments were supporting the regime as part of the
so-called 'war on terror', using Syria as a site to torture terror suspects.
Armed with US-British military equipment, Assad's regime murdered pro-
democracy demonstrators during the Arab Spring, as did Britain and
America's allied governments in Bahrain, Yemen and elsewhere.

Chemical weapons have been one of the main propaganda weapons in
the war. Britain knows all about the deadly effects of sarin because in
1953, scientists at the UK Ministry of Defence's biochemical warfare lab,
Porton Down, administered sarin to British soldiers 'to find out how much
nerve agent it took to penetrate a military uniform before it could kill',
says an MoD report paraphrased by Audrey Gillan in the *Guardian*. The
victim was 20-year-old Ronald Maddison. The young man's body was
returned to the family in a bolted steel coffin. When Maddison's father
demanded to see the body, he was sworn to secrecy about the extent of
his son's injuries under the Official Secrets Act.[20]

Having demonstrated the lethality of sarin by testing it on its own
soldiers, the government started selling chemicals to dictators all over the
world, including Assad's father, Hafez. Then-British Foreign Secretary

---

[18]Marco di Lauro, 'BBC mistakenly runs dated Iraq photo to illustrate the syrian
(sic) massacre', 9 June 2012, http://www.marcodilauro.com/blog/bbc-mistakenly-
runs-dated-iraq-photo-to-illustrate-the-syrian-massacre/.

[19]'Remembering Iraq: The Occupation Ten Years On', Axis of Logic, 18 March 2013,
http://axisoflogic.com/artman/publish/Article_65 480.shtml.

[20]Audrey Gillan, 'Inquiry into nerve gas cover-up', *Guardian*, 20 August 1999,
https://www.theguardian.com/uk/1999/aug/20/audreygillan.

William Hague admitted that in the 1980s, British chemicals were not only sold to Syria but probably ended up in Assad's stockpiles. The report was put on the wires (Press Association) but not picked up by most mainstream papers. Hague says: 'In the early 1980s, the exported chemicals were not subject to any international or UK export controls'. Exports of products used in the manufacturing of weapons continued. Hague admits to 'an export of ventilation fans by a UK company to Syria in 2003 ... Syria appears to have diverted these fans for use in a chemical weapons facility'.[21]

Even more appalling, America trained the anti-Assad terrorists in how to use chemical weapons. On 9 December 2012, an unnamed US official and several diplomats told CNN that America and 'European allies' were using private contractors to train anti-Assad terrorists in how to 'handle' chemical weapons sites and materials. The CNN report says: 'Syrian President Bashar al-Assad seems to be backing off, at least for now, on the possible use of chemical weapons'.[22]

With no British diplomats in the affected areas, how did the UK come to suspect that chemical weapons had been used, unless the anti-Assad terrorists being trained and organized by the UK made the allegations?

Chemical weapons and alleged chemical weapons have been used frequently in Syria. The UN counts 16 occasions in 2013 alone. As some of the anti-Assad terrorists possessed chemical weapons, it is unclear as to who used what and when. We can be sure, however, that both sides used the real or staged attacks (depending on the event) as propaganda against the other. What follows is not a comprehensive assessment of Syria's chemical weapons (scholars and the UN have provided such studies in separate works). Rather, it provides cases of BBC disinformation and selective reporting.[23]

---

[21]William Hague, 'Statement on the Historical Role of UK Companies in Supplying Dual Use Chemicals to Syria', FCO, 9 July 2014, https://www.gov.uk/government/speeches/statement-on-the-historical-role-of-uk-companies-in-supplying-dual-use-chemicals-to-syria.

[22]Elise Labott, 'Sources: U.S. helping underwrite Syrian rebel training on securing chemical weapons', CNN Security Clearance, 9 December 2012, http://security.blogs.cnn.com/2012/12/09/sources-defense-contractors-training-syrian-rebels-in-chemical-weapons/comment-page-5/.

[23]For instance: United Nations Mission to Investigate Allegations of the Use of Chem-

Because it suited the political agenda of covering up crimes committed by the anti-Assad terrorists, the BBC inverted reality and implied that a real chemical attack was invented by the Assad regime. In March 2013, Syria experienced its first chemical weapons attack since the onset of war. According a UN report on eight out of 16 alleged chemical weapons attacks in 2013 alone, the Syrian government and foreign opposition governments (led by the US, Britain and France) both reported the alleged event to the UN. The first attack was alleged to have taken place on 19 March in Khan al-Asal during the Battle of Aleppo. The UN report draws no conclusions as to the perpetrators. It concludes from samples that chemical weapons were indeed used. The BBC News Online report (published before the UN inquiry) states: 'there is scepticism about the chemical attack claims', namely from an unnamed 'chemical weapons monitoring body' and 'the US', which 'said there was no evidence that they had been used'. The BBC therefore implied that it was fake news.[24]

Next came a possibly staged attack. The BBC was quick to report its authenticity. In late March or early April 2013, government helicopters were alleged to have dropped poison gas on civilians in Saraqueb. After quoting a number of unnamed witnesses, BBC News Online quoted ex-UK Joint Chemical Biological Radiological and Nuclear Regiment Commanding Officer, Hamish de Bretton-Gordon. As an ex-British military officer speaking against the Assad government Bretton-Gordon is hardly a credible, impartial source. Having reviewed witness allegations, Bretton-Gordon is reported as saying: 'I gauge that they're not making it up'. Clearly the BBC is appealing to people's respect for authority by inserting such an opinion into a supposedly serious piece of journalism. However, the UN investigation found no conclusive evidence: 'The United Nations Mission was not able to conduct an on-site visit and was therefore not able to collect any primary information on munitions. The information

ical Weapons in the Syrian Arab Republic, 'Report on the Alleged Use of Chemical Weapons in the Ghouta Area of Damascus on 21 August 2013', http://www.un. org/zh/focus/northafrica/cwinvestigation.pdf.

[24] United Nations Mission to Investigate Allegations of the Use of Chemical Weapons in the Syrian Arab Republic, *Final Report*, 2013, https://unoda-web.s3.amazonaw s.com/wp-content/uploads/2013/12/report.pdf. BBC, 'Syria crisis: 'Scepticism about chemical attack claims'', 19 March 2013, http://www.bbc.co.uk/news/av/world-midd le-east-21851327/syria-crisis-scepticism-about-chemical-attack-claims.

gathered from the interviews with the source close to the opposition could not be corroborated by the United Nations Mission'.[25]

# SELECTING SOUNDS & IMAGES

The BBC was caught selectively editing the audio of an interview with a Syria-based medical doctor. In July 2013, the BBC was filming in a Syrian hospital when children wounded in a nearby bomb attack were admitted. Dr Rola Hallam was interviewed wearing a surgical mask. In the original unedited footage, she told the BBC (pauses represented with ellipses):

> I need a pause because it's just absolute chaos and carnage here...umm... we've had a massive influx of what look like serious burns... Er... it seems like it must be some sort of chemical weapon, I'm not really sure, maybe napalm, something similar to that. Um so we are trying to do a bit of triage and stabilisation. We've got a lot of walking wounded who are managing to manage OK but obviously within the chaos of the situation it's very difficult to know exactly what's going on.[26]

In the August 2013 broadcast entitled, *Syria in Crisis*, the audio is edited by the BBC. Because Dr Hallam wears a surgical mask, the editors could easily edit her audio without disturbing the visual content. She is broadcast as saying:

> it's just absolute chaos and carnage here...umm... we've had a massive influx of what look like serious burns... Er... it seems like it must be some sort of napalm, something similar to that [...] but obviously within the chaos of the situation it's very difficult to know exactly what's going on.[27]

---

[25]BBC, 'Syria conflict: BBC shown 'signs of chemical attack'', 16 May 2013, http://www.bbc.co.uk/news/world-middle-east-22549 861. United Nations Mission to Investigate Allegations of the Use of Chemical Weapons in the Syrian Arab Republic, *Final Report*, op cit.

[26]OFCOM Broadcast Bulletin, Issue 288, 21 September 2015, https://www.ofcom.org.uk/__data/assets/pdf_file/0017/50 507/issue_288.pdf.

[27]Ibid.

In September 2013, the footage was broadcast again as part of the BBC's *Saving Syria's Children*. This time, the audio of the same Hallam footage has been edited as follows:

> it's just absolute chaos and carnage here we've had a massive influx of what look like serious burns [...] it seems like it must be some sort of chemical weapon, I'm not really sure.[28]

Following a chemical attack in August 2013, the US intelligence services showed 13 videos of alleged victims from across Syria, which numerous chemical weapons specialists said are likely to be fake (more below). The videos were shown to the Senate Intelligence Committee. The government website confirms that the videos were taken from social media and posted by anti-Assad rebels. The CNN report is a perfect case of double-think: that the video is real and the atrocities committed by Assad, but we can't prove who did it or verify the authenticity of the video. Other than planting seeds of doubt, confirming more bias and painting a general anti-Assad media canvas, what was the point of the story?[29]

Washington correspondent Jake Tapper said: 'CNN has obtained videos that were shown ... to members of the Senate Intelligence Committee in a classified briefing'. The videos were then selectively released by the government to the media. This is a case of inherent bias, i.e., the media reporting what the government wants you to think. 'These videos ... were presented to the Senators by the intelligence community as having been verified as authentic by the intelligence community'. But the intelligence community is not only known for lying (about Iraq, Libya, Saddam's links to al-Qaeda, the anthrax attack in 2001 which turned out to be an inside job, etc.), it has psychological warfare units who specialize in psychological operations designed for propaganda purposes.[30]

'It is a sarin gas attack', says Tapper, who then says in the next sentence: 'CNN cannot independently verify the authenticity of these videos, but we're reporting on them because we have verified that the Obama administration is showing them to Members of Congress'. So if the intelligence services and government say they're true, they must be. Tapper then

---

[28]Ibid.

[29]CNN uploaded by Buzz Source, 'Graphic Videos of Syrian Chemical Attack Victims', YouTube, 8 September 2013, https://www.youtube.com/watch?v=PUQDWm7GwZo.

[30]Ibid.

explains why the intelligence services are showing the videos to Congress: 'they hope to build a case to support military strikes against the Assad regime'. So CNN admits that—real or not—the videos are being used as pro-war propaganda. Tapper also reiterates that it is impossible to tell who perpetrated the attacks allegedly shown in each video.[31]

When asked by activists why the BBC doesn't show images of casualties from British and American airstrikes, the typical response is that the BBC adheres to the 'social responsibility model', where graphic images are not shown for fear of causing distress to audiences. However, when enemies commit atrocities, the social responsibility model goes out the window. After the US intelligence services compiled and released the footage, a montage was broadcast on the BBC evening news purporting to show sarin gas victims: corpses, the dying, young men convulsing and foaming at the mouth and children wearing respiratory masks.[32]

# WHAT SOME EXPERTS SAY

While the media used visuals to shock the public into supporting more violence against Syria, few print media and online media questioned the veracity of the images. The *New York Times* reported: 'The videos, experts said, ... did not prove the use of chemical weapons, which interfere with the nervous system and can cause defecation, vomiting, intense salivation and tremors. Only some of those symptoms were visible in some patients. Gwyn Winfield, editor of CBRNe World, a journal that covers unconventional weapons, said that the medics would most likely have been sickened by exposure to so many people dosed with chemical weapons –

---

[31] Ibid.

[32] It was shocking to see looped footage of Gaddafi's supposed death on the BBC, as it was to see alleged chemical weapons attacks in Syria. We were invited to gloat in the sodomy and murder of the elderly man and reel in horror at the alleged chemical weapons murders. No such footage of children blown into small pieces by US-British drones is ever broadcast, even though photos can be easily found online. But it's not just the BBC. ABC News, for instance, broadcast the gruesome alleged murder of Gaddafi in a 'we got him!' tone, reflecting Hillary Clinton's reaction: 'We came, we saw, he died'. ABC News, 'Moammar Gadhafi Dead Video: Last Moments Alive Caught on Tape in Sirte: WARNING GRAPHIC VIDEO', YouTube, 21 October 2011, https://www.youtube.com/watch?v=sGm492qVEzA.

a phenomenon not seen in the videos'.[33]

Agence-France Presse quotes Paula Vanninen, director of the Finnish Institute for Verification of the Chemical Weapons Convention: 'I am not totally convinced because the people that are helping them are without any protective clothing and without any respirators ... In a real case, they would also be contaminated and would also be having symptoms'. Dr Jean Pascal Zanders says: 'I have not seen anybody applying nerve agent antidotes ... Nor do medical staff and other people appear to suffer from secondary exposure while carrying or treating victims'. Professor Alexander Kekule of the Institute for Medical Microbiology at Halle University, Germany, 'said the symptoms did not fit with typical chemical weapons use as the victims did not appear to be suffering pain or irritation to their eyes, nose and mouth'.[34]

Israel's leading newspaper, *Haaretz*, quotes Dan Kaszeta, a private consultant and former Officer of the US Army Chemical Corps: 'None of the people treating the casualties or photographing them are wearing any sort of chemical-warfare protective gear ... and despite that, none of them seem to be harmed ... [T]here are none of the other signs you would expect to see in the aftermath of a chemical attack, such as intermediate levels of casualties, severe visual problems, vomiting and loss of bowel control'. The newspaper also quotes UK Ministry of Defence consultant, Steve Johnson of Cranfield University: 'from the details we have seen so far, a large number of casualties over a wide area would mean quite a pervasive dispersal. With that level of chemical agent, you would expect to see a lot of contamination on the casualties coming in, and it would affect those treating them who are not properly protected. We are not seeing that here'.[35]

The UN confirms the use of sarin in eastern Ghouta in August 2013, but not in western Ghouta. In an interview with RT, the UN High Representative for Disarmament Affairs, Angela Kane, confirmed that the Syrian government did allow an unprompted investigation in Ghouta. Kane said that the UN team was removed due to fatigue and then tried to re-enter to 'different premises'. Kane confirmed that witnesses were all vetted by

---

[33]Quoted in my *Britain's Secret Wars* (2016, Clairview Books), pp. 168-70n32.
[34]Ibid.
[35]Ibid.

the anti-Assad terrorists. Kane was asked why the UN will not arrange for autopsies to be performed on the alleged victims. She replied: 'a dead body can't tell you anything. Can't tell you how the person died. How the person was affected. How the person suffered'.[36]

# CONCLUSION

The coverage of Syria has not been successful in driving support for war among Britons or Americans; hence the Tory-Liberal coalition government's defeat in Parliament in 2013 when they tried to launch an air war against Assad. But as Britain is a rogue state, its leaders decided to bomb anyway. Coverage has been successful in keeping from the public the fact that it is a proxy war fought by Muslim fanatics allied with the West.

---

[36]UN, op cit. Kane interviewed by Oksana Boyko, "No sarin detected in West Ghouta environment, only in human samples' – UN's Angela Kane', RT, YouTube, 3 October 2013, https://www.youtube.com/watch?v=CcfIj6WLqRk.

# Part III: The battle

# Introduction

There is a battle raging at the top: and ordinary people on the bottom suffer the consequences.

*Neoliberalism*: This roughly translates as the incremental privatization of public assets, the internationalization of volatile money markets, the global circulation of labour to fill skills gaps and the favouring of finance over manufacturing and production. The political and economic effects are complicated. The middle class can survive, but it is weakened and has to work longer for stagnant wages. Children of the middle class have fewer life chances than their parents. The poor suffer the most under economic neoliberalism. But the rich (those earning annual six-figures, or in the case of expensive cities like London, double that) typically do very well out of neoliberalism: they enjoy tax breaks, opportunities to invest in publicly-paid-for-services and reductions in the rights of their staff. Wealth is concentrated in fewer pockets. One of the results is voter disengagement. Under neoliberalism, whoever is in power we end up with the same results, so voters have few party loyalties.[1]

*Slow neoliberalism*: One branch of the elite wants to continue pursuing global economic neoliberalism, but slowly. Advocates of slow neoliberalism favour *status quo* politics: left-wing governments moving to the centre; the formation of policy through supranational institutions, including the EU and multilateral investment deals and the World Trade Organization. They advocate their agenda by appealing to fear of change; that in the absence of familiarity, the far-left and far-right will take over.[2]

*Fast neoliberalism*: Another sector of the elite thinks that the slow model is too slow. Call them Brexiteers and Trumpites, after the hedge funds that bankrolled Britain's vote to leave the EU and, of course, Donald Trump. They feel that supranational institutions—like the EU—are far too politicized and, as a result, slow the workings of neoliberalism

---

[1]See my *The Great Brexit Swindle* (2016, Clairview Books).
[2]Ibid.

by imposing regulations on financial institutions. Advocates of fast neoliberalism want to move ahead, despite a slow global recovery from the Crash of 2008. They advocate their agenda by quietly sponsoring far-right 'nationalists' (who are not really nationalists), like UKIP and Trump.[3]

The ideological effects of neoliberalism on the general public are also complicated. The North American Free Trade Agreement (NAFTA 1994) is an example of a multilateral neoliberal economic policy. NAFTA was signed by America, Canada and Mexico. It guaranteed the rights of corporations, particularly American ones, over people. By the time China acceded to the World Trade Organization in 2001, the combined effects of Chinese steel and Mexican manufacturing resulted in mass lay-offs in US production factories in what analysts call the rustbelt (or Trumpland). But Mexicans fared no better. Millions of Mexican farmers undermined by US agricultural products imported under NAFTA rules flocked to the USA. This led to anti-immigrant operations, like Bill Clinton's border wall. The successive Republican and Democratic parties continued these policies and attempted to expand them globally with the Trans-Pacific Partnership; a NAFTA-style deal concerning mostly East Asian countries.[4]

Meanwhile at home, regulations were gradually eroded, laying the basis for the Financial Crisis and taxpayer-funded bailouts. The slow neoliberals felt that NAFTA, TPP and meek economic regulations should be pursued. The fast neoliberals and general publics alike thought otherwise. Fast neoliberals wanted to dismantle TPP and NAFTA because they fail to tackle hidden taxes on US corporations. They packaged this policy for domestic voters as their patriotic desire to want to bring business back to America: and Donald Trump was their main salesman. This political advert also tapped into the very real anger people felt about jobs being undermined; the trouble was, the angry constituents blamed the wrong targets: migrants and liberals. A similar pattern was repeated in France with the far-right Marine Le Pen. Those of the far-left (which happens to be the majority of Americans and Europeans on most issues, from nationalization to universal healthcare to halting aggressive wars) simply couldn't get their candidates (Sanders in the US) elected because those

---

[3]Ibid.

[4]See my *President Trump, Inc.* (2017, Clairview Books).

candidates were working within the machinery of their centrist political institutions (the Democratic Party in the case of Sanders), who blocked them at every turn. As Trump said, he's so rich that he could simply use the Republican Party machine as a Trojan Horse.[5]

So, where does fake news come in?

The so-called liberal establishment media (BBC, CNN, *Guardian*, *New York Times* et al.) tended to support the centrist status quo candidates and their positions (like Macron in France, whom they ridiculously painted an 'outsider', the Remain camp in the UK's EU referendum, Clinton in the US, etc.). The slow neoliberals were happy with this position, the fast neoliberals were not. Men (and most of them were men) including hedge fund billionaire Robert Mercer, PayPal-founding billionaire Peter Thiel and virtual reality entrepreneur near-billionaire Palmer Luckey weaponized social media as a way of whipping up support for Trump in the US and Brexit in the UK by influencing sites like Reddit and creating sites like Breitbart News, which had the effect of spreading Islamophobic, xenophobic and misogynistic views in support of Trump and Le Pen in France.[6]

Both the slow neoliberals and their status quo media feel threatened by the fast neoliberals and their rebellious media. In the ensuing battle, both have lobbed the charge that the other is 'fake news'. Both sides have cited multiple cases of fakery against the other; and often the charges are true.

But ordinary people are stuck in the middle of this. They continue to get spoon-fed status quo propaganda by the slow neoliberals about social issues, the economy and foreign policy by the status quo media. But they also get sucked into manufactured controversies (like the Obama 'birther' story[7]) by the fast neoliberal libertarian alternative media. In the digital haze are thousands of other sites containing news, analysis, truths and lies from a range of positions.

In this final part of the book, I look at who owns the media, both traditional and internet. Who accesses it and how it apparently came to lose

---

[5]Ibid.

[6]Ibid.

[7]A claim spread by Donald Trump and others, that Obama was born in Kenya, not in the US state Hawaii and was therefore an illegitimate president.

significance. The decline of the status quo media due to online alternative media is largely a myth, I argue. Even online, people continue to get the bulk of their news from the wires and large corporations. They tend to consult alternative media, left and right, to reinforce their own biases (echo chamber). The chapters also look at how hedge funds and state-spies have infiltrated and manipulated social media. How new economic clickbait models are making it even harder to tweeze apart truth and lies. And status quo media attempt to maintain their credibility by offering alleged fact-checking pages to their websites, like the *Washington Post* with its Four Pinocchios for the biggest liar or the BBC with its Reality Check factoids that sometimes appear during broadcasts.

# Chapter 9

# Mainstream: 'News is a way of making money'

*This chapter is about mainstream media: who owns it, how it operates and why public trust in media in America and Britain in particular has declined over the last 20 years. I look at what concerns most Americans, Britons and Europeans and demonstrate how the media barely reflect these concerns. The chapter presents nine principles of media control which, it is argued, prevent the mainstream from reporting relevant events and, crucially, reporting events in a manner relevant to most audiences.*

It is well-known that most people hate and distrust government. Less well-known is that trust in mainstream media (excluding the gutter tabloids, which have always been distrusted) has also declined. On levels of trust in government, Eurobarometer reports that on average 62% of Europeans distrust their parliaments and 64% distrust their governments; the figures vary slightly year to year. In the UK, 'politicians remain the profession least trusted by the British public, below estate agents, journalists and bankers'. Britons trust clergy and police more than politicians, which implies that most Britons would rather live in a theocratic police state.[1]

---

[1] European Commission, 'Public opinion in the European Union', Standard Eurobarometer 83, Spring 2015, http://ec.europa.eu/public_opinion/archives/eb/eb83/eb83_f irst_en.pdf.

In the UK, 'politicians remain the profession least trusted by the British public, below estate agents, journalists and bankers'. Britons trust clergy and police more than politicians, which is worrying. Gideon Skinner and Michael Clemence, 'Politicians are still trusted less than estate agents, journalists and bankers', Ipsos-MORI, 22 January 2016, https://www.ipsos-mori.com/researchpublic ations/researcharchive/3685/Politicians-are-still-trusted-less-than-estate-agents-journ alists-and-bankers.aspx#gallery[m]/1/.

For more on the UK, see also my *Human Wrongs* (2018, Iff Books).

Turning to America: Since polls were first taken in 1958, Pew reports: 'The public's trust in the federal government continues to be at historically low levels. Only 19% of Americans today say they can trust the government in Washington to do what is right "just about always" (3%) or "most of the time" (16%)'.[2]

But what concerns most people? A Flash Eurobarometer survey identified (by order of importance) unemployment, healthcare, immigration, the economy, education, business opportunities, crime and the environment as leading concerns for Europeans, including Eastern Europeans. A Gallup poll suggests shared interests, indicating that most Americans consider dissatisfaction with government, the economy, healthcare, unemployment, the federal deficit, declining morals, hunger/homelessness and education as their main concerns.[3]

Media play a significant role (exactly how to measure it is impossible, given the current parameters of analysis) in shaping people's perceptions about the economy, war, migration, etc. In addition to the immediate public concerns noted above (health services, migration, etc.) there are persistent and general issues which affect all of us in some way: climate change; Islamic terrorism (because the West invades the Muslim-majority Middle East for its oil and provokes terrorist responses); neoliberalism (which has discredited centrist politics and polarized politics into the far-right and progressive-left); and, of course, the key to solving many of these problems: activism. How are these issues covered by the media and do they reflect reality and other people's opinions?

*On climate change coverage:* Reuters reports: 'In general the UK and the US print media quoted or mentioned significantly more sceptical voices than the other four countries. Together they represented more than 80% of the time such voices were quoted across all six countries'. The six countries where analysts studied climate-related news content are Britain, the

---

[2]Pew Research Center, 'Beyond Distrust', 23 November 2015, http://www.people-press.org/2015/11/23/1-trust-in-government-1958-2015/. On the gap between political parties and how their represent people, see Gallup, 'Democratic, Republican Identification Near Historical Lows', 11 January 2016, http://news.gallup.com/poll/188 096/democratic-republican-identification-near-historical-lows.aspx. At the time, just 26% of Americans identified as Republican and 29% Democrat.

[3]Flash Eurobarometer 427, 'Europcom 2015: Far beyond the average', European Commission, October, 2015, http://ec.europa.eu/COMMFrontOffice/PublicOpinion/ind ex.cfm/Survey/getSurveyDetail/instruments/FLASH/surveyKy/2102.

US, France, Brazil, India and China. Even in more sensible, non-British-US media, 'the absolute number of articles which included sceptical voices increased for all but one (*Le Monde* in France) of the twelve [major] newspapers over the two [analysed] periods'.[4]

*On Islamophobia:* a study by the University of California–Berkeley Center for Race and Gender quotes Media Tenor: 'Fourteen years after the September 11 terrorist attacks, U.S. TV news audiences continue to receive high levels of reports about terrorism while news coverage as a whole frames Muslims in an extremely negative light'.[5]

*On media portrayals of neoliberal 'free markets' as the best system:* Dr Joanna Redden of Cardiff University concludes: 'mainstream news coverage narrows and limits the way poverty is talked about in a way that reinforces the dominance of neoliberalism and market-based approaches to the issue'. Redden goes on to say: 'Interviews with journalists, politicians, researchers and activists collectively indicate that getting media coverage is essential to gaining political attention in both countries', namely the UK and Canada—two neoliberal economies whose media she compares.[6]

On media portrayals of activists, particularly demonstrators: Douglas M. McLeod of the University of Wisconsin–Madison School of Journalism and Mass Communication writes that with few exceptions, 'coverage' of protest in the USA generally disparages protesters and hinders their role as vital actors on the political stage. The lack of respect for the value of social protest inherent in such coverage has created frustration among the protesters, which has in turn contributed to dysfunctional confrontations', usually between rival demonstrators and/or state forces.[7]

---

[4]James Painter, 'Poles Apart: The international reporting of climate scepticism', University of Oxford, Reuters Institute for the Study of Journalism, November 2011, https://reutersinstitute.politics.ox.ac.uk/sites/default/files/Poles%20Apart%20 the%20international%20reporting%20of%20climate%20scepticism.pdf.

[5]Council on American-Islamic Relations and UC Berkeley Center for Race and Gender, *Confronting Fear: December 2013-December 2015: Islamophobia and its Impact in the United States, 2016 Report,* http://crg.berkeley.edu/sites/default/files/Final% 20Report-IRDP-CAIR-Report2016_0.pdf.

[6]Redden, *The Mediation of Poverty: The News, New Media and Politics* (2011, Goldsmiths College), University of London, Dep. of Media and Communications (doctoral thesis), http://research.gold.ac.uk/6540/1/MED_thesis_Redden_2011.pdf.

[7]Douglas M. McLeod, 'News Coverage and Social Protest: How the Media's Protect Paradigm Exacerbates Social Conflict', *Journal of Dispute Resolution*, 2007, Vol. 1,

# NINE STRUCTURAL PROBLEMS

There are, arguably, nine reasons for media rigidity in terms of various biases: privatization, hierarchical structures, ownership concentration, limitations on resources, legal constraints, infiltration by agents, censorship, intimidation and exclusion. Some overlap, like intimidation and censorship:

1) *Privatization.* The majority of media are for-profit corporations serving the interests of their shareholders, including the publicly-funded British Broadcasting Corporation. The BBC is Chartered by the Crown and serves first and foremost the interests of the monarch. Its Governors (now known as Trustees) are selected by Parliament and often consist of businesspeople. In 1998, the former controller of editorial policy at the BBC, John Wilson, said: 'News is a way of making money ... No one believes that news and journalism are simply a service to democracy'. The public continues to pay the license fee, as Director-generals reduce staff and pay themselves salaries of £400,000+ per annum. After the resignation of a sports personality was given precedence over the deaths of two British soldiers, former war correspondent Martin Bell said: 'The BBC has set itself adrift in a world of trivia', in keeping with the MoD's long-range projection about the change in media content, to which we shall return.[8]

A partial list of BBC Governors from the 1996–2006 period alone reveals whose interests are disproportionately represented by the Corporation (none of the following represented their institutions during their time at the BBC): Gavyn Davis (Goldman Sachs); David Scholey (the Bank of England, J. Sainsbury, Vodafone); Sir Christopher Bland (Booz and Co.); Adrian White (Biwater); and Baroness Hogg (the BG Group. The BG Group once made an as-yet unrealized deal with the Palestinian Authority to allow Israel, which is occupying Palestine, to take gas from the substantial field off the coast of Gaza. There is no implication that BG acted unlawfully). In 2007, the BBC was restructured, and the Governors replaced with Trustees, many of whom, as Cromwell and Edwards note, represent elite interests: Jeremy Peat (RBS); Diane Coyle (the Competi-

---

http://scholarship.law.missouri.edu/cgi/viewcontent.cgi?article=1529&context=jdr.
[8]Wilson and Bell quoted in Nick Davies, *Flat Earth News* (2008, Vintage).

tion Commission); Rotha Johnston (the Allied Irish Bank); and Anthony Fry (Credit Suisse). And so it continues today. In 2016, for instance, then-PM David Cameron 'personally intervened' (FT) to ensure that a former head of HSBC bank, Rona Fairhead, could serve as chair of the BBC Trust.[9]

The Institute for Government (2010) states: 'Although almost 10m people still buy a newspaper every day [in Britain], people ... get most of their news from the television ... [T]he capacity of commercial broadcasters such as ITN, Channel 4 or Sky to do much in-depth coverage is increasingly attenuated by financial pressures', the report continues. 'The effect is to make the BBC – and what one participant called the "BBC world view" – increasingly dominant with little chance for the public to access alternatives'. As we shall see, most people continue to get their news from mainstream sources, like the BBC, even though they use the medium of the internet.[10]

There are examples of direct manipulation of media by corporations:

Over the last few decades, 80% of real estate editors in the USA have threatened to pull ads from newspapers due to negative coverage of their sector after the Crash. Sixty-two percent of representatives from the American Agricultural Editors Association also reported threatening to withdraw ads due to negative coverage, with nearly 50% actually pulling an advert from a newspaper at one time or other. Procter & Gamble was the largest TV advertiser. In a 1960s' memo, the company advised TV executives: 'There will be no material that may give offense, either directly or by inference, to any commercial organization of any sort'. Astonishingly, it even notes that 'writers should minimize the 'horror aspects' [of conflict reporting]', and that '[m]en in uniform shall not be cast as heavy villains'. It also said that TV should champion businesspeople, ministers, priests 'and similar representatives of positive social forces'. TV should promote the 'basic conception of the American way of life': buying stuff. The memo goes on: 'no material on any of our programs ... [should] in

[9]BBC, 'Full list of boards of governors of the BBC', 2006, http://downloads.bbc.co.uk/ historyofthebbc/board_of_governors.pdf. For the post-2007 list, see Cromwell and Edwards, *Newspeak in the 21st Century* (2009, Pluto).

[10]Jill Rutter, 'Are our media threatening the public good?', Institute for Government, February 2010, https://www.instituteforgovernment.org.uk/sites/default/files/publi cations/Are%20our%20media%20threatening%20the%20public%20good.pdf.

any way further the concept of business as cold, ruthless, and lacking all sentiment or spiritual motivation'.[11]

In other words, the Procter & Gamble memo advocates fake news by omission and the blandification of mainstream TV. Between 1963 and 2008, Procter & Gamble owned Folgers coffee. The company pulled TV ads due to negative coverage of Folgers in a single state: WHDH, Boston, which alleged that revenues from the coffee were linked to bloody civil war in Latin America.[12]

2) *Hierarchies.* As corporations, shareholders choose the boards of directors of media companies, who in turn choose editors, who in turn control to a large extent journalists' output. Information that will threaten the interests of a given corporation is often silenced or neutralized by the addition of official statements or the excision of content. Professor Greg Philo studied the mainstream media after the Financial Crisis of 2007–08 and concluded that with few exceptions, alternative economists, poor people, labour unions and others representing the majority were simply given zero airtime. 'News is a procession of the powerful … When the credit crunch hit, we were given a succession of bankers, stock-brokers and even hedge fund managers to explain and say what should be. But these were the people who caused the problem'. As if to prove Philo's point, he submitted his findings to the *Guardian*'s Comment is Free page, whereupon the editor Matt Seaton rejected it on that the grounds that Philo's article was 'a piece of old lefty whingeing about bias'.[13]

3) *Concentration of ownership.* America's national and to a large extent local news is controlled by a few corporations who own and run satellite and cable news and entertainment. At the time of writing: TimeWarner owns Turner, which owns CNN. Disney owns ABC and 21st Century Fox. Comcast owns NBCUniversal, which owns CNBC, MSNBC and NBC. National Amusements owns Viacom, which owns CBS and CBS News. News Corporation owns Fox and Sky News. UK national print media are owned by a handful of corporations: Associated Newspapers (*Daily Mail* and *Mail on Sunday*), Guardian News & Media (*Guardian* and *Observer*), Independent Print (*The Evening Standard, i, The Independent,* and *The*

---

[11]C. Edwin Baker, *Advertising and a Democratic Press* (2014, Princeton University Press), pp. 54-56.

[12]Ibid.

[13]Cromwell and Edwards, op cit.

*Independent on Sunday*), Mirror Group Newspapers (*Daily Mirror, Mirror on Sunday* and *The People*), News International (*The Sun, The Times, The Sunday Times*), and the Telegraph Media Group (*The Telegraph* and *The Sunday Telegraph*).[14]

Consolidation has grown. A report published in the 1990s by the University of Wollongong (Australia), on British, American and European media noted that 'Robert Hersant, imprisoned for collaborating with the Nazis, owns newspapers whose combined circulations include one third of France's readers of national papers and two fifths of Poland's readers. In Italy, Silvio Berlusconi owns three television channels and three pay TV channels as well as newspapers and magazines'. It concludes that '[a]bout 80% of the press in Britain is controlled by only four corporations and the situation is similar for broadcast media'.[15]

On European Union ownership, media specialist Professor Sarah Venturelli notes that, 'While the rationale for information-infrastructure policy professed commitment to [European] Community common interests such as competitiveness, education, employment, culture, and democracy, the actual provisions of EU policy and law largely reflect the competing private needs and requirements of global and transnational communications entities over market share and conditions of investment'. In a paper published by the Edinburgh Law School, Professor Rachael Craufurd Smith notes that since 2000, both New Labour and the succeeding Tory-Liberal regime 'have pursued a vigorous policy of media ownership deregulation' in the UK, 'even in areas where regulatory bodies such as Ofcom have voiced concerns'. The Media Ownership (Radio and Cross-media) Order 2011 'removed all remaining restrictions on media accumulations at the local level'.[16]

4) *Limiting access to sources*. Between 1986 and 2000, the National Union of Journalists' 8,000-strong membership was reduced by half, as

---

[14]Ashley Lutz, 'These corporations control 90% of the media in America', *Business Insider*, 14 June 2012, www.uk.businessinsider.com/these-6-corporations-control-90-of-the-media-in-america-2012-6 and Media Reform Coalition, 'Who owns the UK media?', October 2015, http://www.mediareform.org.uk/who-owns-the-uk-media.

[15]University of Wollongong Australia, 'Media Ownership Concentration', no date, http://www.uow.edu.au/~sharonb/STS218/media/ownership/concentration.html.

[16]Rachel Craufurd Smith, 'Is the UK 'Media Plurality Test' fit for purpose?', CFOM, 15 July 2011, http://www.cfom.org.uk/2011/07/is-the-uk-media-plurality-test-fit-for-purpose/.

403 local newspapers were closed across the UK. The closures were a
boon for buyer-corporations, including Johnston Press, which allegedly
made £117 million in 2004 alone, largely from axing local media. Local
media often bought their stories from freelancers, employed by agencies
like Anglia Press, Calyx of Dorset, Mid Staffordshire News, Raymond's
of Derby and White's of Sheffield. Like local newspapers, local agencies
also closed *en masse*. In 1992, 200 companies owned local newspapers.
By 2005, just ten companies owned 74% of local papers. Journalists were
absorbed into the neoliberal culture, working up to five hours longer each
day without overtime pay.[17]

In *Flat Earth News*, award-winning journalist Nick Davies notes that
75 percent of news reaching the British public (65 television and 80 print)
derives from just three sources: the Associated Press (AP), the Press Association and Reuters. Davies states that Reuters is influenced at high
levels by MI6 and the AP by the CIA. He further notes the reliance upon
public relations firms in a form of fast-news called 'churnalism'. By 2008,
the number of public relations specialists employed in the UK (48,000)
exceeded the number of registered journalists (45,000). Overworked, un-
derpaid and undermined by editors, journalists often simply rely on copy
handed to them by PR people. According to research conducted by the
University of Cardiff, just 20 percent of print news is entirely original.[18]

5) *Legal restrictions*. Britain has some of the worst libel laws in the
world; certainly the worst in the West. Britain's libel laws have closed
down newspapers, been condemned by the UN and (following amend-
ments) eliminated common law defence. They even make it a *defence*
to state an opinion but a potential *offence* to state a fact. We also find
European-level media regulation skewed in favour of big business and technology:[19]

Members of the European Parliament are significantly influenced by
the Eurolobby. Shortly after the MoD published its prediction of 'Declining News Quality', the EU adopted the Audiovisual Media Services
Directive (2007). The Directive 'provides less detailed and more flexible
regulation and modernizes rules on TV advertising to better finance au-

---

[17]Davies, op cit.
[18]Ibid.
[19]On the UK, see my *Human Wrongs* (2018, Iff Books).

diovisual content'. The Directive professes to ensure 'the independence of national media regulators'. Several liberalizing factors undermine the pluralist assertions, however, including the 'embrace [of] all forms of audiovisual commercial communications, such as sponsorship, product placement [and] teleshopping'.[20]

This also includes 'short reporting', allegedly to complement IT. In reality, to limit information and reduce evidence and argument to sound bites. Giving people the illusion that they are getting more news, the regulatory frameworks ensure they get less. In a book sponsored by the Spanish government and published for European policymakers, social control theorists Hess and Scheerer observe that 'the exponential growth of "information" (mostly trash) ... may make people as disorientated as traditional information'. Sir Nicholas Hewitt, President of the Newspaper Society, said that he wanted '[s]horter stories, more fun and plenty of variety'. Dr Chris Paterson found that the sports content of the European news service APTN was 1 percent in 1995. By 2000, it had leapt to 25 percent. In Europe after the passing of the AVMSD, it exploded.[21]

6) *Infiltration by agents.* In case privatization, concentration, hierarchical structures, legal restrictions and monopolization doesn't suffice, agents of influence are strategically placed in newspapers and broadcast media. At least one CIA agent works in every major American newspaper and magazine at any given time, often in a senior position. The CIA even owns foreign newspapers. The US Congressional Pike Committee (1978) found that *at least* over one quarter of the CIA's secret budget was for 'media and propaganda', and that in a single year, the Agency spent $265 million on propaganda—equal to the combined budgets of the three big wire services: the Associated Press, Reuters and United Press International. In addition, the CIA placed agents in the foreign bureaus of AP and UPI. Reuters, they said, was MI6 territory, where agents are placed in high positions.[22]

7) *Censorship.* Britain's Defence, Press and Broadcasting Advisory

---

[20] European Commission, 24 May 2007, IP/07/706, http://europa.eu/rapid/press-re lease_IP-07-706_en.htm?locale=en. Hewitt and Paterson in Davies, op cit.

[21] Sebastian Scheerer and Henner Hess in Roberto Bergalli and Colin Sumner (eds.), *Social Control and Political Order: European Perspectives at the End of the Century* (1997, Sage), and Davies, op cit.

[22] Ibid.

Committee 'oversees a voluntary code which operates between the UK Government departments which have responsibilities for national security and the media. It uses the Defence Advisory (DA)-Notice System [now DSMA-Notice] as its vehicle'. Put simply, in Britain's 'democracy', the government send letters/emails to editors telling them not to publish certain stories. If editors do publish what they are advised not to, they could face arrest under the Official Secrets Acts.[23]

The D-Notice system prevented the public from knowing anything about MI6's training, arming, funding and protecting of the Islamic *mujahideen* (now re-branded 'al-Qaeada') from 1979 to 1989. The goal was to 'draw the Russians into the Afghan trap', in the words of Zbigniew Brzezinski, Jimmy Carter's National Security Advisor and Trilateral Commission director.[24]

State censorship has prevented Britons from learning about the suffering of the Irish. In 1987, the BBC's *My Country: Right or Wrong* was subject to an (unsuccessful) injunction. In 1988, the Home Secretary invoked unlawful state-censorship powers to ban the appearance on British television of any Sinn Féin, Ulster Defence Association or Irish Republican Army representative, even in matters not relating to terrorism, thereby preventing the appearance of documentaries such as *Ireland: A Television History* and *The Troubles*.[25]

8) *Intimidation.* In case all that isn't enough, the government occasionally resort to overt totalitarianism and arrest journalists and whistleblowers. David Miranda, now-husband of ex-*Guardian* journalist Glenn Greenwald, was detained in 2013 by the British police for allegedly carrying files about the Edward Snowden leaks. This followed the arrest of two SAS men who attempted to leak to the mainstream media a report on the Afghanistan War and the plans for post-NATO reconstruction of Libya. In 1979, the *Sunday Times* was investigated by MI5 for publishing Cabinet Committee documents. A few months later, *The Times* was investigated by the same agency for publishing information on nuclear weapons. MI5 also investigated *The Economist* in 1981 for publishing details of planned public spending. In 1983, Foreign Office clerk Sarah

---

[23] Website of the DA Notice System, archived on 30 July 2015, dnotice.org.uk.

[24] John K. Cooley, *Unholy Wars* (2002, Pluto).

[25] Hugo de Burgh, 'Thirty years of British investigative journalism' in Burgh (ed.), *Investigative Journalism* (2000, Routledge), pp. 52-68.

Tisdall was imprisoned for exposing information on the deployment of cruise missiles in Britain to the *Guardian*.[26]

In the same year, Raymond Williams, an MoD civil servant, was imprisoned for passing documents to *The Observer* regarding weapons procurement. Also in that year, a Department of Employment official was sacked after details of a conversation with the Master of the Rolls appeared in *Time Out*. MI5 investigated the events. In 1986, *The Observer* and the *Guardian* were served with injunctions after publishing portions of Peter Wright's *Spycatcher*.[27]

In 2002, MI5 agent David Shayler was imprisoned for exposing MI6's role in the murder of civilians in terrorist attacks in Libya. The police even arrested a student colleague of Shayler's, Julie Ann Davies who had nothing to do with the case. In 2004, GCHQ employee, Katharine Gun, was arrested for allegedly helping to expose information regarding the Anglo-American spy network at the UN Security Council. In 2006, Neil Garrett, an ITN journalist, was arrested after obtaining a police report on the murder of Jean Charles de Menezes. And so on.[28]

9) *Exclusion/marginalization*. Feminists (with the exception of high-profile people like former CIA asset Gloria Steinem),[29] environmentalists, unions, community workers, peace activists, anti-racism campaigners, volunteers—in fact anyone working to make the world a better place—are almost entirely excluded from participating in national and local medias. As I've concentrated so much on the US, Britain and Europe, let's take the example of Australia and how the national media treat Aborigines;

---

[26] *Guardian*, 'Glenn Greenwald's partner detained at Heathrow airport for nine hours', 19 August 2013, https://www.theguardian.com/world/2013/aug/18/glenn-greenwald-guardian-partner-detained-heathrow.  Jon Ungoed-Thomas, 'Special forces soldiers held over secrets leak', *The Times*, 10 April 2011, https://www.thetimes.co.uk/article/special-forces-soldiers-held-over-secrets-leak-dwqv5tzgkdc.  For Tisdall et al., see Michael Clarke, *British External Policy-making in the 1990s* (1992, Macmillan).

[27] Clarke, op cit.

[28] BBC, 'Student 'astonished' at secrets arrest', 7 March 2000, http://news.bbc.co.uk/1/hi/uk/668 663.stm.  Neil Garrett, 'The cost of telling the truth', *Guardian*, 15 May 2006, https://www.theguardian.com/media/2006/may/15/mondaymediasection.jean charlesdemenezes.

[29] Steinem's admissions occurred in the context of information released during the course of investigations into the JFK assassinations.  Uploaded by Cory Morningstar, 'Gloria Steinem Discussing Her Time in the CIA', YouTube, 19 April 2012, https://www.youtube.com/watch?v=4HRUEqyZ7p8.

in short, they ignore and exclude Aboriginal peoples. When not ignored, they are denigrated.

In the early-1990s, Jakubowicz et al. published a study on racism and the media, drawing on information from the Office of Multicultural Affairs. They found that national media portray Australians overwhelmingly as a blond, blue-eyed stereotype. The typical Australian in the media mythology is highly Anglicized, the report said. Nearly two decades later, Ewart and Beard write that the 'marginalisation' of ethnic minorities 'has been a continuing significant feature of the Australian mediascape'. Citing the work of others, Ewart and Beard concur that part of the marginalization is due to the 'absence' of ethnic minorities 'from news and current affairs stories'. In more than half of the cases studied in the Phillips Report (2011), there are 'no ethnic minority faces at all, not even incidentally in the background'. When they do appear, they are demonized. For example, the BBC reported a fake news story about paedophilia in Aborigine communities.[30]

A 2007 BBC story repeated claims by the Northern Territory government, alleging 'a "disturbing" trend of child-on-child abuse'. The commission blamed poverty and alcohol. The allegations went on: five-year-olds prostituted for drugs, Aborigine men exposing children to pornography and on and on. In the real world, to quote John Pilger:

> In May [2008], barely reported government statistics revealed that of the 7,433 Aboriginal children examined by doctors as part of the "national emergency", 39 had been referred to the authorities for suspected abuse. Of those, a maximum of just four possible cases of abuse were identified. Such were the "unthinkable numbers". They were little different from those of child abuse in white Australia.[31]

On other occasions when Aboriginal peoples are featured in Australian media, they are usually depicted as criminals and drug addicts. The devastating documentary *Australia's Shame* (2016) exposes psychological and

---

[30] Jacqueline Ewart and Jillian Beard, 'Poor Relations' in John Budarick and Gil-Soo Han (eds.), *Minorities and Media: Producers, Industries, Audiences* (2017, Palgrave Macmillan), pp. 165-94.

[31] BBC, 'Aborigine child sex abuse 'rife'', 15 June 2007, http://news.bbc.co.uk/1/hi/world/asia-pacific/6756515.stm. John Pilger, 'Under cover of racist myth, a new land grab in Australia', *Guardian*, 24 October 2008, https://www.theguardian.com/commentisfree/2008/oct/24/australia-aborigine-howard-rudd.

physical abuse of children in state-run prisons, notably Don Dale. Children, many of them Aborigines, were held in isolation without food or water for an indefinite period in Don Dale's so-called Behavioural Management Unit. When one boy escaped from his torture (15 days of solitary confinement), following a guard's failure to lock the door, six boys were tear-gassed by the adult male guards. The national reporting spread fake news by claiming that the boys were 'rioting', when in fact only one tried to escape his torture.[32]

# WHO TRUSTS THE MAINSTREAM?

Unsurprisingly, decades of structural flaws resulting in the kind of elite nonsense documented above have led to growing dissatisfaction among mainstream news consumers in the US, Britain and Europe.

Does fake news and the far-right-linked 'alternative media' dominate public opinion? Does it threaten democracy any more than an untrusted media and untrusted succession of governments across the UK, America and Europe? Trust in media and the mainstream's credibility has declined. This is because mainstream media are simply not credible. The mainstream barely reflects the concerns of its consumers. Consequently, growing numbers turn to alternative sources and the mainstream's information monopoly weakens. Or does it?

Above, I note the concentration of media ownership in the UK. Most Britons agree that media should be democratized. According to YouGov, 74% agree that media owners should be based in the country of origin (in this case the UK) and pay full taxes. 71% agree with placing limits on media ownership. Compulsory ownership rules, such as independent editors, are advocated by 61% of respondents. 64% support an inquiry into the relationship between advertisers and media. 51% support a tax on media profit to fund local journalism.[33]

According to YouGov, the following percentages of people in the UK trusted the following institutions in 2003: BBC 81%, ITV 82%, broad-

---

[32]Mary Fallon, *Australia's Shame* (2016, ABC Australia).

[33]Media Reform Coalition, 'Poll shows strong support for action on media ownership', 1 April 2015, http://www.mediareform.org.uk/get-involved/poll-shows-strong-support-for-action-on-media-ownership.

sheets 65%, local MPs 44%, Labour politicians 25%, 'mid-market' papers
(e.g., *Daily Mail*) 36%, civil servants 26%, Conservatives 20% and tabloids
14%.[34]

In the UK, journalists and editors were caught in a scandal, hacking
people's phones and email, as well as searching their bins for stories. As
Nick Davies documents in *Flat Earth News* (2008), this behaviour is commonplace. The government finally took action, particularly against Rupert Murdoch, because some of his papers started stepping on big toes:
Lords, bankers and the royal family. By 2011, 74% of Britons thought
that media outlets sometimes or frequently lie to audiences. 55% agree
that media content 'has been dumbed down in recent years'. A report by
Public Broadcasting Service UK Trust (2011) finds that in the UK, 64%
of adults consider television the most trustworthy media, with support
mostly for the BBC. Only 38% trust newspapers. '[W]ebsites saw a high
level of trust (55%)', says the report. This excludes blogs, with only 9%
trusting them. Only 15% trust news from Facebook and Twitter. In the
US, by comparison, most people trust the newspapers more than TV. But
even there, trust by the year 2011 was low: 44% trust newspapers, 42%
trust TV, 18% trust blogs and 19% trust social media.[35]

As part of the hacking scandal ('Hackgate'), it was revealed that several
high profile entertainers working for state-television had not only abused
children on a large scale, but had support from the state, including the
police, in the form of cover-ups. The abuse had gone on for decades.
(*Newsnight* reportedly shelved a story on the abuse. This was revealed
by women's campaign groups in their evidence to the Leveson inquiry.
This evidence helped push the media to start publishing stories about
the abuse.) Hackgate and the abuse cover-up further eroded trust in the
media establishment and in the state. A 2012 YouGov poll finds that
'[f]or the first time since YouGov started tracking public trust in British
institutions, more people distrust BBC journalists (47%) than trust them
(44%)'. Compared with the 2003 poll above, levels of trust by 2012 were as
follows: BBC 44%, ITV 41%, broadsheets 38%, local MPs 37%, Labour
politicians 23%, civil servants 21%, Conservative politicians 19%, 'mid-

---

[34]Peter Kellner, 'The problem of trust', YouGov, 13 November 2012, https://yougov.co.
uk/news/2012/11/13/problem-trust/.

[35]Hannah Thompson, 'Trust in the media', YouGov, 14 November 2011, https://yougov
.co.uk/news/2011/11/14/trust-media/.

market' newspapers (e.g., *Daily Mail*) 18% and tabloids 10%.[36]

By 2014, trust in the media had shrunk to the point where 64% of Britons trust Wikipedia compared to 61% who trust BBC journalists. 55% trust ITV journalists, 45% trust print media journalists and unsurprisingly only 13% trust tabloid journalists.[37]

In the USA, trust in mainstream media has also declined. It peaked in 1976, when 72% of the population trusted what they heard in the media. Twenty years later, trust was as low as 53%. With occasional, slight increases the trend has been in decline. By mid-2015, it was as low as 32%. Among Republicans (i.e., mostly middle class Americans who were more likely to vote Trump), trust in media had reached a record low of 14% by 2016. Gallup reckons that Republicans identified with Trump (or at least against Clinton) and the more the media criticized Trump and praised Clinton, the more Republicans distrusted them. Analysing the trend away from mainstream media, Dr Jonathan McDonald Ladd writes: 'Media distrust is consequential. It changes the way people acquire information and form political preferences'.[38]

One example is the empowerment of Donald Trump. 'Overall, it leads to substantial information loss among the mass public'. 'Information loss' usually means that government and propaganda doesn't work. 'Those who distrust the media both resist the information they receive from institutional news outlets and increasingly seek out partisan news sources that confirm their pre-existing views'. Ladd goes on to say that one result is that 'these individuals are less responsive to national policy outcomes, relying more on their political predispositions to form beliefs and preferences'. Academics call this the echo-chamber effect, where people are drawn to radio and internet personalities, like Rush Limbaugh, who reinforce their beliefs, often with factoids and outrights lies. '[D]eclining media trust is a contributing factor to the polarization of the American political system'.[39]

---

[36]Kellner, op cit.

[37]William Jordan, 'British people trust Wikipedia more than the news', YouGov, 9 August 2014, https://yougov.co.uk/news/2014/08/09/more-british-people-trust-wikipedia-trust-news/.

[38]Jonathan M. Ladd, *Why Americans Hate the Media and How It Matters* (2012, Princeton University Press).

[39]Ibid.

# CORBYN: A CASE-STUDY IN FAKE NEWS

When all of the above factors combine, we should expect that media reactions to political candidates who reflect the wishes of the majority of
Britons and not the wishes of big business will reflect the latter's concerns
about the prospects of their losing power: lies, slander, exaggeration and
negative reporting. In general, the media act as a weapon to alienate
people from their own interests.

Jeremy Corbyn has a long record as a Member of Parliament for the
British Labour Party, representing Islington North, London. Corbyn has
consistently voted against abusive domestic legislation (such as social security cuts) and criminal foreign policies (including wars waged in the name
of humanitarian intervention). Crucially, Corbyn has voted against his
own party on numerous occasions; the so-called New Labour government
led by the right-wing Tony Blair and Gordon Brown. Most of Corbyn's
views on domestic issues and foreign policy (except his views on nuclear
weapons and immigration) are shared by the general public. So, either
some 70% of the British public is far-left or both main parties (pre-Corbyn
Labour and the Tories) are far to the right of most people.[40]

Corbyn was elected leader of the Labour party by a quarter of a million
Labour supporters, many of them dismissed by Blairite Labour politicians and centrists as 'Marxist entryists'—people who actually think the
Labour party should be left-wing, working class and representative of common concerns. Despite unfounded allegations of systematic anti-Semitism
and misogyny in the party and attempted coup attempts by rival leaders,
Corbyn survived and went on to rob the Tories of an outright majority
in the 2017 general election. But mainstream media on all sides spread a
great deal of fake news about Corbyn. It makes an important case study
because for the first time since Harold Wilson, or even arguably since the
end of World War II, ordinary people elected a progressive leader who
pledged to take 'a bit more' from the rich in order to spread wealth more
equitably.[41]

---

[40] Jeremy Corbyn, They Work for You, https://www.theyworkforyou.com/mp/10 133/jere
my_corbyn/islington_north.

[41] Heather Stewart, 'Tom Watson sends Corbyn 'proof of Trotskyist Labour infiltration'',
*Guardian*, 10 August 2016, https://www.theguardian.com/politics/2016/aug/10/tom-
watson sends-corbyn-proof-of-trotskyist-labour-infiltration. BBC News, 'Chakrabarti

The first year of Corbyn's leadership was exciting for the downtrodden and terrifying for the privileged. At last, a politician was giving a voice to the voiceless. He was talking about issues that matter. Any pretense of media objectivity vanished as corporate owners, centrists and right-wingers panicked. Ordinary working people might actually enter politics and start changing the system to suit their needs, not the desires of the upper 1%.

In 2015, the London School of Economics Media and Communications Department analysed the content of eight British newspapers for a two-month period. 'Corbyn was represented unfairly by the British press through a process of vilification that went well beyond the normal limits of fair debate and disagreement'. Anti-Corbyn sources were used more than neutral or pro-Corbyn sources and Corbyn's own voice was often missing. '[B]oth the broadsheet and tabloid press' treated Corbyn 'with scorn and ridicule', portraying Corbyn 'as a friend of the enemies of the UK'. The press became an 'attack dog' instead of a 'watchdog', the authors conclude. Anyone who challenges the status quo is subject to mainstream media abuse, the authors continue. It reflects a 'disturbing trend' in journalism.[42]

On Corbyn, the authors divide their analysis between positive, neutral and negative reporting. When it comes to negative stories, they include critical tones which are normal in a 'watchdog' media and antagonism, which is more attack dog. The attack dog technique has 'three components': 'lack of voice or misrepresentation', 'scorn, ridicule and personal attacks' and through 'association'. Across the eight papers, 56% gave Corbyn no voice. Even in the left-wing papers, only 40% feature statements by Corbyn, which is due to the high number of opinion columns. By excluding Corbyn's statements from articles about him, media delegitimize his politics.[43]

In total 57% of all articles were critical or antagonistic. Sixty-seven percent of opinion pieces were critical/antagonistic. Perhaps of equal im-

---

inquiry: Labour not overrun by anti-Semitism', 30 June 2016, http://www.bbc.co.uk/news/uk-politics-36672022.

[42] LSE, 'Journalistic Representations of Jeremy Corbyn in the British Press: From Watchdog to Attackdog', 1 July 2016, https://www.lse.ac.uk/media@lse/research/pdf/JeremyCorbyn/Cobyn-Report-FINAL.pdf.

[43] Ibid.

portance is style. The right-wing papers (which outnumber the left-wing papers in number and circulation) voiced more pronounced antagonistic criticism. Between September and November 2015, the *Sun*'s coverage was 80% negative (including watchdog and attack dog). Almost no coverage was positive and about 20% neutral. Seventy-five percent of the *Express*'s coverage was antagonistic, 10% was neutral and zero was positive. Of the *Telegraph*'s coverage, more than 30% was antagonistic, almost none was positive and less than 15% neutral. Less than 35% of coverage in the *Daily Mail* was neutral, with 65% negative or hostile and the remaining positive. Seventy-five percent of the *Evening Standard*'s coverage in that period was negative, with slightly more positive reporting than the other right-wing tabloids.[44]

Of the left-wing papers, just over 10% of the *Independent*'s coverage was positive, with a small neutral majority. Interestingly, the diehard Labour-supporting *Daily Mirror* contained more negative coverage (including antagonistic) than the *Guardian*, at close to 35%. This outweighed the *Mirror*'s positive reporting of Corbyn, at over 20%. The rest was neutral. The *Guardian* had slightly fewer positive things to say about Corbyn at under 20% (most of which came from the war-supporting Owen Jones and the nuclear arms-supporting Paul Mason). The majority of *Guardian* coverage was neutral. The *Mirror*'s failure to boost Corbyn's profile shows that its editorial interests are not really with working and unemployed people but with the broadly left status quo. Were it not for the *Guardian*'s two clear Corbyn supporters, that paper's coverage would have been almost entirely neutral with a degree of hostility.[45]

The three left-wing papers get the lowest circulation of all the major UK papers. This means that as far as print media is concerned, the public not only got mostly hostile news about Corbyn, even readers of the 'left' found little support for his policies.

The sources of information on Corbyn are equally interesting. The results reveal that the media mainly relied on anti-Corbyn opinions within the Labour party. This suggests that media were looking for excuses to reinforce the status quo against Corbyn by siding with his opponents in the Labour party, even though ordinarily media support the Tories.

---

[44]Ibid.
[45]Ibid.

This suggests that media owners and editors felt threatened by Corbyn's grassroots class activism and looked for status quo centrists within the party to legitimize their own anti-Corbyn bias. By the time Labour elected Corbyn as its leader, the Liberal Democrat party was all but over, having lost most of its seats. So excluding the largely irrelevant Lib Dems, by far the fewest sources for information about and opinion of Corbyn were the unions. This demonstrates that where people directly engage in politics and control over their work (i.e., through unions), they are excluded from media which seek to de-activate them and delegate political decisions to the managerial class.[46]

Corbyn was frequently slurred as 'loony', 'unrealistic', 'radical', 'Marxist' and 'unpatriotic' in left media.

On Remembrance Sunday 2016, when the nation was supposed to be mourning the fallen and remembering those who sacrificed their lives for our freedoms in the Great Wars, the radical communist lunatic Jeremy Corbyn burst into dance. Corbyn disrespected the fallen and shamed the nation. Or so the *Mail Online* and *Sunday Sun* reported when they published a photo of Corbyn appearing to jig.[47]

The photo was taken by veteran photographer Steve Back, who earned a reputation for snapping cabinet members holding classified documents in their hands. With Corbyn prancing around at the sombre event, Back got a scoop. The media narrative of Corbyn as a Britain-hater was further cemented. The trouble with the photo is that it was fake. Corbyn was walking with war veteran, George Durack, and making some moves as if he was telling a story. Back or someone had cropped the image to exclude Durack and the fact that both men were walking through a gate. By removing the background, Back made Corbyn's walk seem as if he was standing on the spot. Each new footstep was likewise cropped and put side by side in a montage. Back Tweeted: 'Corbyn attends Remembrance Sunday and breaks into a dance – showing no respect for the event whatsoever – disgraceful'. When the uncropped images surfaced and Back was

---

[46]Ibid.

[47]Chris York, 'Jeremy Corbyn Uncropped Remembrance Sunday Pictures Show Labour Leader Talking To War Veteran', *Huffington Post*, 14 November 2016, http://www.huffingtonpost.co.uk/entry/jeremy-corbyn-dancing-remembrance-sunday_uk_58299981e4b09ac74c52d3be.

called out, he Tweeted: 'I witnessed him break into a dance'. Even if that is true, the context was removed by Back's cropping and montage.[48]

The real disrespect is the right-wing using a Remembrance service to attack political rivals.

What was also disrespectful was PM David Cameron's poppy scandal. In 2013, Cameron posed for a generic 'official' photo in a suit and tie. On Remembrance Sunday 2015, the same photo was used by Cameron's managers who digitally added a red poppy (a symbol of remembrance) to the old photo. Aside from the two images being otherwise identical, the poppy was very poorly photoshopped. It was slightly too big and more pixelated than Cameron's jacket, suggesting that it had been added from a lower-resolution image. Number 10 Downing Street fessed up to the lie and removed the photo.[49]

The Media Reform Coalition conducted a study of the same 8 newspapers and their coverage of Corbyn's first week as leader. It finds that 60% of articles were negative, 13% positive and 27% neutral. Of the news articles—as distinct from opinion pieces—6% were positive. Sixty-percent of editorials were negative. In the *Sun* and *Sun on Sunday*, 32 out of 36 articles were negative. Of the *Daily Mail* and *Mail on Sunday*'s articles, 50 out of 52 stories were negative. Turning to editorials, 100% of the *Express*, *Mail* and *Sun*'s stories were negative.[50]

Almost a year later, the Media Reform Coalition updated their research with Birkbeck University. This time, research included broadcast media. There is a '[s]trong tendency within BBC main evening news for reporters to use pejorative language' in reference to both Corbyn and his supporters. Both BBC and ITV headlines and content were biased towards Corbyn's critics. The state-run BBC News was twice as likely to feature unchallenged criticism than its commercial rival, ITV. 'Corbyn himself made

---

[48]Ibid.

[49]Matt Dathan, 'David Cameron mocked after Downing Street admits Photoshopping poppy on to his Facebook profile picture', *Independent*, 2 November 2015, http://www.independent.co.uk/news/uk/politics/david-cameron-mocked-after-downing-street-admits-photoshopping-poppy-on-to-his-facebook-profile-a6718636.html.

[50]Media Reform Coalition, 'The Media's Attack on Corbyn: Research Shows Barrage of Negative Coverage', 26 November 2015, www.mediareform.org.uk/press-ethics-and-regulation/the-medias-attack-on-corbyn-research-shows-barrage-of-negative-coverage.

almost daily public statements and responses' to the leadership crisis, so bias was avoidable.[51]

After alleged Islamic terrorists murdered 128 Parisians in late-2015, the BBC aired an interview with Jeremy Corbyn. The BBC's political editor, Laura Kuenssberg, claimed that she asked Corbyn about a police shoot-to-kill policy in order to prevent a Paris-style attack in the UK. 'I am not happy with a shoot to kill policy in general', he was quoted as saying. What Corbyn also said is that as PM, he would indeed order security forces onto the streets in the event of a terror attack. That part of Corbyn's statement was excised from the broadcast. A BBC Trust report concludes that '[it] was wrong in this case to present an answer Mr Corbyn had given to a question about "shoot to kill" as though it were his answer to a question he had not in fact been asked'. Ironically, the BBC News Online article reporting the Trust's findings was tucked away in the Entertainment and Arts section of the website.[52]

This didn't stop the Tories from using the shoot-to-kill clip out of context in their anti-Corbyn campaign video propaganda published on YouTube.

Like his far-right American counterpart Donald Trump, Corbyn began complaining about 'fake news' in the mainstream. After the BBC reported erroneously rumours about Corbyn stepping down as leader, Corbyn said: 'I'm really surprised the BBC is reporting fake news'. The *Telegraph* used this story to spread more fake news: that Corbyn was inspired by Donald Trump. Writing in the *Telegraph*, Michael Deacon wrote an article subtitled '...Corbyn really is copying Donald Trump'.[53]

---

[51] Justin Schlosberg, 'Should he stay or should he go? Television and Online News Coverage of the Labour Party in Crisis', Media Reform Coalition and Birkbeck University, July 2016, http://www.mediareform.org.uk/wp-content/uploads/2016/07/Corbynresearch.pdf.

[52] BBC News Online, 'Laura Kuenssberg report on Jeremy Corbyn inaccurate, says BBC Trust', 18 January 2017, http://www.bbc.co.uk/news/entertainment-arts-38666914. Lizzie Dearden, 'Jeremy Corbyn accuses BBC of reporting 'fake news' when challenged on resignation rumours', *Independent*, 9 February 2017, http://www.independent.co.uk/news/uk/politics/jeremy-corbyn-bbc-fake-news-trump-reignation-rumours-labour-party-leader-clive-lewis-brexit-bill-a7570721.html.

[53] Michael Deacon "Fake News!', Yes Jeremy Corbyn really is copying Donald Trump', Telegraph, 9 February 2017, http://www.telegraph.co.uk/news/2017/02/09/fake-news-yes-jeremy-corbyn-really-copying-donald-trump/.

# CONCLUSION

The mainstream has failed to sustain the trust of the public in the USA, but the 'respectable' mainstream (BBC, *Guardian*) continues to win the trust of British audiences. The mainstream has succeeded in diversifying in the internet age, with the *Independent*, for instance, publishing solely online with a business model generated from online advertising.

# Chapter 10

# The internet: 'Content will be opinion-based'

*The mainstream media claim that fake news is delivered to consumers primarily via digital media, particularly the internet. This chapter is about the development of fake news on the web, attempts to manipulate information on the part of elites (particularly intelligence organizations) and the growth of online sources. The chapter argues that the commercialization of the internet was designed to make it a personal-marketing tool, and that marketing includes all types of information, real and false.*

The internet emerged from the US military and was transferred to the private sector. In the 1950s, the US established the Advanced Research Projects Agency (ARPA) to develop hi-technology for military use. One department, the Information Processing Techniques Office (IPTO), was funded to research computer sciences in US universities with the aim of creating a Command and Control Research structure. Out of this system emerged the ARPANET. J.C.R. Licklider was director of the IPTO. His role was connecting the Pentagon's supercomputers to a global network. By 1962, Licklider and his colleague Welden Clark had published a paper, perhaps the first to formally propose what became the internet: *On-Line Man Computer Communication.*[1]

A few years later, Donald Davies of Britain's National Physical Laboratory coined the term 'packets', referring to information. ARPANET scientists used Davies's packet-switching theories. In 1969, Bolt, Beranek and Newman launched a version of ARPANET, including its four Interface Message Processors (IMPs) connecting computers at the universities

---

[1] M. Mitchell Waldrop, *The Dream Machine: J.C.R. Licklider and the Revolution That Made Computing Personal* (2002, Penguin).

of California–LA, California–Santa Barbara and the University of Utah. Each node contained IMPs. ARPANET's Network Control Protocol allowed users to access computers and printers in foreign locations. By the 1970s, David D. Clark, senior research scientist at the MIT Laboratory for Computer Science, was moving the ARPANET forward and by the early-1970s, UCLA ARPANET specialist, Jonathan B. Postel, had proposed the official domain names .net, .edu and .com.[2]

Around the same time, packet switching was enabled via radio waves and satellites through SATNET. The similar TELNET (the first Public Packet Date Service) allowed users to connect commercial applications with the ARPANET and related, Hawaii-based ALOHANET through telephone cables. Once Norway and the UK were added to the network, two protocols were adopted: the Transmission Control Protocol and the now-famous Internet Protocol (IP, hence IP address). In 1979, the USENET went online. Invented by Truscott, Ellis and Belovin, it involved email, protocols and dial-up.[3]

By the 1980s, the Pentagon had divided ARPANET into that and MIL-NET, the latter being used solely for ultra-secure military applications. The National Science Foundation (NSF) contracted the Merit Network, IBM and the State of Michigan to upgrade the operating systems for business use. The first transatlantic fibre-optic cables were installed, connecting France to the USA. By 1989, numerous countries, including Australia, Israel, Puerto Rico and the UK were connected to the NSFnet, with William Wulf proposing ideas for collaboration to enable the rapid sharing of scientific results and data. Tim Berners-Lee of CERN helped construct a distributed hypermedia server (which he called the world wide web), allowing different forms of information to be shared via a variety of software, including Uniform Resource Locators (URLs), Hypertext Transfer Protocols (HTTPs) and Hypertext Markup Languages (HTMLs).[4]

---

[2]Matthew Lyon and Katie Hafner, *Where Wizards Stay Up Late: The Origins of the Internet* (1998, A Touchstone Book).

[3]Ramesh Bangia (ed.), *Dictionary of Information Technology* (2010, Laxmi).

[4]Office of Science and Technology Policy, *A Research and Development Strategy for High Performance Computing*, 20 November 1987, https://science.energy.gov/~/media/ascr/pdf/program-documents/archive/Reports_leading_to_national_high_perform ance_computing_program.pdf.

The Web became the main system for using the internet. By the 1990s, the information explosion shifted the Web and Net from being a clunky, slow, difficult to navigate, esoteric networking system to an economically efficient (even profitable) and marketable entity. By the mid-1990s, the website Jerry and David's Guide to the World Wide Web was established (before becoming Yahoo!). Internet carriers for personal computers and business machines included British Telecom, France Telecom, Deutsche Telekom and other European telecoms companies. By that time, nearly 40 million people worldwide were online. By the late-1990s, Larry Page and Sergey Brin were working on a search engine, BackRub (which became Google). By the year 2000, there were 361 million internet users in 60 countries and ten million web domains registered. A year later, Jimmy Wales and Larry Sanger founded Wikipedia. By 2010, Zuckerberg, Saverin, Moskovitz and Hughes out-performed MySpace with their Facebook social networking site. Other giants (Amazon, PayPal, Twitter and YouTube) were also founded.[5]

The internet is and always was a construct of the deep state and wealthy people, mainly in the USA. It is therefore not surprising that despite its enormous potential for informational enlightenment and progressive, status quo–challenging social networking, the architecture and principal owners of the internet and its major websites seek to use it as a tool of social control and profit-making.

# WHO USES THE NET & WHY?

People aged between 18 and 34 are more likely to use the internet than older people. They are also likely to use the net more frequently and use social media. Internet usage is also biased to gender, particularly in Africa where men are more likely to access it. Most internet users are better educated than non-users. This is of interest because, as we saw in chapter 1, elites like to keep a so-called educated intelligentsia within a narrow propaganda system which supports their power. On the other hand, educated persons outside the intelligentsia may use their access to information and wide-ranging education to challenge existing power

---

[5]Debal K. SinghaRoy, *Knowledge Society: New Identities in Emerging India* (2014, Cambridge University Press), pp. 137-39.

systems. Consequently, it is important for controllers to feed educated internet users with status quo news while crying foul over alternative fake news.[6]

By the year 2013, a median of 45% of individuals living in so-called emerging economies used the internet. Two years later, 54% reported using it. In so-called developed countries, 87% use it. In so-called developed countries, a median of 68% own a smartphone, compared to 37% in the so-called developing world. Highest internet usage by percentages are South Korea 97%, Australia 93%, Canada 90%, USA 89%, the UK 88%, Spain 87%, Israel 86% and Germany 85%. Interestingly, 76% of all internet users in the 40 countries surveyed by Pew report using social media, notably Twitter and Facebook. In regions with least internet access (Latin America, Africa and the Middle East), social media use is highest. So, in Europe 65% of users report regularly using Facebook and Twitter, as do 71% of US users. In the Middle East, however, 86% of those who use the internet regularly use social media. In Latin American, it is 82% and in Africa 76%.[7]

One explanation could be the comparative lack of community and communitarianism in Europe and the USA, which are highly consumer-orientated, compared to countries in Africa and the Middle East, which are far poorer in terms of average incomes. This is also important to this study, because as documented elsewhere, social media users in other countries are susceptible to manipulation by US intelligence services which may want to overthrow former allies or current, unfriendly regimes. Social media can also act as a tool to keep people in status quo societies, like Europe and America, disengaged from political activism. Fake news could act as a tool to polarize activists between progressives and far-righters.[8]

Is a majority or even plurality of news consumers using online resources to access status quo–threatening alternative media? Not according to the data.

---

[6] Jacob Poushter, 'Smartphone Ownership and Internet Usage Continues to Climb in Emerging Economies', Pew Research Center, 22 February 2016, http:// www.pewglobal.org/2016/02/22/smartphone-ownership-and-internet-usage-continues-to-climb-in-emerging-economies/.

[7] Ibid.

[8] Ibid.

The top ten most popular websites for 2016 were: Google, YouTube, Facebook, Baidu (a Chinese search website), Wikipedia, Yahoo!, Google (India), Reddit, Qq (a Chinese messaging company) and Taobao (a Chinese online shopping site). An AOL survey of 55,000 consumer interactions finds that the eight main reasons (or 'content moments') for internet use are: inspiration (looking for new ideas), knowledge (staying up-to-date with information), seeking answers or advice (e.g., about DIY or beauty), comfort (seeking support), connection (with others, such as communities), well-being (to improve mood), entertainment and social updates (as opposed to more generic informational updates). In the USA and Europe, the most common searches include news items, including 'Trump' and 'Hillary Clinton', as well as so-called trending terms such as Powerball (lottery), Prince (who died in the year surveyed), Hurricane Matthew and Pokémon Go (all top search terms for 2016).[9]

## A THREATENED MONOPOLY?

Most people who get their information online go to the mainstream news providers, like the BBC, CNN and the MSN sites which carry newswire articles by Reuters, etc.

According to a 2016 Pew survey, 59% of Americans want unbiased news, with a minority wanting news that reflects their political views. But most Americans consider politics a low news priority. Between 2004 and 2012, most Americans considered the following their top news priorities (from top to bottom): weather, crime, community, sports, health, local government, central government, science/technology, business and, finally, international affairs. Fortunately, entertainment came last, even though

---

[9]Sangeetha Shanmugham, 'Why do you use the internet?', World Economic Forum, 24 October 2016, https://www.weforum.org/agenda/2016/10/why-do-you-use-the-internet. Alex Gray, 'These are the world's most popular websites', World Economic Forum, 10 April 2017, https://www.weforum.org/agenda/2017/04/most-popular-websites-google-youtube-baidu/. TIME, 'Here Are the Most Popular Google Search Terms of 2016', 14 December 2016, www.time.com/4598647/most-popular-google-search-2016/+&cd=2&hl=en&ct=clnk&gl=uk. Pew Global, 22 February 2016, http://www.pewglobal.org/files/2016/02/pew_research_center_global_technology_report_final_february_22__2016.pdf. Alexa, 'The top 500 sites on the web', http://www.alexa.com/topsites/category/News.

celebrity news takes up a lot of time and space.[10]

Pew reports that growing numbers of people are getting their news on-line, as well via phones and tablets. This has clearly threatened print media, says Pew, and is gradually threatening TV media. However, we should remember that by 2012, the top online news sites were (most popular first): Yahoo!, Google News, CNN, local news sites, MSN, Fox, MSNBC, *New York Times*, AOL, *Huffington Post*, Facebook, ABC, *Wall Street Journal*, BBC, *USA Today*, internet service providers ESPN, *Washington Post* and The Drudge Report. This shows that although print media has technically declined, the 'mainstream' still dominates the web. Yahoo! and Google get almost all of their news from the three main agencies, who also sell to the major newspapers: Associated Press, Press Association and Reuters. Fox and the rest are still big online players. The only 'alternative' site mentioned in the Pew survey 2012 is Drudge (more on which later).[11]

In just two years (2010–12), the percentage of Americans who got their news from social media jumped from 9% to 19%. Social media is especially used by people under 30 as a source of news. Within a single percentage point, almost as many under-30s accessed news via social media as accessed it on television. Among all age groups, 68% of Americans got their news from television in 1991. By 2012, that had shrunk to 55%. In 1991, 56% got their news from newspapers. By 2012, it had fallen to 29%. In 1991, 54% got their news from the radio, compared to 33% in 2012. When polls were taken in 2002 of social media users, the percentage who accessed news was 24. By 2012, it had leapt to 39%. In TV, the biggest casualty in the rise of social media was CNN, whose share of regular audiences fell from 24% of Americans in 2008 to 16% in 2012. Interestingly, the far-right Fox News and centrist MSNBC held steady. It is worth noting, however, that the average age of the average Fox viewer is 70.[12]

---

[10]Michael Barthel and Jeffrey Gottfried, 'Majority of U.S. adults think news media should not add interpretation to the facts', Pew Research Center, 18 November 2016, http://www.pewresearch.org/fact-tank/2016/11/18/news-media-interpretation-vs-facts/.

[11]Jacob Poushter, 'Smartphone Ownership and Internet Usage Continues to Climb in Emerging Economies', Pew Research Center, 22 February 2016, http://www.pewglobal.org/2016/02/22/smartphone-ownership-and-internet-usage-co ntinues-to-climb-in-emerging-economies/.

[12]Ibid.

By 2012, 20% of Americans were getting their news direct via mobile technology. This may seem small, but it is large when considering that at the time, few Americans used social media like Twitter and Facebook. Above, I note the monopoly of local UK news by few companies. In the US, the audience share of regular local TV declined from nearly 80% in 1992 to 48% in 2012. The percentage of regular nightly network news viewers declined from 60% in 1992 to 27% in 2012. The percentage of Americans who regularly get their news online rose from 1% or less in 1996 to 46% by 2012. Print media share fell from 41% of Americans who read print media in 2002 to 23% who read it in 2012 (or 29%, according other analysis in the same poll). However, regular print media viewers accounted for 38% of the share in 2012 (down by 54% in 2004).[13]

Above, I note the mainstream share of online news. The Pew survey also finds that Twitter users seem 'more closely connected to professional journalists and news organizations than their social networking counterparts'. So, it would seem that the mainstream was hoping to simply use the internet as an extension of its power.

From the most popular to the least, here are the top 20 news websites for 2016. Only one is a so-called alternative site (Reddit), which is in fact a news sharing site, so it includes mainstream and alternative news: *Wall Street Journal, USA Today,* Reuters, *Bloomberg, Times of India,* AccuWeather, Fox News, Yahoo! News, *Forbes,* Weather.com, Google News, *Huffington Post, India Times, Washington Post,* BBC News Online, *Guardian, New York Times,* CNN and Reddit. So, the idea that the mainstream is losing its monopoly over information is false. The medium has changed, i.e., from print to online and TV to online, but the news-creators largely remain the same, with a few 'alternatives' (such as Drudge or InfoWars) competing with the mainstream for hits.[14]

# THE CHANGING NATURE OF TRUTH

As we've seen above, the internet came out of the military sector. We've also seen how the mainstream media has shifted to broadcasting/publishing on the internet. In 2007, the UK Ministry of Defence

---

[13] Ibid.
[14] Alexa, op cit.

published a lengthy report projecting trends out to the year 2036. The report discusses what it calls 'declining news quality', the rise of opinion- and entertainment-based content and the changing nature of 'truth'. It says that due in part to pervasive internet usage, '[t]he truth will not always be based on objective analysis but on what "is believed"'. Much of what the report predicted is coming true today.[15]

The report says: 'The expansion of commercial and unofficial, web-based applications will challenge the primacy of traditional corporate tele-visual and print based formats'. It goes on to say that, '[s]imilarly, the emergence of "citizen-journalists" operating independently of traditional Main Stream Media (MSM) outlets will participate actively across the whole future media environment, fuelled by widespread access to the suc-cessor technologies to digital audio-visual recording devices, such as digital video cameras and camera-phones'. This is an important point because, in order to counter independent journalists, the mainstream supports (by giving them a platform) citizen journalists who usually support the main-stream version of events, such as those behind Bellingcat.com (which largely publishes anti-Russian propaganda) and Metabunk.org (which mo-stly debunks conspiracy theories).[16]

'Advocacy-journalists', ranging from pressure groups to terrorists, will 'stage the news events that they cover and compete in political processes', the report continues. 'MSM will feed off these sources, but also use these techniques themselves, encouraging a trend away from traditional editorial functions, responsibility and quality control'. In this way, the mainstream is trying to look more radical and less mainstream. 'Given these trends, governments in "closed" societies', like Saudi Arabia and North Korea, 'will find it increasingly difficult to control the spread of news and infor-mation, especially where there is a shift to internationalized or shared sources'. Ergo, 'closed societies' are more susceptible to manipulation by CIA-backed 'Twitter' revolutions.[17]

In the UK, the general election 2017 was sold to the public as an elec-tion about Brexit: PM Theresa May claimed she wanted a 'strong hand' (i.e., political support from the public) to enter negotiations in Brussels

---

[15]Ministry of Defence (UK), 'Strategic Trends Programme: 2007-2036', 23 January 2007 (3rd), Swindon: DCDC.

[16]Ibid.

[17]Ibid.

about Britain leaving the EU. The real issues concerning the public were immigration, healthcare, jobs and the economy. Brexit was a secondary issue. The Tory party understood their lack of popularity among the general public and decided to follow the US presidential model in promoting Theresa May as a leader, instead of the party as a whole. The plan backfired and the ruling Tory government lost its outright majority, but remained in power because it achieved a plurality (in terms of percentage of voters). The media were complicit in this technique by allowing May a well-controlled media platform instead of bringing issues to the front of their coverage.[18]

The UK MoD report predicted the rise of exactly this kind of deception: 'The power and ubiquity of the media will increase the tendency towards populist and personality-based politics in democratic electorates, with confidence in politicians centred on administrative and executive competence rather than issues'. During the election 2017, Labour Party leader Jeremy Corbyn played against this game and stuck to issues, many of them non-Brexit. In this way Corbyn broke through the fake news paradigm; and it worked: Corbyn's approval ratings increased and, following her handling of a series of disasters including terror attacks and a major fire in London, May's ratings declined. Even before the series of disasters, the media went into overdrive to demonize Corbyn, particularly with regards to competence more than issues. The report goes on to say: 'Governments, political parties and administrative organs will be subject to pervasive scrutiny and challenge by individuals and groups, who will form a constantly shifting pattern of pressure and lobby groups at the expense of monolithic political parties in democratic societies'. It also notes that '[t]his will be fed by, and will encourage, informal groupings, communitarian solutions to local problems and the spread of libertarian and individualistic values'. Interesting last point:[19]

When Donald Trump came to power, a lot of people in the so-called conspiracy community (including people who believe that 9/11 was an inside job) were shocked to see people like Alex Jones of InfoWars taking Trump's side. Where previously Jones had exposed government crimes

---

[18]Carl Baker et al., 'General Election 2017: full results and analysis', House of Commons Library, Commons Briefing papers CBP-7979, 22 September 2017, http://researchbriefings.parliament.uk/ResearchBriefing/Summary/CBP-7979.

[19]MoD, op cit.

(with a mix of truth and lies), Jones began following Trump 100% in blaming Muslims for terrorism (whereas before Jones would expose Western intelligence service complicity in terrorism) and denigrating the Black Lives Matter movement as an international communist plot against American freedoms. We shouldn't be surprised about Jones's sea change because, as part of the so-called alternative media, Jones was simply following the 'libertarian and individualistic values' predicted in the MoD report.[20]

The MoD's projection (out to 2040) reiterates the predicted changing nature of truth:

'The information environment will become increasingly crowded, with a proliferation of traditional web-page based sites, instant messaging and voice over Internet Protocol applications, and new forms of social media'. It goes on: 'Information will increasingly be transient in nature, generated and tailored to meet need, provide the context to queries, and interact with cyberspace by these and more advanced mediums'. Crucially, it notes that, '[a]s a consequence it will become progressively more difficult to identify sources and validate the information that has been provided'. As a result, '[a]ccess to personal data, and its subsequent exploitation, will have to be safeguarded with commitments to protect user privacy and control'. With regards to truth: 'The majority of new content will be 'opinion-based', rather than formed through objective analysis and peer review, and may start to alter collective perceptions of truth'.[21]

The report also notes that people will get more news from the internet than from newspapers: but it doesn't say whether the source of information will be net-based mainstream news or alternative news. 'The impact of mobile phone videos posted on the Internet has transformed public confidence, scrutiny and interaction with institutions, forcing official organisations to respond to micro-events perceived to be of disproportionate significance to the public'. This is significant because government forces and/or business could create seemingly alternative, independent news sources which are in fact fronts promoting distraction stories to keep the public interested in comparative trivia while real issues go unreported.

---

[20]The Alex Jones Channel, 'Alex Jones Attacked by Communist BLM – Jones FIGHTS BACK!', 19 July 2016, https://www.youtube.com/watch?v=yxPJgMrjAJ4.

[21]MoD (UK), 'Strategic Trends Programme: Out to 2040', 4 February 2010 (4th), Swindon: DCDC.

One of the admissions of the report is: 'The traditional media will continue to attempt to shape the opinion of the general populace and will sell themselves on their trust, integrity and reliability'. This, contrasted with supposedly more diverse media, will result in the echo-chamber effect, wherein consumers will be less inclined to believe media unless it reflects their own opinions and biases. 'This will affect the profile of people who access media changing them from passive consumers to more cynical multiple source users who will take their opinion from many areas and form an opinion based on those they trust, and their own experience'.[22]

## MIND MANIPULATION

A few years ago, several websites and individuals published a leaked collaborative programme by the so-called Five Eyes: America, Australia, Britain, Canada and New Zealand. These countries host huge US spying bases and eavesdrop on most of the world's communications: phone calls, texts, emails, purchased items and webpages visited. In the digital age where members of the public are no longer limited geographically and restricted to using snail mail, the British Ministry of Defence and US National Security Agency (NSA) have targeted online hacktivist groups and even political groups, like the far-right English Defence League (EDL). Led by Britain's Government Communications Headquarters (GCHQ), the programme is called the Joint Threat Research Intelligence Group (JTRIG).[23]

The leaked internal documents seem centrist in that they rhetorically oppose the far-right EDL as well as foreign hackers and online criminals. But in reality, the so-called security services have a long record of infiltrating, disrupting and spying on progressive movements. It is therefore possible that these papers were strategically leaked to get the public onside

---

[22]Ibid.

[23]Mandeep K. Dhami, 'Behavioural Science Support for JTRIG's (Joint Threat Research and Intelligence Group's) Effects and Online HUMINT Operations', Human Systems Group, Information Management Department, Defence Science Technology Laboratory, 10 March 2011, http://www.statewatch.org/news/2015/jun/behavioural-science-support-for-jtrigs-effects.pdf and Glenn Greenwald, 'How covert agents infiltrate the internet to manipulate, deceive, and destroy reputations', 24 February 2014, https://theintercept.com/2014/02/24/jtrig-manipulation/.

by supporting online infiltration of the EDL and other extremist groups. It is worth taking the papers with a pinch of salt and reading between the lines: that everyone, not just hackers, crooks and thugs, is a potential JTRIG target.[24]

One leaked JTRIG report from 2011 states: 'JTRIG staff use a range of techniques to, for example, discredit, disrupt, delay, deny, degrade, and deter'. Techniques used by JTRIG operatives include: 'uploading YouTube videos containing persuasive messages; establishing online aliases with Facebook and Twitter accounts, blogs and forum memberships for conducting HUMINT [human intelligence] or encouraging discussion on specific issues; sending spoof emails and text messages as well as providing spoof online resources; and setting up spoof trade sites'. So, if you're an activist who appears to be making bizarre or criminal online posts or videos, perhaps it's really a JTRIG operative?[25]

The report advocates applying social, cognitive and neurosciences to online manipulation methods: 'social cognition, attitudes, persuasive communications, conformity, obedience, interpersonal relationships, trust and distrust, and psychological profiling'. Work should draw on research from 'advertising and marketing, and from criminology (i.e., crime prevention)'. The MoD's Defence Science and Technology Laboratory (DSTL) is advised to develop a programme which 'measures the generalisability of specific social influence techniques across cultural groups representative of the types of targets of interest to defence and security organisations so that techniques can be applied appropriately'. DSTL, according to the report, should create a programme to assess 'the feasibility of compiling psychological profiles based on information available about the individual on the internet so that those conducting online HUMINT operations can compile and exploit such profiles'. Interestingly, the report categorizes 'online HUMINT and effects' as 'doing things in cyberspace to make something happen'. In other words, provocateurism.[26]

---

[24]Ibid.
[25]Ibid.
[26]Ibid.

JTRIG even goes so far as to advocate creating fake online digital publications. We have already seen the issuance of a fake ISIS edition of *Dabiq* (which the fake news-promoting BBC quoted as real). JTRIG advocates '[p]roviding spoof online resources such as magazines and books that provide inaccurate information (to disrupt, delay, deceive, discredit, promote distrust, dissuade, deter or denigrate/degrade)'. This would make framing people easy. Extremist articles appearing to be written by individuals who are later blamed by the media for alleged assassinations, for instance, could be used to indict innocent victims and frame them for events perpetrated by the deep state. In previous chapters, I have documented how easy it is to fake photos and film. 'Staff suggested that the success of an operation may be threatened by factors such as the: ... Lack of photographs/visual images of online aliases'.[27]

It is easy for the secret services to create entirely fake terrorists, the only proof of whose existence being a photo or two created from 1s and 0s on a design programme, and 'leaked' to the newswires which could then report them as if they are real. To give an example of how easy this could be, artist Kyle Lambert created a perfectly realistic digital image of the actor Morgan Freeman from scratch, using only a finger-paint (or finger-drawing) app on an iPad. Unless told that Lambert had digitally painted Freeman, nobody could guess that it was not a photograph. In addition, a scientific study into beauty appreciation involved the creation of digital composites of really-existing people, i.e., a pair of eyes from one person, a nose from another, etc., and added them to a third person's head, creating a fake but very attractive fourth person who was then rated the most beautiful of all the images. Had one of these fake composites been flashed on-screen by a news programme blaming them for a terror attack, we would never know that the person doesn't really exist.[28]

Back in 1996, 28-year-old Martin Bryant allegedly murdered 35 people in Australia's first mass-shooting. In order to make Bryant look insane, newspapers later admitted manipulating photos of his eyes to bring out the whiteness. It would appear that *The Australian* manipulated the image

---

[27]Ibid.

[28]Kyle Lambert, 'Morgan Freeman', Kyle Art Studio, 2013, http://www.kylelambert .com/gallery/morgan-freeman/. *Telegraph*, 'Are these the most beautiful faces in the world?', 30 March 2015, http://www.telegraph.co.uk/news/11502 572/Are-these-the-most-beautiful-faces-in-the-world.html.

(which it denies doing) and other outlets used it, leading to a court order against the papers. Others included *The Age*, the Australian Broadcasting Corporation (TV) and Hobart's *Mercury*. Specialist Geoff Turner writes:

> The coverage ... raised several important questions about journalistic practice. Of particular concern was the use by the [Rupert] Murdoch media and others of pictures of the accused, Martin Bryant. In one newspaper, the *Australian*, manipulation of the picture to lighten the eye area left Bryant looking quite deranged, which the paper said was not intentional. However, given that the picture took up a sizeable part of the paper's front page under the heading "Face of a killer", with the drop-head "Violent loner spooked locals", this was unfortunate at the very least, and the newspaper apologised to its readers on the front page next day.[29]

Returning to JTRIG, whose stated aim is to do such things online: it's not only monitoring and spoofing. JTRIG also advocates '[i]nterrupting (i.e., filtering, deleting, creating or modifying) communications between real customers and traders (to deny, disrupt, delay, deceive, dissuade or deter)'. In addition to spoofing, it also suggests using what it openly calls propaganda; '[p]ropaganda techniques include: Using stereotypes; substituting names/labels for neutral ones; censorship or systematic selection of information; repetition; assertions without arguments; and presenting a message for and against a subject'.[30]

There are half a dozen such leaked documents which go beyond advocacy and specify strategies. Just bear this in mind when considering alternative 'news' sites and trolls online.

## CONCLUSION

It would appear that, for all the hype, the alternative media have made only a small dent in the mainstream's armour. The most-visited news websites remain either mainstream or spinoffs.

---

[29]Geoff Turner, 'News media chronicle, July 1995 to June 1996', *Australian Studies in Journalism*, Vol. 5, 1996, pp. 265-311.

[30]Dhami, op cit. and Greenwald, op cit.

# Chapter 11

# Algorithms – 'The Harvey and Irma of journalism'

*Much of this book has exposed the lies of the 'mainstream' media and the failure of anti–fake news pundits to admit that the most influential 'fake news' tends to come from the so-called mainstream. But fake news is also a tool of so-called rebel elites, like Trump and his supporters. This chapter examines who is responsible for web-based fake news and outlines some of their motivations. It analyses those who claim to fact-check and debunk fake news. In conclusion, a false paradigm has been established by elites of different stripes; one side of which is the fake news mainstream, the other is the fake news alternative media. Potential voters are polarized and elite systems continue to dominate. We need a genuine, grassroots people's media opposed to both sides of the dialectic.*

Sir Harold Evans, former Editor of *The Times*, caused a storm (last pun of the book) with his comments that the duopoly of Facebook and Google, which allow fake news to spread, were the 'Harvey and Irma of journalism', referring to the devastating hurricanes.[1]

But fake news creates a dialectic. The mainstream, status quo–supporting media allege, correctly on many occasions, that the alternative, mostly-online media are fake news. The alternative media make the same allegation against the mainstream. More often than not, both mainstream *and* alternative are fake news to a greater or lesser extent, depending on how one defines fake news. In the broadest sense, the mainstream tends to omit crucial information from the public and

---

[1]Harold Evans, 'Sir Harold Evans backs Press Gazette Duopoly campaign: 'Facebook and Google are the Harvey and Irma of journalism'', *Press and Gazette*, 11 September 2017, http://www.pressgazette.co.uk/bbcs-jon-sopel-says-it-is-wrong-some-journalists-have-become-donald-trumps-opposition/.

narrow the spectrum of debate to the point where alternative voices are excluded. The alternative news, conversely, tends to take a grain of truth and stretch it into disinformation or else invent claims entirely.

Much of the alternative media are run by wealthy, sometimes mega-wealthy, politically-motivated individuals whose aim is to alienate fake news readers from their own interests by exaggerating the importance of largely irrelevant issues. The mainstream, which are more often than not transnational corporations, seek to limit audiences to fixed viewpoints. Fake news polarizes audiences to support either the mainstream or the alternative news, depending on their personal preferences and biases. Either way, we are getting fake news. Let's turn to current thinking on fake news, what it is and how to counter it.

## FAKE NEWS & SCHOLARSHIP

Chapter 1 of this book argued in part that the intelligentsia of any culture has to internalize and believe the lies and alleged values of the leaders and culture they serve. It is more important to convince the managerial class of its own right to rule than it is to convince the lowly subjects at the bottom who feel the weight of their oppression every day. The recent burst of literature on fake news from the intelligentsia draws unsurprising conclusions: with few exceptions, fake news is something 'they' do (ISIS, Russia, China, far-right politicians); the fake news 'we' do (mainstream media, status quo political parties, big business, the military) is only ever accidental or due to rogues operating within the given system. Consider the recent books about fake news:

'There exists a hierarchy of information sources', says Dr Daniel Levitin, a psychologist, in his critique of fake news and post-factualism. Naturally, those at the top are most trustworthy. In order to identify 'truth', he writes, one must be aware that '[t]wo sides to a story exist when evidence exists on both sides of a position. Then, reasonable people may disagree about how to weigh that evidence and what conclusion to form from it'. This is exactly the kind of changing nature of truth hypothesis predicted by the UK Ministry of Defence. In any situation, there are any number of 'sides', i.e., contexts and ways to evaluate evidence. Reducing analysis to two sides is a classic Platonic dialectic technique which, as we have seen in Chapter 3, results in bounded choice and inductive reasoning.[2]

A common theme among mainstream critics of non-mainstream fake news is the targeting of alternative political systems rather than reflections on one's own. Levitin generates his own fake news by claiming that Yugoslavia was 'communist', as opposed to saying that its wretched dictators used the slogans of communism in order to portray themselves in a utilitarian light. This has the effect of reinforcing the anti-communist propaganda prevalent in the USA, so that when genuine socialistic politicians like Bernie Sanders stand for president, they can be associated with tyrannies like the Soviet Union. 'NBC reported on a thriving community of "fake news" fabricators in the town of Veles, Macedonia'. Levitin felt the need to add: 'This region was in communist Yugoslavia until 1991'. The irony of quoting NBC criticizing fake news was lost on Levitin.[3]

For Levitin, appearance is important. If something appears to be traditional, it can be trusted more readily than if something looks radical. As young people tend to make political change more than old people, this would appear to be a subtle way of denigrating anything new as a threat: 'In the old days, factual books and news articles simply looked authentic, compared to a screed that some nut might have printed in their basement'. But now thanks to the internet, '[a] crank website can look as authentic as an authoritative, fact-checked one'. And how, exactly, does one 'fact-check' the mainstream, which often gets its sources from government officials?[4]

If something is coming from the US government, it is probably true, says Levitin. Why would they lie? 'It pays to familiarize yourself with the [web] domains in your country because some of the domains have restrictions, and that can help you establish a site's credibility for a given topic'. Levitin implies that experts and people in authority cannot lie, as long as they are our leaders. They can only make mistakes. 'Venerable authorities can certainly be wrong', he says: 'The U.S. government was mistaken about the existence of weapons of mass destruction (WMD) in Iraq in the early 2000s'. Evidence is redundant.[5]

---

[2]Daniel J. Levitin, *Weaponized Lies: How to Think Critically in the Post-Truth Era*, (2017, Penguin).
[3]Ibid.
[4]Ibid.
[5]Ibid.

Journalist and author Matthew D'Ancona is demonstrably wrong when he refers to our time as 'a new phase of political and intellectual combat', as we saw in the early chapters of this book. D'Ancona laments that 'ugly populism' is 'shak[ing] ... democratic orthodoxies and institutions'. To translate: people are asserting themselves and trying to take power from elites whose neoliberal policies have harmed their living standards. D'Ancona's basic thesis is that one should believe in the established mainstream media, otherwise so-called '[c]onspiracist websites and social media' adopt a distorted form of Kantian logic: 'Dare not to [know]'.[6]

Like this author, BBC presenter Evan Davis directs us to history, including lies and the exposing of lies in the age of Henry VIII and Victorian literature. Davis denounces what he calls 'bullshit'. This includes 'any form of communication – verbal or non-verbal – that is not the clearest or most succinct statement of the sincere and reasonably held beliefs of the communicator'. Davis further develops his parametres: 'lying is bullshit; trying to deceive without lying is bullshit; and the myriad forms of padding that are designed to impress, obfuscate or attract attention are also bullshit'.[7]

Naturally, when it comes to Iraq—the acid test for honesty—Davis spins his own fake news and 'bullshit', writing that the intelligence which led to war 'simply turned out to be faulty and so in that sense I think it is fairer to say that the war was based on a mistaken premise rather than a lie'. Despite the mountain of well-documented evidence to the contrary, Davis holds fast to the belief that the establishment (whoever they may be at any given time) cannot lie and commit crimes on the basis of a lie: they can only make mistakes.[8]

## ACTIVISM & THE INTERNET

Activism occurs when dominant elites fail to implement policies conducive to the interests of oppressed groups. How has the internet changed activism? The answer to this question is complicated. When disaffected and

---

[6]Matthew D'Ancona, *Post-Truth: The New War on Truth and How to Fight It* (2017, Random House).

[7]Evan Davis, *Post-Truth: Why We Have Reached Peak Bullshit and What We Can Do About It* (2017, Little, Brown).

[8]Ibid.

oppressed peoples needed to organize and push back against the establishment throughout history, they did not need the internet. In today's online culture, it is expected that activists in richer countries will use online media to organize protests, share information and spread propaganda.

Activism predates the internet. The organizers of the Peasants' Revolts (1381 and 1524) didn't need to post messages on Facebook. But few would deny the power of instantaneous, global communication in organizing events. Needless to say, the government and its agencies, including the military and deep state, have always had a keen interest in the uses of the internet for social agitation and resistance. In their view, the internet, and particularly social media as a tool of change, is a double-edged sword. People's lives can be monitored by the state in real-time and target governments can be attacked by dissident populations using social media, as seen in Cuba and across North Africa. But populations can gather unprecedented amounts of good information on governments and use social media to engage in actions counter to government-corporate interests.[9]

BURN! was set up in 1995 by undergraduates at the University of California–San Diego as a way of monitoring real-time web activities related to global activism. The website appeared to be aimed at anarchists and included information about/posts by the Chicano Press Association, Anarchist Communist Federation, Anarchy Now!, the Anti-Censorship Campaign and the Black Ribbon Campaign.[10]

Before long, BURN! was allegedly attracting the attention of groups on the arbitrary US terrorism list, including the Kurdish PKK, Revolutionary Armed Forces of Colombia (FARC) and Basque Homeland and Freedom. These groups saw BURN! as a way of communicating their ideas to young Americans who might find sympathy with their plight.[11]

The site was subsequently disbanded.

---

[9] On Cuba, see Manuel Roig-Franzia, 'USAID effort to undermine Cuban government with fake 'Twitter' another anti-Castro failure', *Washington Post*, 3 April 2014, https://www.washingtonpost.com/lifestyle/style/usaid-effort-to-undermine-cuban-government-with-fake-twitter-another-anti-castro-failure/2014/04/03/c0142cc0-bb75-11e3-9a05-c739f29ccb08_story.html?utm_term=.ba143c414bb0. On the Middle East and North Africa, see Chapter 1 of my *Britain's Secret Wars* (2016, Clairview Books).

[10] BURN!, website, archived 1996, http://burn.ucsd.edu/.

[11] Todd Wolfson, 'Activist Laboratories of the 1990s', *Cultural Studies*, 2014, (28)4, pp. 657-75.

Also in the mid-1990s at the Massachusetts Institute of Technology, numerous individuals, some of them connected to private industry, established an organization called Cypherpunks, also known as Cyberpunks. Many of the individuals associated directly or indirectly with the organization used MIT's professional website to post information about their views and goals, some of which are illegal. Why were the posts not removed? For example, on the MIT Computer Science and Artificial Intelligence Laboratory website, Timothy C. May published his *Crypto Anarchist Manifesto*, which states: 'crypto anarchy will allow national secrets to be trade freely and will allow illicit and stolen materials to be traded. An anonymous computerized market will even make possible abhorrent markets for assassinations and extortion'.[12]

When the internet became marketable and affordable to certain sectors of the progressive left, it was used as a useful tool to organize protests against neoliberal corporate globalization. Primarily young people organized a series of protests across the US and Europe to oppose corporate globalization. A large 'free trade' deal was stopped due in large part to internet-based activism. The text of the proposed, corporate-drafted Multilateral Agreement on Investment was leaked online. This brought enough attention to the treaty to raise sufficient concern among unions and environmental groups over unregulated capital, that politicians, particularly in France, were compelled to reject the treaty.[13]

The Global Carnival Against Capitalism in June 1999 coincided with the Group of Eight meeting in Germany. The slogan, *Our Resistance is as Transnational as Capital*, captured the mood of an integrated people's globalization enabled by the instant-spread of information. Of course, there had been transnational protests long before the internet, information about which had been spread by newspapers, pamphlets and word of mouth (the 1848 demonstrations, for instance). The internet enabled protestors to keep pace with corporate and political activities. New, cheap surveillance tools like camcorders enabled the demonstrators to document

---

[12]Timothy C. May, 'The crypto anarchist manifesto', no date, MIT CSAIL Groups, http://groups.csail.mit.edu/mac/classes/6.805/articles/crypto/cypherpunks/may-crypto-manifesto.html.

[13]Gordon Laxer, 'The defeat of the Multilateral Agreement on Investment: National movement confront globalism' in Laxer and Sandra Halperin (eds.), *Global Civil Society and Its Limits* (2003, Palgrave Macmillan), pp. 169-88.

police brutality in ways never before possible.[14]

But social media is a weapon. The CIA set up fake Twitter-type accounts in Cuba so that the Americanized middle-class could organize against the state-controls of the Castro regime. In the Middle East and North Africa, the US targeted specific regimes—Ben Ali in Tunisia, Mubarak in Egypt and especially Gaddafi in Libya—with social media. This was easier than in Cuba because millions of Arabs wanted political change in the form of democratization in their countries. The proof of the US plan can be found in various military documents, including one which talked of 'manufacturing democracy' in the region and another (sponsored by the RAND Corporation) which talked about hijacking genuine democratic movements like *Kifaya* in Egypt.[15]

US-allied Arabs can use social media as tools to attack regimes the US doesn't like by reporting back to Western mainstream media sources the atrocities of the given regime. The novelty of the new media has a powerful effect on Western audiences whose critical thinking capacities can be limited by the very fact that the information is being presented by new medias.[16]

# THE DEATH OF THE BLOG?

Blogger Kevin Drum says that the main 'currency' of bloggers used to be links from social traffic. But since Facebook came along, absorbing much of the traffic, traditional bloggers 'just don't deliver the numbers'. Blogging conversations became swamped with multi-person blogs, making them 'choppier and harder to follow'. Drum also notes that mainstream outlets using the internet 'started co-opting nearly all of the high-traffic bloggers'. Drum himself was employed by *MoJo*. Ezra Klein was hired by the *Washington Post* and went on to edit Vox. Steve Benen (an intern for Bill Clinton) went on to work for the *Washington Monthly*. Pro–Iraq War 'liberal' Harvard graduate Matthew Yglesias wrote for *The American Prospect*, *Atlantic* and *Slate*.[17]

---

[14]Wolfson, op cit.

[15]See note 9, above.

[16]Ibid.

[17]Kevin Drum, 'Blogging Isn't Dead. But Old-School Blogging Is Definitely Dying', *Mother Jones*, 31 January 2015, http://www.motherjones.com/kevin-drum/2015/01/

You might have noticed by now that many of these bloggers already came from privileged financial backgrounds and simply moved up the social ladders into the 'liberal' mainstream media.

Jeet Heer is an editor at the *New Republic*. His view on blogging is worth quoting at length. 'Blogging was where those of us who didn't trust the Bush administration's push to war' with Iraq in 2003 through blogging 'got alternative takes from Juan Cole, Marcy Wheeler, and other informed sources'. So far, so good: use the internet to question the mainstream media. 'Or if we were conservatives, blogging was where we fisked (remember fisking?) the lamestream media'. Fisking refers to blogs which undermined the position of Robert Fisk, one of the bravest and greatest foreign correspondents who has spent much of his life in the Middle East to bring the horrors of war on all sides to audiences in the UK and the world more generally. (The *New Republic* is biased in favour of Israel's foreign policy.)[18]

'Blogging was where a new wave of feminism was born on sites like Jezebel (a surviving Gawker Media property), launching writers like Irin Carmon and Anna Holmes'. Feminist? Really? Does Jezebel deal with issues of ethnicity, poverty and institutional oppression? If so, in what ratio to their coverage of celebrity news? 'But blogging wasn't just for the young. It also energized older writers (Andrew Sullivan, Mickey Kaus)', says Heer, 'and gave them a much larger audience than they'd had before'. Like the Drum story, we learn that many bloggers were already blogging from an establishment mindset ('pro'-Israel, anti-Republican but also anti-progressive left and 'feminist' within narrow limits).[19]

In true *New Republic* fashion, Iran is a target. In making the case that Twitter and other big social media outlets wiped out traditional blogging, Heer notes that Iranians were able to blog about how awful their governments are via the wonders of US-created social media.[20]

Heer again reinforces the notion that 'classic', old-school bloggers are in fact cornerstones of the establishment. He cites as 'classic' bloggers who espouse 'political wisdom' Brad DeLong (sic—J. Brad DeLong), Digby

---

blogging-isnt-dead-old-school-blogging-definitely-dying/.

[18] Jeet Heer, 'What were blogs?', *New Republic*, 24 August 2016, https://newrepublic
.com/article/136 272/what-were-blogs-death-gawker-blogging.

[19] Ibid.

[20] Ibid.

and Corey Robin. DeLong is a Harvard graduate who worked as Deputy Assistant Secretary for Bill Clinton's Treasury Secretary, Lawrence Summers; one of the many economists who engineered the financial crisis of 2008. Again, readers following this blog are trapped in the dialectic between hating Republicans and loving neoliberal Democrats like DeLong.[21]

Digby turns out to be Heather Digby Parton, a promoter for the Trans-Alaska Pipeline System. Corey Robin is a Yale University graduate and Professor. Robin has conducted valuable research into 'conservatism' as an elite reaction to social progress. But Robin has also written on the alleged problems of the progressive left.[22]

# HOW THE ESTABLISHMENT HIJACKED THE INTERNET

As citizen journalism, blogging has been largely destroyed by three factors: 1) big money (e.g., Robert Mercer quietly funding Breitbart), 2) the usurpation of blogs by establishment institutions (e.g., the BBC setting up blogs on its website to publish reports by dissidents in foreign countries) and 3) advertising (e.g., mainstream owners setting up spin-off websites which appear to operate outside the mainstream news paradigm and end up taking hits away from independent bloggers).

Arguably, the first blog was Justin Hall's *Justin's Links from the Underground* (1994), later Links.net. It offered tours of the world wide web. By the mid-2000s, blogging (web logging) had entered the lexicon and tens of thousands of individuals from all over the world were at it, including individuals working within the establishment. By offering 'free' webspace (meaning that eventually bloggers agreed to have adverts placed on their blog pages), sites like BlogSpot and Wordpress made it easy to post lengthy items online.[23]

In 2005, Dr D. Calvin Andrus of the CIA's Directorate of Support, wrote about the dangers posed to US military operatives and government policy in general by bloggers and blogging. In the past, journalists, including freelancers, risked life and limb to jot down their experiences and

---

[21] Ibid.
[22] Ibid.
[23] Justin's Links, www.links.net.

take film and/or photographs. The correspondents had to fly home or at least send their reports back by fax or snail mail, not to mention get their photos developed chemically. But in the age of the blog, conscientious reporters, like Dahr Jamail, could and did risk life and limb and send instant information, including digital pictures, around the world in seconds via their blogs.[24]

Andrus writes: 'Intelligence Community (IC) ... is faced with the question of how to operate in a security environment that, *by its nature*, is changing rapidly in ways we cannot predict. A simple answer is that the Intelligence Community, *by its nature*, must change rapidly in ways we cannot predict' (emphases in original). Andrus goes on: 'From ... self-organized response[s] will emerge the adaptive behavior required of the Intelligence Community'.[25]

Andrus shows that the intelligence services use blogs among themselves. The mainstream propaganda machine has also used blogs for journalism and psychological operations, if indeed the two can be separated. BBC journalists Chris Vallance and Kevin Anderson both spoke of the importance of blogging in Iraq, specifically as a means of connecting with Iraqis and occupying forces. Vallance explained how difficult it is to interview a person who has recently witnessed a bombing, but the witness is 'able to record something and email it'.[26]

Blogs are also used by elites to target enemy governments by encouraging dissident populations to write critical reports via blogs; the cases of Iran and China are prominent ones, where the BBC used as sources blogs written by Iranian and Chinese citizens sympathetic to US interests. The young Nobel Laureate, Malala Yousafzai, for instance, started as an anti-Taliban blogger in Pakistan for the BBC.

---

[24]D. Calvin Andrus, 'The Wiki and the Blog: Toward a Complex Adaptive Intelligence Community', *Studies in Intelligence*, 49(3), pp. 63-69. Daniel Bennett, *Digital Media and Reporting Conflict: Blogging and the BBC's Coverage of War and Terrorism* (2013, Routledge), p. 70.
[25]Ibid.
[26]Ibid.

# MAINSTREAM GOES 'ALTERNATIVE'

With a lot of money behind them—from business groups, entrepreneurs and advertising revenues—news corporations have spun out into the web. With well-known journalists, access to social media and highly professional-looking site designs, these establishment organizations operating under the guise of progressive alternative news have taken hits away from independent journalists and bloggers.

Some of the most popular 'progressive' websites are BuzzFeed, *Daily Beast*, *The Hill*, *Politico* and *Salon*. But who owns them, how do they make money and how did they become so popular?

Exemplifying the incestuous nature of the internet-business-progressive liberal agenda, BuzzFeed was established in 2006 by Jonah Peretti and John S. Johnson. Before long, Kenneth Lerer of the *Huffington Post* started investing in BuzzFeed. The company then hired Ben Smith of *Politico* to expand the site's journalism content. The editors and owners deny the allegation, but one could make a case that BuzzFeed engaged in fake news by generating initial revenue from native advertising: a type of advertising where adverts are disguised as articles. Since then, BuzzFeed has generated tens of millions of dollars in revenue from equity firm General Atlantic, NBCUniversal and Comcast, setting the company's value at $1.7bn.[27]

*The Daily Beast* was established in 2010 by Lady Evans CBE, a graduate of Oxford and one-time *Vanity Fair* and *New Yorker* editor. It is owned by IAC/InteractiveCorp (est. 1995). It gets one million visitors per day. IAC is worth $3.14bn and boasts 150+ brands. Their brands include Ask, CollegeHumor.com, *Daily Burn* and Vimeo.[28]

The *Huffington Post* gets around 80 million hits a month. It was co-founded by Republican businesswoman Arianna Huffington, millionaire far-righter Andrew Breitbart and others, supposedly in response to the growth of right-wing online media, such as Drudge report. The fact that Huffington and Breitbart established their 'liberal' *Huffington Post*, yet espouse(d) right-wing views, means that they are (or in the case of Breit-

---

[27]Reuters, 'NBCUniversal doubles stake in BuzzFeed with $200 million investment', 21 November 2016, https://www.reuters.com/article/us-buzzfeed-equityfinancing/nbcun iversal-doubles-stake-in-buzzfeed-with-200-million-investment-idUSKBN13G27V.

[28]IAC, 'The Daily Beast', no date, http://iac.com/brand/daily-beast.

bart were) either pure businesspeople or shrewdly creating an online dialectic to polarize opinion. The *Huffington Post* was sold to AOL in 2011. Verizon bought AOL via Oath Inc. in 2015.[29]

*Politico* (USA) is generally right-wing. It gets over 25 million unique monthly hits and is a political platform, publishing mainly online but also in print and broadcasting on television and radio. It was established in 2007 by two ex–*Washington Post* employees and is based in Virginia and features former CIA agent Alex Finely as a contributor to its *Politico Magazine*.[30]

The liberal *Salon* was founded by ex–*San Francisco Examiner* (SFE) staff, notably David Talbot, in 1995 following the strike at the SFE. By 2003, *Salon* was over $80m in debt and was selling stock for 5 cents.[31]

*Slate* was established in 1996 by *New Republic* editor, Michael Kinsley. It started out as an offshoot of Microsoft's portal, MSN. *The Washington Post* (Graham Holdings Company) purchased *Slate* in 2004. *Slate* made its money from hosting ads and introduced a paywall for certain content in 2014. Has *Slate* spread fake news? It generates hits via its counterintuitive *Slate Pitches* page, where journalists write obviously illogical headlines and readers have the pleasure of discovering how the journalist could back up their claims with peculiar logic.[32]

*Vice* was founded in Canada in 1994 as the *Voice of Montreal* by Suroosh Alvi (a filmmaker), Gavin McInnes (an anti-Semitic Knight of Columbus) and Shane Smith (a now-billionaire entrepreneur). *Vice* started life as a Government of Canada–funded project before making deals (particularly in the video sector) with Intel, Viacom, YouTube and HBO. (In 2017, I reached out to one of *Vice*'s journalists, Phil Miller; an excellent researcher who works on British state crimes. I suggested that the two of us work together on issues of human rights and foreign policy. Miller responded with a patronizing email criticizing my book *Britain's Secret*

---

[29] Alex Pareene, 'The stupid saga of Andrew Breitbart and the Huffington Post', *Salon*, 24 March 2011, https://www.salon.com/2011/03/24/huffpo_breitbart/.

[30] Alex Finley, C-SPAN, 13 May 2017, https://www.c-span.org/video/?428365-6/washington-journal-alex-finley-discusses-cia-future-spying.

[31] Scott Rosenberg, 'The San Francisco Examiner, 1887-2000', *Salon*, 21 March 2000, https://www.salon.com/2000/03/21/examiner/.

[32] Michael Kinsley, 'My history of Slate', *Slate*, 18 June 2006, www.slate.com/articles/news_and_politics/slates_10th_anniversary/2006/06/my_history_of_slate.html.

*Wars* on the basis of a single source he didn't like and falsely accusing me of 'paraphrasing' his 'work at length'.)[33]

## SOME MEGA-RICH GO 'ALTERNATIVE'

We have seen how the so-called progressive mainstream media (or status quo mainstream) spun out internet sites and how they and social media destroyed bloggers. Another nail in the coffin is the entrepreneurial initiatives of wealthy, far-right individuals, notably Matt Drudge, Alex Jones and Andrew Breitbart. But who is behind the rise of the online, fake news–spreading far-right, or alternative (alt-right) as they are often known?

*Drudge Report* was founded in 1995 by Matt Drudge as an email news source. It is notable for breaking the Bill Clinton sex scandal story in 1998. Drudge worked with Charles Hurt, who works at the right-wing *New York Post*, and the late Andrew Breitbart of the liberal *Huffington Post* and later the far-right Breitbart News. Drudge Report made money from subscriptions and now makes money from advertising. The site has 3 million hits a day.[34]

*The Daily Caller.* This site was established by Tucker Carlson, the son of Richard W. Carlson, an ex-LA news anchor, US Ambassador to the Seychelles, president of the Corporation for Public Broadcasting and director of Voice of America; the latter being a well-known outlet for US propaganda targeted at other countries. Carlson's step mother is the Swanson foods heiress. Carlson worked for right-wing publications funded by the Heritage Foundation and Hoover Institute. By 2016, Carlson was one of Fox News's most watched presenters, with his show, *Tucker Carlson Tonight*. *The Daily Caller* was financed by the Evangelical Christian businessman, Foster Friess, who managed the $15bn investment firm, Friess Associates. The site gets over 30 million hits a month.[35]

---

[33]Gavin McInnes, 'La Raza VS. The Knights of Columbus = "the race" VS. "charity, unity, fraternity, patriotism."', *Twitter*, 8 June 2016, https://twitter.com/gavin_m cinnes/status/740728763139424 256?lang=en-gb.

[34]DrudgeReportArchives.com.

[35]Joel Meares, 'The Great Right Hype', *Columbian Journalism Review*, July-August 2011, http://archives.cjr.org/feature/the_great_right_hype.php.

*Breitbart News*. Hedge fund billionaire Robert Mercer and his daughter Rebekah not only financed the Trump campaign and Breitbart News (to the tune of $10m in 2011 alone), but the Mercers reportedly arranged for one of its former editors, Steve Bannon, to work in Trump's cabinet. Robert and Rebekah spent $13.5m in donations to organizations supporting Republican Ted Cruz. After Cruz dropped out, their funding went to Trump. *Bloomberg* alleges that Rebekah met Trump's daughter Ivanka and her husband, Jared Kushner. Rebekah reportedly suggested that Trump employ Breitbart editor Steve Bannon as his chief strategist.[36]

*Reddit* was founded in 2005 as a news aggregation/sharing/rating and community forum site. In 2014, a pool including Peter Thiel invested millions of dollars in the website. Thiel (worth over $2bn) is the founder of PayPal and a major Facebook investor. He is a staunch Trump supporter whose book on technology start-ups, *Zero to One* (2014), inspired the Trump team's use of social media in the election campaign. After Thiel invested in Reddit, users established a subreddit called /r/The_Donald.[37]

Palmer Luckey is an entrepreneur worth $700m. In 2014, he sold his Oculus virtual reality start-up to Facebook for $2bn. Luckey started posting on Reddit's /r/The_Donald in an effort to raise funds for a non-profit entity called Nimble America. Under the username NimbleRichMan, Luckey wrote: 'I am a member of the 0.0001% ... I have supported Donald's presidential ambitions for years. I encouraged him to run in the last election ... I have already donated significant funds to Nimble America ... I will match your donations dollar for dollar'. 'Shitposting' is a term used to describe forum posts and threads that take a subject off-topic and include generic abuse. It has been used by Trump supporters as a propaganda weapon against Hillary Clinton. KnowYourMeme.com notes that one of its Trump-supporting moderators allowed Palmer Luckey's Nimble America to get some free advertising, noting the success in shitposting. The site confirms that in September 2016, 'moderator TehDonald [sic] of the /r/the_donald subreddit submitted a post promoting ... Nimble America, remarking that the community had "proven that shitposting is powerful and meme magic is real." Meanwhile, Redditor NimbleRichMan [i.e., Luckey] submitted a /r/the_donald post asking for help defeating Hillary

---

[36]See my *President Trump, Inc.* (2017, Clairview Books).
[37]Ibid.

Clinton by donating to Nimble America'.[38]

# RISE OF THE FACT-CHECKERS

No dialectic would be complete without one side's opposite. In this case, the status quo mainstream under the guise of fact-checking reaffirms its own credibility by exposing the lies and exaggerations of the other side, like those mentioned above. But who fact-checks the fact-checkers and what authority to do they have to call themselves fact-checkers, given that we are all susceptible to bias?

Snopes and the other self-professed fact-checking websites share a common theme: they debunk claims that come from the bottom-up (or ones that appear to come from the bottom up. As we have seen, wealthy entrepreneurs (the top) are sponsoring many astroturf sites (ones that appear to come from the bottom)). In other words, Snopes rarely considers debunking, for instance, top-level government claims, except those of the far-right Trump.

Snopes was first active in 1995, founded by David Mikkelson. The parent company is Bardav, Inc. Mikkelson has connections with the US State Department. The US Embassy Switzerland and Liechtenstein describes Snopes.com as 'a leading U.S.-based resource for debunking rumors and false information'. At a lecture co-convened by the Embassy, Mikkelson discussed 'media literacy, rumor research and the importance of trustworthy sources'. Trustworthy means whatever the status quo government says is true. The fact that the US Embassy is uncritically sponsoring a talk by Mikkelson implies that the US State Department endorses his work.[39]

Mikkelson is a successful entrepreneur and Snopes.com has a working business model. It generated revenues from Proper Media, until the latter claimed a contested 50% ownership of Snopes. Mikkelson raised $600,000 in just a few days of a crowd-funding effort. Mikkelson also has a colourful

---

[38]Ibid.

[39]US Embassy in Switzerland and Liechtenstein, 'Public Lecture at the House of Electronic Arts in Basel on April 27 from 18:00 – 19:00', no date circa March 2017, https://ch.usembassy.gov/david-mikkelson-co-founder-snopes-com-speaker-urban-legends-rumor-research/?_ga=2.65835 566.1654884 985.1509096 797-1956873 248.1 509096 797.

personal life which has crossed over into his company's finances, according to allegations which he denies.[40]

As we might expect, Snopes.com tends to protect centrist government claims by failing to investigate and debunk them. For instance, there are just 21 entries for 'Libya' (late-October 2017 search). Some of those entries are Associated Press reports and not directly related to the NATO destruction of the country, i.e., an Associated Press report of the queen of the UK calling the alleged perpetrator of an alleged terrorist attack in the UK 'wicked'. There is no debunking of the Obama-Clinton claims that Gaddafi was going to launch an 'ethnic cleansing' and thus justified US military attacks on the country. There is no debunking of the claim that NATO engaged in high-precision bombing to minimize civilian casualties. There is no debunking of the claim that the US and wider NATO forces had UN authorization to attack Libya.[41]

Snopes.com also appears to engage in psychological operations by shifting the parameters of discussion in subtle ways. Take the example of weapons of mass destruction (WMD) in Iraq: Snopes has nothing to say about the lies of the Bush administration and the gullible/greedy Democrats who claimed to believe them. The Snopes.com article says that their list produces alleged statements by Democrats found online. They were 'made by Democratic leaders about Saddam Hussein's acquisition or possession of weapons of mass destruction'.[42]

The Democrats clearly lied about Hussein's nonexistent WMD programme. The Snopes.com article doesn't deny this, instead it seeks to shift the point of debate from point $a$ exposing Democrats' lies to $b$: are the quotes in or out of context? Rather than exposing the lies of the powerful, both Republicans and Democrats, and the human costs of those effects, the Snopes article manages the information compiled by research online.[43]

---

[40]David Folkenflik, 'Who's The True Boss Of Snopes? Legal Fight Puts Fact-Check Site At Risk', NPR, 26 July 2017, http://www.npr.org/2017/07/26/539576 135/fact-checking-website-snopes-is-fighting-to-stay-alive.

[41]Associated Press, 'The Latest: Queen Meets Victims, Calls UK Bombing 'Wicked'', 25 May 2017, https://www.snopes.com/2017/05/25/latest-queen-meets-victims-calls-uk-bombing-wicked/.

[42]Snopes.com, 'Weapons of Mass Destruction Quotes', 16 February 2015, https://www.snopes.com/politics/war/wmdquotes.asp.

[43]Ibid.

PolitiFact was basically founded by the *Tampa Bay Times* newspaper, with connections to the Poynter Institute, in 2007. It has spread its own fake news, particularly about Iraq, as we shall see. The organization and its offshoots, like Truth Squad, have received funding from the Bill & Melinda Gates, Ford and Knight foundations. Other organizations that have donated include the Collins Center for Public Policy, the Craigslist Charitable Fund and the Reynolds Journalism Institute. The Collins Center is now defunct. The Reynolds Journalism Institute is part of the University of Missouri and partnered with Apple, AT&T, Google and, among others, the *Washington Post*.[44]

Craigslist is a company specializing in classified advertising. Though it denies the claims, it has been accused of facilitating child sex trafficking and illegal dog-breeding by having lax rules on advert posting. The staff have since worked with the FBI to stop illegal actions.[45]

What about content?

In trying to debunk a 'meme' that Bill Clinton had the same policy of regime change concerning Iraq and Saddam Hussein as his Republican successor, George W. Bush, PolitiFact.com's Keely Herring and Louis Jacobson write: 'Clinton was hardly friendly toward Hussein, but he did not take actions to use military might to oust the Iraqi leader from power'. They omit that part of the Clinton-Hussein un-friendship was the US-British genocide of over one million Iraqis as part of the illegal blockade (1990–2003). The authors omit that US-British naval forces were involved (i.e., military action) and that the stated aim was to push Iraqis to overthrow Saddam Hussein. The report does mention the no-fly zones, but fails to mention that they were illegal and, according to a leaked UN report, mostly involved bombing Iraqi civilian targets, including jetties and farms. The propaganda also goes on to paint Clinton as a humanitarian by selectively quoting the Iraq Liberation Act of 1998, which, say the authors, was designed to send aid to pro-democracy groups. They fail to

---

[44] Aaron Sharockman, 'Who pays for PolitiFact?', 6 October 2011, http://www.politif act.com/truth-o-meter/blog/2011/oct/06/who-pays-for-politifact/.

[45] FBI News, 'Craigslist robbers', 20 March 2017, https://www.fbi.gov/news/stories/craigslist-robbers. See also Associated Press, 'Craigslist founder Craig Newmark isn't closing site's 'erotic' section', *Daily News*, 25 April 2009, http://www.nydailynews.com/news/world/craigslist-founder-craig-newmark-isn-clos ing-site-erotic-sectio n-article-1.361 830.

mention that under Clinton terrorists were being trained by the CIA to attack Iraqi civilian targets suspected of having pro-regime sympathies (as Patrick Cockburn reported at the time).[46]

In one of the more appalling cases of fake news pedalled by PolitiFact, the organization claims that Saddam Hussein sought WMD after his capture by US forces. Their source for this claim? George Piro of the FBI in a *60 Minutes* interview. Do the authors have capacity for critical thinking, i.e., not to believe second-hand claims made by an occupying force? Furthermore, what jurisdiction did the FBI (America's internal criminal investigation unit) have to question the leader of a foreign, sovereign state over a policy that is a matter for the United Nations and its inspection regimes? The article is titled, *Hussein did say he hoped to get WMD*. What it should be called is, *FBI agent alleges that Hussein claimed he wanted WMD, having been captured by illegally occupying US forces which had destroyed his country and killed a million people with sanctions in the 1990s and then unleashed 'shock and awe' bombing against civilians. And by the way, what are the FBI doing interrogating the head of a sovereign state?*[47]

Admittedly, the truthful headline would not have been so catchy.

We can find other examples of this kind of deception. To give one more: PolitiFact claims that Iran is not complying with its obligations to the International Atomic Energy Agency which, due to alleged Iranian intransigence, cannot verify whether its illicit materials are designed for a WMD programme.

When it comes to tit-for-tat minutia about how the US should be run—a class-based, liberal (centrist-Democratic) society vs. a highly class-based illiberal (right-Republican) society, PolitiFact is quick to side with the Democrats. When it comes to more important matters, such as nuclear proliferation, non-intervention in foreign countries and exposing the lies of the 'liberal' mainstream media which tend to be pro-war, PolitiFact is

---

[46]Keely Herring and Louis Jacobson, 'Meme says Bill Clinton, George W. Bush had basically the same policy on Iraq', PolitiFact, 6 June 2015, http://www.politifact.com/truth-o-meter/statements/2015/jun/16/facebook-posts/meme-says-bill-clinton-george-w-bush-had-basically/.

[47]Angie Drobnic Holan, 'Hussein did say he hoped to get WMD', PolitiFact, 5 June 2008, http://www.politifact.com/truth-o-meter/statements/2008/jun/05/john-mccain/hussein-did-say-he-hoped-to-get-wmd/.

quick to side with either party which can demonize alleged US enemies.[48]

On Iran and the IAEA, one article states: 'The IAEA published a report ... that said Iran wasn't giving the agency the level of access and information required to verify that all nuclear activity in Iran is peaceful – a violation of their obligations as signatories of the Nonproliferation of Nuclear Weapons Treaty'. However, the article omits the likelihood that, being a puppet agency of the US empire (to a degree, not entirely, of course), the IAEA is a politicized organization, which according to analyses published in the *Bulletin of Atomic Scientists* has for years overstepped its legal authority. According to the *Bulletin* in a 2012 study (by Daniel H. Joyner): 'the director general's report also applies two additional and separate legal standards – "to provide credible assurance about the absence of undeclared nuclear material and activities in Iran, and therefore to conclude that all nuclear material in Iran is in peaceful activities"' (sic). The report continues: 'I think that the two additional legal standards are ultra vires, or beyond the authority, of the IAEA to apply to Iran and to be the basis for investigations and assessments by the IAEA'.[49]

Another report (by Andreas Persbo) asks, 'does Iran's Safeguards Agreement require the IAEA to verify that materials have been placed in nuclear explosive devices? No, not at all'. Persbo concludes: 'Another way of putting it is to say that the IAEA simply employs *standards agreed with Iran* to investigate and assess the country's compliance with its Safeguards Agreement, and that the agreement should be kept' (Persbo's emphasis). But the US has imposed crushing sanctions on Iran to force it to agree with IAEA and other demands.[50]

---

[48] A search for negative stories yields more results for Republicans than for Democrats on PolitiFact.

[49] Lauren Carroll, 'Liz Cheney: Iran not meeting nuclear reporting obligations', PolitiFact, 22 March 2015, http://www.politifact.com/punditfact/statements/2015/mar/22/liz-cheney/liz-cheney-obama-iaea-iran-agreement/.

[50] Andreas Persbo, 'Agreements should be kept', *Bulletin of the Atomic Scientists*, 1 November 2012, https://thebulletin.org/iran-and-bomb-legal-standards-iaea-0. Daniel H. Joyner, 'Overstepping bounds', *Bulletin of the Atomic Scientists*, 30 October 2012, https://thebulletin.org/iran-and-bomb-legal-standards-iaea-0.

# WHO YOU CALLIN' FAKE?

Who's to say what's fake? What are the parameters for defining an entire organization as fake news? For instance, should the BBC with its reputation for lying and spreading misinformation be completely written-off as 'fake news'? Should Global Research, which publishes good material alongside poor material, also be dismissed as fake?

The label 'fake news' is a dangerous one. In the first place, powerful institutions, such as mainstream media and popular online sites, use and abuse the term. There is no democratic input from ordinary citizens in determining what is or is not fake news. Ergo, a minority of influential institutions selects what is and is not fake. Second, the broad brush term can be used to discredit individuals and organizations. Third, having been labelled fake news by the powerful, other powerful institutions (such as media colleagues or web service providers) uncritically co-label organizations fake news (group-think). Four, how much material should be fraudulent before a given organization is entirely written off as fake?

As we shall see, one influential group (in this case FakesNews-Watch.com) can influence others (in this case Google) who could then harm third parties (in this case AlterNet) by labelling them 'fake news' and using algorithms to divert traffic from their sites.

FakeNewsWatch.com appeared a few years ago, doesn't identify its members and divides 'fake news' into three categories: parody (e.g., *The Onion*), clickbait (e.g., BeforeItsNews.com, they claim), and hoax sites (e.g., ClickHole.com). According to Whois Details, FakeNewsWatch.com is registered by Linwood Jarratt of Round Lake Beach, Illinois. Jarratt is a Republican and political candidate. *The Daily Herald* describes Jarratt as '[o]ne of the founders of the Lake County Tea Party'. According to the Heartland Institute, Jarratt is project manager for the Center for Transforming Education and 'Jarratt has presented analysis on Common Core and education choice on Fox News, Breitbart, ABC Chicago and multiple radio outlets and newspapers across the United States'. So, a guy writing for news organizations spreading their fair share of fake news (e.g., Breitbart) smears others (e.g., Global Research) as fake news?[51]

---

[51] FakeNewsWatch.com.HostDir, 'Fakenewswatch.com Website and Hosting Information', no date, http://fakenewswatch.com.hostdir.org/. The Heartland Institute, 'Lennie Jarratt', https://www.heartland.org/about-us/who-we-are/lennie-jarratt. *Daily Her-*

On the website, there is no content analysis, no real-to-fake content ratios and no statements from both sides of the debate: just pure smear. FakeNewsWatch.com lists its sources. They include FortLiberty, which writes: 'A small group of morally-challenged individuals have discovered that there is a great deal of money to be made by publishing fake news articles'. It goes on to say that '[t]hese rags publish ridiculous headlines like "Monsanto is Killing Your Children", "Ukrainians Worship the Devil", and "Hillary Clinton's Secret Affair with Vladimir Putin". These inflammatory headlines are then promoted though social media sites like Facebook and Twitter'. Notice that the alleged headlines cited by the site tacitly support big agribusiness (Monsanto), US coups (in Ukraine) and the status quo politics of contemporary America (Clinton). 'They are actually doing a worse job than the mainstream media – something many of us once thought impossible', says the site.[52]

But, organizations linked to FortLiberty include: American Enterprise Institute, Americans for Prosperity, the Cato Institute, Center for Security Policy, the Club for Growth, FreedomWorks and the Heritage Foundation. Many of these organizations are right-wing, but not too far right. Many supported the Tea Party before it splintered into the clickbait alt-right. They have sought to push Democrats further right and advocate so-called 'free market' liberal internationalism led by the USA and its corporations, whereas the far-right elites want nationalism but of a bastardized kind.[53]

The people defining what is or isn't 'fake news' have their own agenda for doing so. Many are right-wing organizations that have sponsored the Republican Party. They are upset by far-right, self-styled paleoconservatism of the Donald Trump–Alex Jones variety. They are losing a number of voters to this fringe. By denouncing alternative media as 'fake news', they presumably hope to bring internet users back into the fold of mainstream news and thus into the corporate-owned left-right paradigm.[54]

FakeNewsWatch.com also cites P2T2 Solutions, which says of itself:

---

*ald*, 'Linwood Jarratt: Candidate Profile', 10 February 2012, http://www.dailyhera ld.com/article/20120131/submitted/301319505/.

[52]FortLiberty, 'Web Sites Which Publish Fake News and Other Hoaxes', no date, http://www.fortliberty.org/hoax-sites.html.

[53]Ibid.

[54]Ibid.

'P2T2 Solutions and P2T Tactical sharing helpful information both Patriotic, Prepping and Tactical to help keep you safe during these troubling
times'. Its YouTube page features videos like, 'Is Obama a Muslim?'. Obviously FakeNewsatch.com doesn't get irony. Above, we've examined the
background and agendas of Snopes and *New Republic*, other sources cited
by the website.[55]

# BEWARE THE BOTS

In addition to all of the above, it is important to recognize the relevance
of algorithms ('bots') in today's social media and news content. Bots
are getting so sophisticated that it is becoming increasingly difficult to
tell which online comments are real and which are bots, which sites are
genuinely popular and which are getting fake hits generated by bots.

Net-based fake news has become a phenomenon. Yet according to public
opinion polls, few Americans have heard of the 'alt-right', the ideological
grouping mainly responsible for online fake news. Donald Trump lost the
popular vote by 2.6 million, but he won the Electoral College vote. In
other words, 'alt-right' voters were numerous enough to give Trump a
plurality in the Electoral College. How do we explain this discrepancy,
that fake news is a phenomenon yet its main champions remain obscure?

It turns out that bots are pushing fake news stories to make them go 'viral' by sharing stories among fake bot accounts ('sock puppets') on social
media. In 2011, a team at Texas A&M University created gibberish-spew-
ing Twitter accounts. Their nonsense could not have possibly interested
anyone, yet soon they had thousands of followers. They found that their
Twitter 'followers' were bots.[56]

In 2017 under a Pentagon grant, Shao et al. analysed 14 million Tweets
spreading 4,000 political messages during the 2016 US Presidential campaign. They found that '[a]ccounts that actively spread misinformation
are significantly more likely to be bots'. Fake news, they say, includes
'hoaxes, rumors, conspiracy theories, fabricated reports, click-bait head-

---

[55]P2T2 Solutions, YouTube page, https://www.youtube.com/channel/UCcXNBn7-
nB1R63DQAVRqNpw.

[56]Emilio Ferrara, Onur Varol, Clayton Davis, Filippo Menczer and Alessandro Flammini,
'The Rise of the Social Bots', *Communications of the ACM*, 59(7), pp. 96-104.

lines, and even satire'. Incentives include sending 'traffic to fake news sites [which] is easily monetized through ads, but political motives can be equally or more powerful'. During the presidential campaign, it was discovered that popularity profiles of fake news are indistinguishable from fact-checking articles.[57]

The authors note that, 'for the most viral claims, much of the spreading activity originates from a small portion of accounts'. The so-called super-spreaders of fake news are likely to be 'social bots that automatically post link to articles, retweet other accounts, or perform more sophisticated autonomous tasks'. Regional vote shares toward Trump did not match the geographical location of (likely) bot accounts. Though it is unconfirmed, it is likely 'that states most actively targeted by misinformation-spreading bots tended to have more surprising election results'.[58]

Ratkiewicz et al. argue that Twitter has a structural bias for fake news due to its '140-character sound bytes [which] are ready-made headline fodder for the 24-hour news cycle'. Ferrara et al. write that bots can 'engage in ... complex types of interactions, such as entertaining conversation with other people, commenting on their posts, and answering their questions'. The authors go on to note that bots 'can search the Web for information and media to fill their profiles, and post collected material at predetermined times, emulating the human temporal signature of content production and consumption', including the time of day when bot activity spikes.[59]

In 2014, the *Guardian* revealed that the UK Ministry of Defence was spending over £60,000 of taxpayers' money on a project called Full Spectrum Targeting. The project was conducted with Detica (a subsidiary of BAE Systems), the Change Institute and Montvieux. 'Emphasis is put on identifying and co-opting influential individuals, controlling channels of information and destroying targets based on morale rather than

---

[57]Chengcheng Shao, Giovanni Luca Ciampaglia, Onur Varol, Alessandro Flammini and Filippo Menczer, 'The spread of fake news by social bots', arXiv, 26 September 2017, https://arxiv.org/pdf/1707.07 592.pdf.

[58]Ibid.

[59]J. Ratkiewicz, M. D. Conover, M. Meiss, B. Gonçalves, A. Flammini and F. Menczer, 'Detecting and Tracking Political Abuse in Social Media', Proceedings of the Fifth International AAAI Conference on Weblogs and Social Media, https://www.mashregh news.ir/files/fa/news/1393/12/24/946 657_331.pdf.

military necessity'. The Cognitive and Behaviour Concepts of Cyber Activities project cost over £310,000 and included Baines Associates, i to i Research and several universities, including Northumbria, Kent and University College London.[60]

# FAKE NEWS, BOTS & THE MAKING OF A PRESIDENT

In 2012, scientists working for the Center for Tobacco Control Research and Education at the University of California and San Francisco exploited nearly 700,000 Facebook users by making them participate in an experiment without their knowledge or consent.[61]

'The experiment manipulated the extent to which people ... were exposed to emotional expressions in their News Feed', says the research paper. The experiment 'tested whether exposure to emotions led people to change their own posting behaviors'. The two parallel experiments involved 1) reducing friends' exposure to positive content and 2) reducing their exposure to negative content. '[F]or a person for whom 10% of posts containing positive content were omitted, an appropriate control would withhold 10% of 46.8% (i.e., 4.68%) of posts at random, compared with omitting only 2.24% of the News Feed in the negatively-reduced control'. The authors go on: 'As a secondary measure, we tested for cross-emotional contagion in which the opposite emotion should be inversely affected: People in the positivity reduced condition should express increased negativity, whereas people in the negativity reduced condition should express increased positivity'.

The results concerning emotional contagion were statistically miniscule, 0.001. But, as the authors, point out: given 'the massive scale of social networks such as Facebook, even small effects can have large aggregated consequences'. This, they theorize, equates 'to hundreds of thousands of

---

[60]Ben Quinn, 'Revealed: The MoD's secret cyberwarfare programme', *Guardian*, 16 March 2014, https://www.theguardian.com/uk-news/2014/mar/16/mod-secret-cyber-warfare-programme.

[61]Adam D. I. Kramera, Jamie E. Guilloryb and Jeffrey T. Hancock, 'Experimental evidence of massive-scale emotional contagion through social networks', PNAS, 111(24), pp. 8788-90.

emotion expressions in status updates per day'.[62]

This is relevant to fake news because it shows how bots can spread fake news and cause emotional contagion among large numbers of potential voters. For example, a negative story about Hillary Clinton—amplified by bots online—could make potential Clinton-voters feel bad and bicker with one another about the significance of voting, while simultaneously reinforcing bonds among pro-Trump voters in their collective opposition to Clinton.

Extending on the information above concerning Robert Mercer, various mainstream sources report that Robert Mercer worked for IBM on technology used to develop its Watson super-computer ('Brown clustering') and Apple's Siri technology. Mercer is a Trump mega-donor. There's no evidence directly connecting Robert Mercer to pro-Trump bots. The companies involved with Mercer, including Cambridge Analytica and Renaissance Technologies, have done nothing illegal. Yet the kind of technologies and services in which they are involved include influencing elections.[63]

Trump has 30 million Twitter 'followers', only half of whom are real; the other 50% are bots. *New York Daily News* spoke to Simon Crosby of Bromium technologies, who explained that some of the Watson technology, allegedly developed by Mercer, 'can quickly build, test and deploy bots or virtual agents across mobile devices or messaging platforms to create natural conversations between apps and users'. Crosby goes on to say that 'arbitrary and ridiculous information [is] spread very quickly, and now to targeted user[s]', who are 'more susceptible to believing it and spreading it'.[64]

One of Trump's first Twitter 'supporters' was a bot called PatrioticPepe. A whole fifth of Twitter accounts tweeting about the election were bots. Hilarity ensues when the organization reporting on this, the *Washington Post*, also reports that the data for fake, Trump-supporting accounts are accrued from Twitter Audit: the website points out that an estimated

---

[62]Ibid.

[63]Carole Cadwalladr, 'Robert Mercer: the big data billionaire waging war on mainstream media', *Guardian*, 26 February 2017, https://www.theguardian.com/politics/2017/feb/26/robert-mercer-breitbart-war-on-media-steve-bannon-donald-trump-nigel-farage.

[64]Adam Edelman, 'The billionaire GOP patron behind Trump's social media bot army', *New York Daily News*, 10 June 2017, http://www.nydailynews.com/news/politics/billionaire-gop-patron-behind-trump-social-media-bot-army-article-1.3236933.

35%+ of the *Washington Post*'s Twitter's followers are also bots. The reporter overcomes this hypocrisy by writing that *The Washington Post*'s percentage of fake followers is lower than that of Trump's.[65]

As I and others have documented, Brexit was in part a psychological operation aimed at the public by mega-wealthy hedge fund managers who want out of Europe. The *Guardian*'s Carole Cadwalladr spoke with Andy Wigmore, communications director at the Leave.Eu campaign. Wigmore was behind the Trump–Nigel Farage meeting and photo op.[66]

Recall the contagion effect measured above. Referring to Brexit, Wigmore explained that (Cadwalladr's paraphrase) 'Facebook was the key to the entire campaign'. Wigmore is quoted as saying, 'using artificial intelligence, as we did, tells you all sorts of things about that individual and how to convince them with what sort of advert', i.e., spread contagion about things that matter to voters, such as immigration, via algorithms.[67]

## 'TACKLING' FAKE NEWS?

One of the effects of allowing the proliferation of far-right alternative media and its subsequent being labelled fake news, has been the knock-on effect of rendering certain progressive websites with the same epithet.

The Trump victory in 2016 shocked and upset certain quarters of the status quo establishment, which put its money on Trump's rival, Hillary Clinton. The real problem is that the American political system is rigged not only against Democrats, but against progressive Democrats. Hillary Clinton, the status quo Democrat, was the second least popular candidate in US history; Trump was the least popular. Public opinion polls suggest that had Clinton and her supporters not sabotaged Bernie Sanders's campaign, Sanders would have beaten Trump. Nevertheless, Clinton won the popular vote by 2.6 million. Trump was elected only by the Electoral College.[68]

---

[65] Philip Bump, 'Welcome to the era of the 'bot' as political boogeyman', *Washington Post*, 12 June 2017, https://www.washingtonpost.com/news/politics/wp/2017/06/12/welcome-to-the-era-of-the-bot-as-political-boogeyman/?utm_term=.44099f069e81.
[66] Cadwalladr, op cit. See also my *The Great Brexit Swindle* (2016, Clairview Books).
[67] Ibid.
[68] See my *President Trump, Inc.* (2017, Clairview Books).

The illusion that Trump was popular with enough Americans to win the Presidency was perpetuated by mainstream media itself. Mainstream media raised enough objection to pressure the big internet providers—Facebook, Google and Twitter—to counter so-called fake news. But, as noted above, certain actors working for wealthy and comparatively influential think-tanks (like the Heritage Foundation) smear news and analysis providers with the label fake news. They lump the far-right and the progressive left together. Citing no examples, evidence or criteria for what is or is not fake news, said organizations appear to have influenced Facebook et al.'s taxonomy.[69]

*Bloomberg* reports that 'Facebook was criticized for allowing misleading information to go viral, potentially resulting in misinformed voters' and thus led to a Trump victory (though, as noted, the real reasons are more complex and institutional). 'One viral hoax, for example, claimed that the Pope had endorsed Trump'. It notes that Facebook 'has created a software algorithm to flag stories that may be suspicious and send them to third-party fact checkers'. Those cited in the recent past include Snopes.com and PolitiFact, which, as we have seen, are as establishment as it gets. So, back to square one.[70]

A couple of months later in October 2017, Facebook added an 'i' button to its news feeds, so that users can assess the origin of the story. For instance, it describes the Associated Press as 'an American multinational non-profit news agency'. Here, we encounter the appeal-to-authority logical fallacy, that because something comes from an authoritative source, it is more likely to be true. Notice that the 'i' button does not describe the AP as being responsible for approximately 30% of all news (with Reuters supplying an additional 30% (approx.)) or that the AP is well-known to be infiltrated by the CIA, as Nick Davies documents in *Flat Earth News*.[71]

Facebook, which has a habit of conducting tests on an unsuspecting public, completed trials in November of the same year. It was a test to put items containing the word 'fake', both real stories and hoaxes/half-truths,

---

[69] Ibid.

[70] Andrew Harrer, 'Facebook Has a New Plan to Curb 'Fake News'', *Bloomberg*, 3 August 2017, http://fortune.com/2017/08/03/facebook-fake-news-algorithm/.

[71] Tom Huddleston, 'Facebook's Latest Attempt at Fighting Fake News Is to Provide Publisher Info', *Fortune*, 5 October 2017, http://fortune.com/2017/10/05/facebook-test-more-info-button-fake-news/.

in order to '[prioritize] comments that indicate disbelief'. This creates a group-think fallacy, that on the basis that the majority of opinion holds $x$ to be correct or incorrect, $x$ is correct or incorrect. The project targeted only a certain number of users, generating annoyance and frustration, says the BBC.[72]

Dr Nafeez Ahmed has documented the CIA origins of Google and its various related companies. Co-founder Eric Schmidt went on to work for the Pentagon's Defense Innovation Board. Perhaps of equal importance (for US military dominance and the hi-tech economy are inexorably linked to big business), Google is a multi-billion dollar giant. It is in its interest, therefore, to promote pro-business agendas, including those of both Trump and his fake news-toting alt-right sponsors and Hillary Clinton and her fake news-spouting status quo mainstream. Genuine people's information, from the ground-up, is a threat to Google as a business and to the Pentagon as a social movement.[73]

In addition to so-called fake news, the practice of clickbait (below) has been censured by Google; except the authorized clickbait sites like Taboola (which the owners stress are not clickbait sites). These include so-called black hat search engine optimization (SEO) practices, wherein those seeking to maximize web hits and thus ad revenue violate search engine guidelines. Sites also feature more ads than information, despite titling pages in a way that entice visits. *Forbes* reports that since March 2017, when Google introduced Fred, a jokingly-named search update—in reality a new algorithm—black hat SEOs and large-ad sites saw up to a 90% drop in traffic.[74]

Importantly, progressive sites previously labelled 'fake news' by those mentioned above took a hard hit. AlterNet says that since June 2017, it has lost 40% of its unique hits, or 1.2 million people per month. This has

[72] Jane Wakefield, 'Facebook's fake news experiment backfires', BBC, 7 November 2017, http://www.bbc.co.uk/news/technology-41900 877.

[73] Nafeez Ahmed, 'How the CIA made Google', *InsurgeIntelligence*, 22 January 2015, https://medium.com/insurge-intelligence/how-the-cia-made-google-e836 451a959e. In two parts.

[74] Rajiv Parikh, 'How To Bounce Back From The Google Fred Algorithm – And Prepare For Future Updates', *Forbes*, 5 October 2017, www.forbes.com/sites/forbesagenc ycouncil/2017/10/05/how-to-bounce-back-from-the-google-fred-algorithm-and-prepar e-for-future-updates/.

also meant a loss in advertising revenue and thus an inability to provide as efficient a news and analysis service. (If I may indulge in another tedious personal example, Emily C. Bell of AlterNet published an analysis of an interview I conducted for my edited book, *Voices for Peace*. Where once the subject of the interview would have appeared in Google News, the Fred algorithm, I assume, prevented it from appearing there. It was only after a website called Truthdig picked up the article that the Truthdig version appeared.)[75]

The World Socialist Web Site (WSWS) has also experienced a crash in hits. The site claims to get over 460,000 hits per day from Google searches. By the end of July, however, the WSWS was receiving just 138,000. The average position of articles fell from 15.9 to 37.2. WSWS produces a chart of traffic metrics. Apparently, the following sites have all seen a sharp decline in hits, ranging from 4.9% in global reach (counterpunch.org) to a stunning 44.9% (the American Civil Liberties Union).[76]

Is this COINTELPRO for the digital age? Affected sites include: Amnesty International, AntiWar, Common Dreams, Consortium News, *Democracy Now!*, Global Research and TruthOut. In previous chapters, we saw that for all the hype, web-based alternative sites on the left and right are swamped by the mainstream and its web-based spin-offs. *Salon* notes that as MSNBC's left-leaning (but within status quo limits) Rachel Maddow enjoys record viewers as part of the cable channel's anti-Trump agenda, 'this new energy on the left has not necessarily helped progressive websites'. It quotes Google engineer Ben Gomes as saying that Google deliberately inserted 'offensive or clearly misleading content' into a number of search results in order to 'help surface more authoritative [i.e., establishment] pages and demote low-quality content'.[77]

---

[75] Don Hazen, 'Editorial: Google's Threat to Democracy Hits AlterNet Hard', AlterNet, 28 November 2017, https://www.alternet.org/media/editorial-googles-threat-democracy-hits-alternet-hard.

[76] Andre Damon and Niles Niemuth, 'New Google algorithm restricts access to left-wing, progressive web sites', WSWS, 27 July 2017, https://www.wsws.org/en/articles/2017/07/27/goog-j27.html.

[77] Ibid. Matthew Sheffield, ' "Fake news" or free speech: Is Google cracking down on left media?', *Salon*, 18 October 2017, https://www.salon.com/2017/10/18/fake-news-or-free-speech-is-google-cracking-down-on-left-media/.

# CLICKBAIT

No chapter on web-based fake news would be complete without a reference to ad-revenue-generated clickbait. Many mainstream sites which chide others for being 'fake news' are not only hypocritical in their refusal to tell the truth about the workings of the world, they are hypocritical in that they host fake news in the form of clickbait.

Google has generated most of its revenue from AdSense. According to the European Union, which by July 2017 had filed three antitrust suits against Google, complained that 'Google has hindered competition by limiting the ability of its competitors to place search adverts on third-party websites' (EU Antitrust Commissioner, Margrethe Vestager). Google Shopping 'unduly favoured its own comparison shopping service in its general search result pages', the EU alleges.[78]

According to the self-styled tracker of fake news and extremist sites, Storyzy analysed 700+ websites on its automated blacklist and found that 90% of those using programmatic adverts are associated with AdSense. Google AdSense amounts to clickbait in that it does not remove sponsored content from websites, but only from certain pages. While Macedonian teenagers and progressives are getting the blame, the usual culprits were found to be using AdSense on alleged fake news and extremist sites, according to Storyzy: Adobe, American Express, AT&T, Dell, Goodyear, Hertz, Microsoft, McDonald's, Toyota, Verizon and Visa. These companies deny any wrongdoing.[79]

One of the worst clickbait culprits, according to critics (a claim denied by the company and its founder), is Taboola. The company was established by ex-Israeli military cyber intelligence entrepreneur, Adam Singolda. '[S]ome Taboola employees are IDF [Israeli Defence Forces] reservists', says the BBC. Taboola reaches one billion people per month and is worth $500m. 'I don't think fake news or any variation of that should exist ... I think there needs to be a human element. I don't think bots can

---

[78]Samuel Gibbs, 'European commission files third antitrust charge against Google', *Guardian*, 14 July 2016, https://www.theguardian.com/technology/2016/jul/14/eur opean-commission-files-third-antitrust-charge-against-google.

[79]Stan Motte, 'How Google AdSense and Brands Continue to Fund Extremist Websites', MediaShift, 8 September 2017, http://mediashift.org/2017/09/google-adsense-allows-ads-extremist-sites/.

solve this one', says Singolda.[80]

The BBC, which cries foul about fake news, gave Singolda a little free advertising; paid for by British licence-fee payers, of course. 'A charming Mr Singolda ... jokes that we only have ourselves to blame. "The problem is that for everyone who hates one piece of content, many others love it, and click on it," he says'. The BBC goes on with more free advertising and boot-licking: 'Taboola is now [2014] looking to secure a fresh multi-million dollar injection of investment, as it plans to expand around the world'.[81]

Finally, the other big ad sponsor is Outbrain. Established in 2006, this time by two ex-Israeli Navy Officers (Yaron Galai and Ori Lahav), Outbrain uses targeted content to maximize interest. It reaches 90% of American internet users and, unlike Taboola, claims to make greater efforts to screen spam. *Wired* reports that Outbrain, Taboola and others mean that '[r]elevant news is increasingly being replaced with fake ads'. *Wired* points to ChangeAdvertising.org which analysed the top 50 news sites. It found that by mid-2016, 82% used 'content ads' from Adblade, Outbrain, Revcontent and Taboola. Of these, 26% were clickbait sites. Of the 26%, nearly nine out of ten were anonymous sites.[82]

The report found that advertisers are also disguising their ads by calling them 'From Around the Web', 'More to Explore' and 'Promoted Links'. This alleged dishonesty is possibly counter to America's Federal Trade Commission's Native Ad Guidelines. They create the tabloidization of the internet, including of the 'respectable' sites that host their ads.[83]

---

[80]Will Smale, 'Taboola: The internet firm at the forefront of 'click-bait'', BBC, 30 September 2014, http://www.bbc.co.uk/news/business-29322 578. Christopher Kompanek, 'Taboola founder Adam Singolda on stopping fake news', *FT*, 22 June 2017, https://www.ft.com/content/101e7236-54d2-11e7-80b6-9bfa4c1f83d2?mhq5j=e5.

[81]Smale, op cit.

[82]James Temperton, 'We need to talk about the internet's fake ads problem', *Wired*, 27 March 2017, http://www.wired.co.uk/article/fake-news-outbrain-taboola-hillary-clinton. ChangeAdvertising.org, 'The Clickbait Report', 2016, https://web.archive.org/web/20170709062 818/http://changeadvertising.org/the-clickbait-report/.

[83]Ibid.

# CONCLUSION

The mainstream has succeeded in spinning off internet venture sites, mostly paid for by advertising. The alt-right has also succeeded as a business model, but failed to reach any more than a fringe of the US electorate. This can be gauged with polls indicating that even majorities or large minorities of Republicans don't believe many of the alt-right's claims.

# Conclusion: Some personal reflections

This book has argued that fake news is everywhere and always has been. If knowledge is power, the most important issue concerning fake news is who has power over whom and how that power is used. By referring to something as fake, it follows that its given opposite is authentic. Authenticity and truth are closely related. If something is authentic it is also, to whatever degree we may judge, truthful. For example: An artefact is discovered and put in a museum (authentic), yet we later learn that the museum has re-coloured the artefact to make it more visually attractive to museum-goers (element of inauthenticity). Seldom do we consider absolute truths: For example, the atomic decay of the artefact means that on one level of interpretation, it is not the same now as it was when it was first made (Ship of Theseus paradox).

## AS PILATE SAID, WHAT IS TRUTH?

Truth depends on individual experience and interpretation. Yet, there are objective truths, though perhaps not 'ultimate' truths. Almost all of us will agree that 2+2=4, yet it is possible to dispute this if we change the parameters of debate:[1]

$$-20 = -20$$
$$16 - 36 = 25 - 45$$
$$4^2 - (9x4) = 5^2 - (9x5)$$
$$4^2 - (9x4) + 81/4 = 5^2 - (9x5) + 81/4$$
$$(4-9/2)^2 = (5-9/2)^2$$

Cancel the powers on both sides:

$$4-9/2 = 5-9/2$$

---

[1] xbasux, '2+2=5 Proof', YouTube, 14 December 2010, https://www.youtube.com/watch?v=XXhbThOITLQ. Thanks to Dr Matthew Watkins.

Cancel (-9/2) from both sides:

4=5 or 2+2=5.

The above equation is a trick. It collapses at $(4-9/2)^2 = (5-9/2)^2$ or $(-1/2)^2 = (+1/2)^2$ or $(-3)^{\wedge 2} = (+3)^2$, which doesn't mean that $-1/2 = +1/2$. So, it doesn't follow that 2+2=5. The trick works only in the context of squaring because positive and negative versions of the same given number square the same. Thus, it is possible to alter perceptions of any 'truth' by changing parameters (like the ancient artefact example). But 99.9% of the time, 2+2 will equal 4 because of the context in which we are discussing and due to shared aims and assumptions.

It follows that most of us can agree that President Donald Trump said (referring to the high school shooting in Florida in February 2018):

> Today we're here with state and local leaders, law enforcement officers, and educations officials [sic] to discuss how we can make our schools safe and our communities secure. And no better time to discuss it than right now. And I think we're making a lot of progress, and I can tell you [sic] there's a tremendous feeling that we want to get something done. And we're leading that feeling, I hope.

With the exception of the transcription error which reads 'educations officials' instead of 'education officials' and the omission of Trump's misspeak ('I can tell you there are... there's a tremendous feeling'), this transcript and the fact that Trump said it is objectively verifiable. Trump doesn't dispute that he said it. There is audio and video of Trump saying it (though audio and video is subject to manipulation and fakery). There are witnesses (though witnesses can be wrong or tell lies). The statement is posted on the White House website. (Although websites can be hacked, the White House has never retracted the statement.) In this context and with the evidence to support it, most of us will agree that Trump said it.[2]

However, the statement becomes dubious and the boundaries between objective verification and subjective verification blur when we contextualize the statement as a matter of interpretation. Most people will agree

---

[2]White House, 'Remarks by President Trump in Meeting with Local and State Officials on School Safety', 22 February 2018, https://www.whitehouse.gov/briefings-statements/remarks-president-trump-meeting-local-state-officials-school-safety/. The White House, 'President Trump Meets with State and Local Officials on School Safety', 22 February 2018, https://www.youtube.com/watch?v=ihVxKNtKPWA.

that Trump meant it and was correct in saying: 'Today we're here with state and local leaders, law enforcement officers, and education officials'. Indeed, Trump and his officials were in the Roosevelt Room of the White House on the day he claimed they were there (as the evidence above supports). State and local leaders, plus law enforcement officers and education officials were present (ditto). Objectivity becomes subjective, however, when we consider the real vs. rhetorical reasons for Trump's meeting, which he claims was 'to discuss how we can make our schools safe and our communities secure'.

Within the context of the then-recent school shooting in Parkland, Florida, most of us will agree that Trump is referring to preventing school shooters from murdering children. There are at least four levels of interpretation: 1) Trump means what he says, 2) Trump doesn't mean what he says, 3) Trump believes he means what he says, 4) Trump doesn't believe he means what he says.

With regards to points 1) and 3), we can call this objective and subjective truth. Trump means to make schools safer (1, objective) and believes he will (3, Trump's subjective belief). With points 2) and 4), we can call it objective and subjective lies. Trump doesn't care about making schools safer but says he does (1, objective lie) and knows that he doesn't care but also knows that he's pretending to care (4, subjective lie). Which of the four points or what combination of the four points is correct? How do we know and how can we prove it? At this point (interpretation), 'truth' becomes more dubious.

Because neuroscience cannot yet enter Trump's brain and prove one way or the other what he believes or thinks, we must include an additional measure of validity, that of time- and logic-based implementation. Trump cannot make schools safe from shooters overnight, yet there are logical steps that can be immediately implemented with executive orders: 1) mandate the security services to act more swiftly on warnings (Nikolas Cruz, the alleged shooter, was known to the FBI), 2) invest more in mental health services (Cruz was alleged to have heard voices), 3) impose restrictions on access to military-grade weapons, especially for persons likely to kill others. It could be, and indeed is, argued by many in the USA that these options are not necessarily desirable in the long-run (for example, if the government one day becomes totalitarian, military-grade weapons might be necessary for self-defence). However, in the single-issue vacuum of school shootings, these measures would reduce the likelihood of shootings.

Is Trump imposing these measures? No. Does this reduce the likelihood that he is objectively serious about making schools safe from shooters? In this context, yes. So, this 'truth' has been difficult to ascertain and has required a logical corollary to determine it. The corollary is time-dependent. Unlike objectively verifying whether Trump said what he said or not, the issue of interpretation cannot be objectively verified from the narrow temporal and spatial frame in which it is uttered (i.e., from the Roosevelt Room). Only time would tell, as the saying goes, if Trump implemented these or similar measures (i.e., evidence that he did or did not act on his claim to want to make schools safer).

Spatial relations are also an issue affecting truth in reporting war and crimes against humanity. Who really knows what is going on in Syria, for example, except the people involved? Here, we must rely primarily on Western sources speaking against their own interests in order to have a context for understanding the cause and effect of the war. For instance, if Western governments say they are supporting anti-Assad 'rebels' to bring democracy to Syria, we should treat their claims with a high degree of scepticism, or better yet dismiss them entirely. It is in their interest to say such things and it is therefore irrelevant. If, however, they admit elsewhere that Assad was refusing to privatize Syria's resources and open the economy to Western businesses, we can treat the claim with less scepticism because it is not in the interests of Western governments to admit this. Unlike the other claim, it makes them look like anti-human imperialists, not the humanitarian interveners they claim to be.

Even then, we must proceed with caution. It was not in the Israeli military's interest to claim that they dropped one million cluster bombs on Lebanon in 2006 (as they claimed) because this contradicts their claim to being the 'most moral army in the world'. I believed the one million claim until I learned that Israel dropped 3.5 million cluster bombs on Lebanon; i.e., they understated the level of destruction unleashed on Lebanon.[3]

---

[3] On the one million claim, see Meron Rappaport, 'IDF Commander: We Fire More Than a Million Cluster Bombs in Lebanon', *Haaretz*, 12 September 2006, https://www.haaretz.com/1.4865651. On the most moral army, see Yuli Novak (former Air Force officer), 'When I served, the Israeli military was the most moral in the world. No more', *Guardian*, 28 July 2014, https://www.theguardian.com/comment

# MAINSTREAM VS. ALTERNATIVE: A DIALECTIC

Historically, fake news emanated from the top down in the form of religious or military propaganda. It continues today. But this is tempered by the rise of so-called alternative media. Class divisions among elites mean that there is no homogeneous 'top'. Some elites support fake news in status quo mainstream media, others support fake news in web-based, so-called alternative media. Either way, the real issues that matter to most people are not presented in a sensible way. The alternative news on both the progressive left and far-right accuses the mainstream of being fake news. The mainstream accuses the alternative left and right of being fake. People are polarized by this dialectic and remain divided.

What is missing from much of the alternative media, as well as the so-called mainstream, is democratization. Ordinary people are not permitted to take part in deciding what should be on the media agenda and how it should be presented. Blogging enabled this for a while in a small yet significant way, but rich people have wiped out bloggers by posing as alternative media. Because the rich can afford to pay charismatic frontmen (most of them are men) and build professional-looking websites, alternative news consumers have gradually moved away from bloggers and turned to elite-funded alternative sites. Some progressives (e.g., TheCanary.co) are trying to rebalance this by adopting business models to generate hits and revenues for their blogs. Yet this model is at odds with their professed progressivism. How seriously can we take a website that exposes corporate abuses in, say, the mining sector, only to host adverts for gold?

As this book has examined, the so-called 'mainstream' is not really *mainstream*, if people's interests and concerns matter. This is why some, particularly younger people, are moving away from the 'mainstream' and looking to alternatives (some of it fake); however, as documented, the mainstream media remain the dominant source of information for most people.

Some alternatives are honest and sincere, others are not. Some have elements of good and bad. For better or worse, public opinion polls consis-

---

isfree/2014/jul/28/israeli-military-most-moral-no-more-outrage-indifference. For the 3.5 million, see House of Commons Foreign Affairs Committee, 'Global Security: The Middle East', Eighth Report of Session 2006-07, HC 363, 13 August 2007, p. 5, https://publications.parliament.uk/pa/cm200607/cmselect/cmfaff/363/363.pdf.

tently suggest that most ordinary people—that is, non-elites—care about the economy, healthcare, the democratic process and immigration. The mainstream (even the so-called liberal mainstream) is often to the right of the population on many issues (even so-called liberal media), by for example giving zero coverage of alternative economists when discussing austerity or fiscal policy. I have therefore used the term 'mainstream' as shorthand for mass media.

# CREDIBILITY & APPEAL TO AUTHORITY: CASE STUDY

In his review of my book *Britain's Secret Wars*, *Lobster Magazine* editor Robin Ramsay claimed that I had spread fake news; though he didn't put it in those words. In pointing out that Britain's military contribution to Sri Lanka is tiny compared to America's, Ramsay failed to understand the moral issue: that even if Britain had sold a single weapon to the Sri Lankan military and trained a single officer, it is still morally and legally culpable of participating in crimes against humanity (with reference to the 2009 ethnic cleansing of Tamils). Ramsay writes of the book in general: 'The plain facts are striking enough but Coles can't occasionally resist bigging them up. Grace Livingstone – a journalist and a good one – becomes "scholar Grace Livingstone"'. This was a mistake. I read and referenced *Inside Colombia* (2003), Livingstone's book published by a university press (Rutgers), and wrongly assumed she was a scholar; she is a journalist by profession. Ramsay mistook my mistake for a conspiracy to exaggerate the claims.

'Early Day Motions in the House of Commons, which are expressions of MPs' opinions and mean little, become "the British Parliament"'. I used the term 'the British Parliament' as shorthand, rather than spelling out what Early Day Motions are and what meaning they have. The purpose was to state a claim and give the reader an idea who was saying it. The crucial issue is not how the Early Day Motions are defined, but rather whether the material in them, and thus in the book, are accurate. Ramsay doesn't even address let alone dispute the accuracy of the claims. The specifics of the sources can be found in the book's endnotes. My attempt at shorthand was taken by Ramsay as a plot to mislead.

'Scratching around for evidence, a couple of times he cites stories in the *Daily Star*, which is hardly a reliable source'. I was not 'scratching around for evidence'. The name of the Libyan individual in question was entered into a search engine and the tabloid article appeared at the top of the page. With regards to the second case, the tabloid quoted British intelligence officials talking about Iran and the price of oil. Ramsay's argument is an appeal to authority fallacy: Would the quotes be more authentic if they came from a respectable source, like *The Times* of London? Neither the Libyan in question nor the intelligence agencies have denied what the tabloid says or refutes the quotes attributed to them.

'Neither, in my view is, is [sic] former LaRouchie William Engdahl'. This is another appeal to authority fallacy. The BBC, for instance, has a reputation for credibility, yet it lies all the time about everything. (By lies, I mean it usually frames stories in such a way as to omit the broader context, giving only elite versions of events.) The question is not whether Engdahl or the BBC or anyone is credible, but whether the given information they provide is true or not. I judged Engdahl's to be true in the case in question. Journalist Phil Miller also chided me for citing the *Executive Intelligence Review* (LaRouche's journal), which he felt damaged my credibility and his own, because I also cite Miller elsewhere in the book. This is a guilt by association fallacy. By this logic (and I don't agree), it could be argued that Miller has damaged his own credibility by working for Vice.com, which produces videos championing David Icke and was founded by an anti-Semite, a fact from which Vice.com wants to distance itself.[4]

(By the way, this subchapter is included to illustrate a point, not to bash Robin Ramsay, with whom I have happily collaborated on a book called *Voices for Peace*, which was edited and published after his scathing review of *Britain's Secret Wars*.)

---

[4] Robin Ramsay, 'Book review: Britain's Secret Wars', *Lobster Magazine*, 72, https://www.lobster-magazine.co.uk/free/lobster72/lob72-britains-secret-wars.pdf. On Miller, Vice.com and anti-Semitism, I refer to Gavin McInnes. See *Times of Israel*, 'Ex-Vice founder: Israelis have 'whiny paranoid fear of Nazis'', 16 March 2017, https://www.timesofisrael.com/alt-right-star-says-israelis-have-whiny-paranoid-fear-of-nazis/.

# FAKE REVIEWS & VIDEO GAMES

Above, I discuss how misinterpretation can lead to allegations of fakery. Here's an amusing example of micro-business hubris: Without my knowledge or consent, one of my publishers posted fake (and of course favourable) reviews of my/their books on a certain well-known online retailer: a simple check to see if the purchase is verified is usually a clue as to whether the review is real or not. Sadly, several prospective buyers found these fake reviews helpful. But fake news can be more serious than mere online dishonesty. Fake news can support war: and war kills, injures and traumatizes. Consider this remarkable episode of fakery from the so-called respectable mainstream:

Part of the barrage of anti-Gaddafi propaganda broadcast to the British public in 2011 during Britain's illegal assault on Libya included an ITV documentary. Entitled, *Exposure: Gaddafi and the IRA*, the documentary purported to show an Irish Republican Army (IRA) video of IRA soldiers (or terrorists as the narrator calls them) shooting down a British helicopter. The narrator says: 'With Gaddafi's heavy machine guns, it was possible to shoot down a helicopter, as the terrorists' own footage of 1988 shows'. The caption reads: 'IRA film 1988'. There was just one problem: the footage was not only totally fake, it was taken from a video game, *ARMA 2*, without the permission or knowledge of the game-makers and not properly attributed.[5]

For the very few sceptical British anti–Libya War audiences and activists (there were three of us in Plymouth UK at the time), the ridiculous documentary tried to make us believe that the war was morally justified by evoking old cases of Gaddafi-IRA collaboration and fabricating new ones. Citing unnamed sources, it claimed that 'even in hiding, Gaddafi's final act of defiance is to send cash to these new [IRA] terror groups'. No sources or evidence necessary.[6]

When the website *PC Gamer* alerted readers to the fact that video game footage had been used, broadcaster ITV said: 'The events featured in *Exposure: Gaddafi and the IRA* were genuine but it would appear that during the editing process the correct clip of the 1988 incident was not

---

[5]ITV, *Exposure: Gaddafi and the IRA*, September 2011.
[6]Ibid.

selected and other footage was mistakenly included in the film by producers'. *ARMA 2*'s developer Bohemia Interactive said that while it was unacceptable to use fake footage in a real show and not even credit it, 'we consider this as a bizarre appreciation of the level of realism incorporated into our games'.[7]

If producers and editors in ITV and its related companies thought they could get away with this, one wonders how much fake footage is out there in the mainstream going undetected.

# 'CHEMTRAIL' CONSPIRACIES: A CASE STUDY

Ironically, one of the newspapers reporting on the video game–ITV incident was the *Daily Mail*. The newspaper has been denounced by Wikipedia for publishing too much alleged fake news about other subjects. Wikipedia now refuses to allow its contributors to use the *Daily Mail* as a source. But Wikipedia is hardly a bastion of credibility. The only time 'I've' ever cited Wikipedia in an article was in 2011 when I wrote a piece for *Lobster Magazine* on the history of weather warfare. (Weather weapons are not a conspiracy theory. See Professor James R. Fleming, *Fixing the Sky* (2010, Columbia University Press).) Without my knowledge or consent, editor Robin Ramsay included a Wikipedia entry for my section on Project Stormfury, the US government's effort to modify hurricanes. (This is an example of how authors can be at the mercy of what editors do. The great Robert Fisk recalls a similar and incomparably more serious event in his book *The Great War for Civilisation* (2005, HarperPerennial), in which an editor slandered the victim of a bombing as a terrorist by changing Fisk's report. A relative later confronted Fisk.)[8]

---

[7]BBC, 'ITV documentary in IRA computer game blunder', 27 September 2011, http://www.bbc.co.uk/news/uk-northern-ireland-15082177. Sara Nathan and Paul Revoir, 'ITV admits it passed off clip from a VIDEO GAME as footage of IRA attack on British helicopter in new flagship news show', *Daily Mail*, 28 September 2011, http://www.dailymail.co.uk/news/article-2042568/ITV-fake-footage-row-new-documentary-passes-game-IRA-gun-attack-British-helicopter.html.

[8]Jasper Jackson, 'Wikipedia bans Daily Mail as 'unreliable' source', *Guardian*, 8 February 2017, https://www.theguardian.com/technology/2017/feb/08/wikipedia-bans-daily-mail-as-unreliable-source-for-website. T.J. Coles, 'Weather weapons: the

This section is about shades of grey in the war between 'fake news'/'conspiracy theory' and 'real news' and truth.

In theory, anybody can edit Wikipedia and even when a consensus opinion is wrong, a Wikipedia entry can claim it as fact. Take the issue of 'chemtrails'. Many people wrongly believe that all of the persistent white lines in the sky are part of a deliberate, covert operation. In fact, most of the white lines are generated by commercial airliners (contrails) as part of the normal aviation process. There is no consensus on what the aim of the supposed covert 'chemtrail' mission is. Some say it is depopulation through chemical poisoning. (If it is, the perpetrators are doing a poor job, considering that world population is fast approaching 9 billion.) Others, more plausibly, say it is a covert geoengineering programme designed to offset climate change by whitening the skies to deflect sunlight and heat. But those in the latter camp provide little evidence. (One such site, GeoengineeringWatch.org, has been labelled fake news, again ironically, by FakeNewsWatch.com.)[9]

The strongest evidence cited by proponents of the theory for the existence of 'chemtrails' is a report published by the US military in 1996 called, *Weather as a Force Multiplier: Owning the Weather in 2025*, which discusses the purposeful generation of condensation trails for shielding operations against satellite observation. The document can still be read on the US military's website (see footnote). As Wikipedia correctly points out in the entry for 'chemtrails', the document was only a theoretical one and contains 'fictional scenarios'.

But the editors of Wikipedia refuse to publish important information on possible real-life 'chemtrails', namely the fact that by its own records, the US Army and Air Force ran a federally-funded programme called Owning the Weather from 1995 to circa 2004, part of which included efforts to sell technology for what they call 'climate change experiments' to the government. (The old Office of the Federal Coordinator for Meteorology e-reports outlining the plans are still available on Archive.org. See footnote

---

dark world of environmental warfare', *Lobster*, 62, Winter 2011, https://www.lobster-magazine.co.uk/free/lobster62/lob62-weather-wars.pdf.

[9]Wikipedia, 'Chemtrail conspiracy theory', https://en.wikipedia.org/wiki/Chemtrail_conspiracy_theory. On alleged depopulation, see for example: Humans Are Free, 'The connection between chemtrails and the depopulation agenda', July 2014, http://humansarefree.com/2014/07/the-connection-between-chemtrails-and.html.

for details.) Like their opponents, the anti-chemtrail theory websites Contrailscience.com and Metabunk.org (both run by ex-video game developer, Mick West) are also not honest enough to publish these documents and say that while most 'chemtrail' theorizing is demonstrable falsity, some of it is not and therefore at least some of the white lines in the sky are indeed likely to be covert geoengineering tests.[10]

# HOW FAKE NEWS SPREADS: A MICROCOSM

Under the perhaps self-deceptive belief that they are guardians of 'real' information, websites like Wikipedia and SourceWatch can be just as a bad as mainstream news in limiting debate. SourceWatch is run by Lisa Graves, a former Bill Clinton administration lawyer who does a good job of exposing big corporations and their links to government. But as one can imagine, when researchers veer too far left and support, say, Bernie Sanders over Hillary Clinton, SourceWatch rubbishes them as 'conspiracy theorists'. Their entry for me, for instance, contains an old biography, which the researchers did not bother to check was outdated. It was plagiarized from my old bio on AxisOfLogic.com and even contained the same spelling errors to prove it. It also had false information, that I 'write' for *New Dawn*, which the website abuses as a 'conspiracy' magazine. The fact is, I've written a single article (unpaid) for *New Dawn* and my work has appeared in the mainstream, including *Newsweek* and the *New Statesman* (also unpaid), as well as in the peer-reviewed journals, *Peace Review* and *Ethical Space*.[11]

---

[10]It can be read here: http://csat.au.af.mil/2025/volume3/vol3ch15.pdf. If it's been removed, try here: https://ia802603.us.archive.org/1/items/WeatherAsAForceMultiplier/WeatherAsAForceMultiplier.pdf. The Office of the Federal Coordinator for Meteorology reports can be read here: https://web.archive.org/web/20150812144558/http://www.ofcm.gov/fedplan/fp-fy97/text/toc.htm. The specific one referring to geoengineering (OFCM, 'Owning the Weather–An Army force multiplier', DoD Weather Programs, Section 4) can be read here: http://www.pipr.co.uk/wp-content/uploads/2017/01/ddwpd.pdf.

[11]On Graves, see Charlie Savage, 'Newest Spy Court Pick Is a Democrat but Not a Liberal', *NYT*, 20 August 2013, http://www.nytimes.com/2013/08/21/us/roberts-varies-pattern-in-choice-for-spy-court.html. SourceWatch, 'T.J. Coles', https://www.sourcewatch.org/index.php/T._J._Coles and https://www.disinfopedia.org/index.php/T.J._Coles. The book in question is *President Trump, Inc.* (2017, Clairview Books).

But all of this was ignored by SourceWatch which sought to paint me as a kook. It ignored all of the positive reviews of my book *Britain's Secret Wars*, including one published in the academic *Journal of Global Fault-lines* (by Matt Alford, who also endorses this book, to declare a potential conflict of interest) and another in the national paper *Morning Star*, and instead cited Ian Sinclair's critique in *Peace News*. SourceWatch spread more fake news by pretending that my book has received no positive reviews from what they would consider credible and respectable sources. I can only imagine that their motivation was that I wrote a book about Donald Trump in which I point out that the Clintons, Obama and other status quo centrists are ultimately responsible for Trump's victory because their greedy politics allowed the political vacuum to be filled by a far-right hatemonger. Until then, SourceWatch had no interest in me. (SourceWatch generally does such good work that I cite their research into the Koch Brothers in my Trump book.)[12]

As an example of how fake news can spread on the internet, Source-Watch's inaccurate entry about me (which even refers to me as 'Cole' in the body of the text) was then copied and pasted into a site called Disinfopedia.org.

The danger with investigatory and monitoring websites like Source-Watch is: few people trust the mainstream news or politicians. Even fewer trust alternative, so-called conspiracy websites. People are therefore looking for a sensible middle-ground. By presenting themselves as that middle-ground, and by the nature of their critiques of both mainstream and non-mainstream sources, such websites appear to be honest and accurate, especially if they appear to come from the progressive left in opposing the actions of the federal government and big corporations. This new internet phenomenon is like a packaged investigation. But who checks the fact-checkers? As a result, the kind of biases and inaccuracies noted above can and do spread. By 2014, Graves's Center for Media and Democracy, Inc. (which publishes as PRWatch) was worth over $1m. Having spread fake news about me, SourceWatch's donations appeal reads: 'Don't let Trump wipe out real news by calling it "Fake!" Keep it real. Give today!'.[13]

---

[12]Ibid.
[13]SourceWatch.org.

# IDENTITY POLITICS

But news consumers are not going to find 'real' answers from the other side either, from the alt-right websites like Breitbart (funded by the billionaire hedge fund manager Robert Mercer) or the madcap InfoWars run by Alex Jones, who admits that he comes from a family which collaborated with the CIA. News consumers will also be hard-pressed to find truth from so-called progressive, independent shows like *Democracy Now!*, which has failed miserably to report the truth about the war in Syria: that it was a proxy war fought by Islamic terrorists (mainly comprised of the Free Syrian Army) organized by the US, Britain and France. *DN!* has been much more preoccupied with reporting the actual and alleged atrocities of Syria's Assad regime than it has with reporting on the atrocities committed by the US-British-backed Free Syrian Army.[14]

By accusing the other side of being fake news, websites and mainstream news only box us into categories and separate us.

The truth is not only a lonely warrior, it is getting purposefully harder to define. Back in 2007, the UK Ministry of Defence published a projection on the future of news and information. As if predicting the case above involving video games, part of the document says that that 'simulation' will be used to 'aid policymaking' and even 'blur the distinction between illusion and reality'.[15]

But as this book documents, letters, photos and film have been faked and doctored by all sides throughout history for political and commercial gain. It is not only elites seeking to control thoughts via religion, education and media. People who cling to identities try to convince you that you are wrong. But they also convince themselves and listen to news that

---

[14]On the funding of the alt-right by billionaires, see my *President Trump, Inc.* (2017, Clairview Books). Alex Jones interviewed on The Opie & Anthony Show, 17 April 2013, https://www.youtube.com/watch?v=bBMXmjVr954. On *DN!*'s awful Syria coverage, see Ann Garrison, 'Peace Activists Confront Amy Goodman on Biased Syria Coverage', Black Agenda Report, 17 May 2017, https://www.blackagendareport.com/activists_confront_amy_goodman_on_-syria. See also a letter by Veterans for Peace, 'We Need Better and More Diverse Coverage on Syria', *Dissident Voices*, 15 April 2017, https://dissidentvoice.org/2017/04/we-need-better-and-more-diverse-coverage-on-syria/.

[15]Ministry of Defence, 'Strategic Trends Programme: 2007-2036', 23 January 2007 (3rd), Swindon.

reinforces their beliefs (the echo chamber effect). To survive the new age of media wars, you have to think critically about everything (including this book), realize that everyone has an agenda (including this author) and consult a wide range of primary material where possible (as this book tries to do).

## WHAT CAN WE DO?

To end with a final personal example of what can be achieved with individual and, more importantly, collective activism:

Back in 2014, Israel launched another of its massive attacks against the Gaza Strip, a territory belonging to Palestinians which Israel continues to illegally occupy (though not with colonizers, as it had until 2005). Following the kidnapping of three Israeli teenagers, Israel launched Operation Brother's Keeper in the Palestinian territories. This prompted Palestinian militias to fire their crude projectiles indiscriminately (and unlawfully) into Israel's mainland. Israel has a legal obligation to end its occupation of Palestinian territories before it can be legally justified in launching armed, defensive attacks against Palestinians. But it refuses to do so and has illegally occupied Palestine since June 1967. As long as Israel remains the occupying power, it has no right to use force against Palestinians outside its borders.[16]

---

[16]Hyde's *International Law Volume III* states: 'A belligerent', e.g., Israel, 'which is contemptuous of conventional or customary prohibitions', i.e. Israel's occupation of Gaza since 1967, 'is *not* in a position to claim that its adversary', i.e., Hamas and affiliated groups, 'when responding with like for like', e.g., rocket fire into Israel, 'lacks the requisite excuse' (emphasis in original). *The Annual Digest and Reports of Public International Law Cases 1948* states: 'Under International Law, as in Domestic Law, there can be no reprisal against reprisal. The assassin who is being repulsed by his intended victim may not slay him and then, in turn, plead self-defense'. In response to the Gaza massacre 2014, international jurist John Dugard said: 'Given the fact that Gaza is an occupied territory, it means that Israel's present assault is simply a way of enforcing the continuation of the occupation, and the response of the Palestinian militants should be seen as the response of an occupied people that wishes to resist the occupation'. Even though the resistance may violate international law (i.e. Hamas targeting Israel's civilians) it does not justify an Israeli attack. It necessitates a full Israeli withdrawal of armed forces and colonizers to the pre-June 1967 borders, otherwise known as 1949 Green Lines. (Dugard interviewed: *Democracy Now!*, 'Can Israel Claim Self-Defense Against the Territory It Occupies? Int'l Jurist John Dugard Says

Following the Palestinian rocket attacks, which killed no Israelis, Israel launched Operation Protective Edge, which it had planned since 2008–09. During the 2008/09 attack, Operation Cast Last, Israeli strategists appeared on Western media boasting about a future Cast Lead II. This turned out to be Operation Protective Edge. In 2014, Israel lost 66 soldiers and six civilians (a seventh Thai person was killed) during Protective Edge. Palestine lost 2,202 individuals, of whom 1,391 were civilian and, says Reuters, including 526 children. This was a massacre, not a war, though less of a massacre than Operation Cast Lead, when Israel lost three civilians and five armed personnel, compared to Palestinians who lost 1,391 in Gaza (13 of whom killed by Palestinians for suspected collaboration): 759 of whom were civilians.[17]

Involved at the time in the Exeter Palestine Solidarity Campaign, I and others protested locally (with stalls, petitions and vigils) and in London on a coach, which demonstrated at the American Embassy (the police blocked access to the Israeli Embassy) and then to the BBC headquarters in opposition of their pro-Israeli reporting. Other protestors camped near local BBC stations. Eventually, the BBC was compelled to report the casualties. For the first time, having endured for weeks, the British public was able to understand the disparity in casualties and thus how much help ordinary men, women and children in Palestine needed.[18]

Let me make it clear that although it has declined in Europe and North America, anti-Semitism is very real and spills over into critiques of Zionism and Israel. Being anti-Zionist is not inherently anti-Semitic. However, large numbers of Jew-haters disguise their prejudices as anti-Zionism. Others are more openly anti-Semitic, for example, posting online

No', 6 August 2014, https://www.democracynow.org/2014/8/6/can_israel_claim_-self_defense_against.)

[17] B'Tselem, 'Fatalities during Operation Cast Lead', no date, http://www.btselem.org/statistics/fatalities/during-cast-lead/by-date-of-event. B'Tselem, '50 Days: More than 500 Children: Facts and figures on fatalities in Gaza, Summer 2014', 26 July 2016, Press Release, https://web.archive.org/web/20171018181530/http://www.btselem.org/press_releases/20160720_fatalities_in_gaza_conflict_2014.

[18] Lizzie Dearden, 'Hundreds protest against 'BBC pro-Israel bias' of Gaza coverage in cities across the UK', *Independent*, 16 July 2014, http://www.independent.co.uk/news/uk/home-news/hundreds-protest-against-bbc-pro-israel-bias-of-gaza-coverage-in-cities-across-the-uk-9609016.html. BBC, 'Gaza crisis: Toll of operations in Gaza', 1 September 2014, http://www.bbc.co.uk/news/world-middle-east-28439404.

comments about the enslavement of goyim and avatars with illustrations of the hook-nosed stereotype clasping their hands. More seriously for Jews, governments are the allies of anti-Semites. The US and Britain allied with the Poroshenko government of Ukraine, which they helped to install. The regime is allied to the neo-Nazi Azov Battalion. The British Tory party is allied to Poland's Law and Justice Party, whose leaders have made anti-Semitic comments.[19]

There was no systematic anti-Semitism on the London protest against Operation Protective Edge. Jews for Justice for Palestine marched in solidarity, as did Hasidic Jews (who have their own anti-Zionist agenda). It is unclear which one, but a single newspaper in the UK claims to have interviewed one Dan Rosenberg, who said of the protests:

> It is horrific what is going on in Gaza. It is collective punishment. I don't know how any human being can stand back while this is happening. But it is difficult being here. We have seen the anti-Semitic attitudes and you feel very threatened and scared, but we feel we have to stand up and represent. I have Jewish friends who wanted to come but they felt uncomfortable being here.

Clearly, this fake news was designed to lessen the importance of the protest, undermine the character and purpose of the protestors and divert attention from atrocities then taking place in Gaza. All dated 9 August 2014, the following papers printed the smear: *Express, Huffington Post, Independent, Mirror, Standard* and *Telegraph.*

I contacted one Natasha Culzac, a reporter for the *Independent*, with the following question: 'Can you please provide evidence (other than Mr. Rosenberg's statement) that the protests in London today (9th August 2014) had elements of anti-Semitism?'. Culzac was kind enough to respond:

> ...I think Mr Rosenberg was referring to the UK, rather than the march. I think he meant that it was hard being at the march while

---

[19]Tom Parfitt, 'Ukraine crisis: the neo-Nazi brigade fighting pro-Russian separatists', *Telegraph*, 11 August 2014, http://www.telegraph.co.uk/news/worldnews/europe/ukraine/11025137/Ukraine-crisis-the-neo-Nazi-brigade-fighting-pro-Russian-separatists.html. *Times of Israel*, 'Concern as controversial rightist party wins Poland's election', 26 October 2016, https://www.timesofisrael.com/concern-as-rightist-party-that-made-auschwitz-joke-wins-polands-election/.

there were/are acts of anti-Semitism going on (in France/some parts of UK), so he felt nervous, not that those acts of anti-Semitism were going on at the actual protest.

At the beginning of the article it also states that it was a peaceful march, so I hope that's evident in the rest of the article.

Apologies for the mix-up. (Email to author.)

The online version of the article was then amended with a square bracket inserted to Rosenberg's quote:

> It is horrific what is going on in Gaza. It is collective punishment. I don't know how any human being can stand back while this is happening. But it is difficult being here. We have seen the anti-Semitic attitudes [elsewhere] and you feel very threatened and scared, but we feel we have to stand up and represent. I have Jewish friends who wanted to come but they felt uncomfortable being here.[20]

The inclusion of Rosenberg's amended statement still sought to mislead and misrepresent the purpose of the protests and the character of the peoples involved (an editorial decision, I assume, not made by Culzac, who seemed sincere), but the amendment nevertheless presents an important, tiny victory that an individual achieved.

Incomparably more significant achievements can and are being made around the world. To make them happen, we must first divorce ourselves from preconceptions before acting alone and with others against lies and injustice, subtle and obvious.

---

[20] Natasha Culzac, 'Israel-Gaza conflict: 150,000 protest in London for end to 'massacre and arms trade'', *Independent*, 9 August 2014, http://www.independent .co.uk/news/uk/home-news/israel-gaza-conflict-thousands-protest-in-london-for-end-to-massacre-and-arms-trade-9659180.html.

# Index

Abbas, Ali, 129
Abbott, Diane, 157, 158
ABC, 93, 123, 152, 172, 186,
    193, 208, 236
ABC News Australia, 152
Abedi, Ramadan, 139
Abedi, Salman, 114
Adams, John, 50
Adblade, 247
Adderall XR, 81
ADHD, 80, 81
Adobe, 246
AdSense, 246
Afghanistan, 96, 106, 124, 125,
    149, 190
AFRICOM, 139
*Age, The*, 216
Agence France-Presse, 154, 155,
    173
al-Assad, Bashar, 52, 129, 137,
    159–169, 171, 172, 174,
    252, 261
al-Assad, Hafez, 167
al-Haideri, Adnan Ihsan Saeed,
    120
al-Hamid, Abd, 44
al-Maliki, Nouri, 118
al-Qaeda, 21, 96–98, 113, 118,
    119, 125–131, 134, 164,
    171

al-Shehri, Waleed, 29
al-Zarqawi, Abu Musab, 113,
    123, 125–127, 130
al-Zawahiri, Ayman, 97
Alexander the Great, 39
Allard, Kenneth, 124
Allende, Salvador, 20
Allied Irish Bank, 185
AlterNet, 236, 244, 245
Alvi, Suroosh, 228
American Civil Liberties Union,
    245
American Enterprise Institute,
    237
American Express, 246
American Legion, 66
*American Prospect*, 223
Americans for Prosperity, 237
Amet, E.H., 89
Amnesty International, 145
Anarchist Communist
    Federation, 221
Anarchy Now!, 221
Anderson, Kevin, 226
Anglia Press, 188
Anselm of Ribemont, 47
Anti-Censorship Campaign, 221
anti-Semitism, 59, 196, 197, 228,
    255, 263–265
AntiWar, 245

Antony, Marc, 37
AOL, 207, 208, 228
Apple, 233, 241
APTN, 189
Arab League, 146
Arab Spring, 28, 60, 164, 165,
    167
Archive.org, 258
Aristophanes, 39
Aristotle, 39, 62
ARMA 2, 256, 257
ArmorGroup, 146
Armstrong, Louis, 92
Ask, 227
Associated Press, 48, 105, 152,
    154, 188, 189, 208, 232,
    233, 243
AT&T, 233, 246
*Atlantic*, 223
Audiovisual Media Services
    Directive [2007], 188
Augustus Caesar, 43
Australian Broadcasting
    Corporation, 216
*Australian, The*, 215, 216
Azov Battalion, 264

Babylon Media, 124
Back, Steve, 199
BAE Systems, 239
Bahrain, 164, 167
Baines Associates, 240
Ball, Lucille, 92
Ball, Maj. Joseph, 106
Bank of America, 16
Bank of England, 104, 184
Bannon, Steve, 230

Barclays, 16
Bartholomew, Peter, 47, 48
Bartlam, Gary, 110
Basque Homeland and Freedom,
    221
Batirashvili, Tarkhan, 128
Bauer, 18
BBC, 20, 23, 26, 29, 57, 60, 61,
    90, 96, 97, 103–105, 109,
    110, 113, 114, 117, 122,
    127, 138, 142, 154,
    159–162, 165–172, 179,
    180, 184, 185, 190–196,
    200–202, 207–209, 215,
    220, 225, 226, 236, 244,
    246, 247, 255, 257, 263
Bedley, Scott, 58, 60–62
Bell Labs, 77
Bell Pottinger, 122, 127, 134
Bell, Martin, 184
Ben Ali, Zine El Abidine, 163,
    165, 223
Benen, Steve, 223
Berg, Nick, 130, 131
Berns, Jeremy, 34
BG Group, 184
Bill & Melinda Gates
    Foundation, 233
bin Laden, Osama, 20, 21, 61,
    96–98, 113, 125–127
Biograph, 90
Biwater, 184
Black Ribbon Campaign, 221
Blackbird, 123
Bland, Sir Christopher, 184
Blumenthal, Sidney, 10
Bogart, Humphrey, 92

Bohemia Interactive Studios, 257
Booz and Co., 184
Brazil, 183
Breitbart News, 26, 116, 179, 225, 227–230, 236, 261
Breitbart, Andrew, 227–229
Brexit, 22, 177, 179, 210, 211, 242
Bright, John, 56
Bromium, 241
Brown, Gordon, 196
Brown's Iron Bitters, 79
Bryant, Martin, 215, 216
Brzezinski, Mika, 10
Brzezinski, Zbigniew, 190
Buchanan Ingersoll and Rooney, 123
BURN, 221
Bush, George W., 61, 96, 118–121, 125, 160, 163, 224, 232–234
BuzzFeed, 227

C.I. Hood Com, 79
Cagney, James, 92
Calhoun, John C., 86
Calyx of Dorset, 188
Cambridge Analytica, 241
Cameron, David, 138, 140, 143, 146, 185, 200
Campaign for Nuclear Disarmament, 104
Capewell, Maj. Gen. David, 158
Carlson, Richard W., 229
Carlson, Tucker, 229
Carlyle Group, 96

Carmon, Irin, 224
Carnegie Endowment for International Peace, 163
Carson, Johnny, 34, 92
Carter, Jimmy, 190
Cato Institute, 237
CBS, 124, 186
Center for Media and Democracy, Inc., 260
Center for Security Policy, 237
Cervera, Pascual, 89
Chalabi, Ahmed, 120
Change Institute, 239
Channel 4, 23, 185
Chaplin, Charlie, 91
Charlemagne, 45, 46
Charles I, King, 51
Chartism, 65
Chávez, Hugo, 152
Cheney, Dick, 160, 235
Chicano Press Association, 168, 188, 208, 221
China, 33, 40, 41, 47, 89, 178, 183, 218, 226
China [ancient], 33, 40–42, 47, 178, 207, 226
Churchill, Winston, 67, 106
CIA, 20–22, 61, 96–98, 103, 105, 120, 126, 160, 188, 189, 191, 210, 223, 225, 228, 234, 243, 244, 261
Clegg, Nick, 140, 143
Cleopatra, 37
clickbait, 12, 22, 23, 26, 180, 236, 237, 244, 246, 247
ClickHole.com, 236
climate change, 17, 182, 258

Clinton, Bill, 61, 96, 178, 223,
    225, 229, 233, 234, 259
Clinton, Hillary, 9, 33, 34, 41,
    140, 146, 153, 166, 172,
    207, 230, 231, 237, 241,
    242, 244, 259
CNBC, 186
CNN, 34, 97, 123, 130, 168, 171,
    172, 179, 186, 207–209
Cohen Group, 124
Cole, Juan, 224
CollegeHumor.com, 227
Collins Center for Public Policy,
    233
Colorado Fuel and Iron
    Company, 15
Colorado National Guard, 15
Comcast, 186, 227
Common Dreams, 245
Competition Commission, 185
Concerta, 81
Connors, Keith, 80
Consortium News, 245
Contrailscience.com, 60, 259
Corbyn, Jeremy, 22, 27, 114,
    117, 196–201, 211
Cordesman, Anthony, 148
Corporation for Public
    Broadcasting, 229
Cotton, Sir Arthur, 56
Cowan, William [Rt. Marine],
    123
Coyle, Diane, 184
Cradle of New Civilization
    Media, 124
Craigslist Charitable Fund, 233
Cromwell, Oliver, 51, 52, 122,

    184–186
Crosby, Simon, 241
Cruz, Nikolas, 251
Cruz, Ted, 230
Cuba, 89, 221, 223
Cudlipp, Hugh, 105
Culzac, Natasha, 264, 265
CyberBerkut, 134
Cypherpunks, 222

D-Notices, 190
Daalder, Ivo, 141
Dabiq, 114, 115, 117, 127, 134,
    215
Daily Beast, 227
Daily Caller, 229
Daily Herald, 236
Daily Mail, 24, 27, 28, 106, 107,
    116, 137, 186, 194, 195,
    198, 200, 257
Daily Mirror Newspapers, 104
Daily Telegraph, 24
Dante, Joe, 92
Davenport-Hill, Florence, 65, 66
Davis, Gavyn, 184
Davis, Mike, 54, 55
de Bretton-Gordon, Hamish, 169
de Menezes, Jean Charles, 191
delebs [dead celebrities], 93
Dell, 246
DeLong, J. Brad, 224, 225
Democracy Now!, 245, 261
Dewey, John, 66, 70
di Lauro, Marco, 166, 167
Digby Parton, Heather, 225
Digby, William, 55
Doublier, Francis, 87, 88

Downing, Wayne A., 124
Dream Quest Images, 94
Dreyfus, Capt. Alfred, 87, 88
Drudge Report, 27, 208, 209,
        227, 229
Drudge, Matt, 229
Drum, Kevin, 223, 224
Dufferin Enquiry [1887], 56
DuPont, 66

Eads, Lt. Col. Timur J., 123
Egypt, 24, 34–37, 108, 163–165,
        223
    ancient, 34–37, 108, 165
el-Sisi, Gen. Abdel Fattah, 165
Elgin, Lord, 56
Emerging Technologies
        International, 123
Emoto, Masaru, 76
Endara, Guillermo, 120
Engel, Natascha, 154, 155
Eurasia Review, 142
Evans, Lady, 227
Evans, Sir Harold, 217

Facebook, 26, 65, 194, 200,
        205–209, 214, 217, 221,
        223, 230, 237, 240,
        242–244
Fairhead, Rona, 185
FakeNewsWatch.com, 236, 237,
        258
Fallon, Michael, 138, 161, 193
FARC, 221
Fawcett, Henry, 55
Fenton, Roger, 86
Finley, Alex, 228

Fisk, Robert, 224, 257
Foley, James, 131, 134
Food and Drug Administration,
        81
Ford Foundation, 233
Ford, Peter, 159–162, 233
FortLiberty, 237
Fox News, 123, 132, 133, 186,
        208, 209, 229, 236
Fox, Liam, 158
Franklin, Benjamin, 50, 51
Frazer Institute, 20
Free Syrian Army, 130, 162, 261
FreedomWorks, 237
Friess, Foster, 229
Fry, Anthony, 185

G8, 222
Gaddafi, Muammar, 10, 52, 60,
        114, 137–140, 142–148,
        150–155, 157, 158,
        163–165, 172, 223, 232,
        256
Galai, Yaron, 247
Gall, Sandy, 106
Gardner, Alexander, 86
Gardner, Col. [Rt.] Sam, 121
Garrett, Neil, 191
Gawker Media, 224
General Atlantic, 227
General Motors, 66
Geneva Conventions, 144, 151
GeoengineeringWatch.org, 258
Germany, 45, 173, 206, 222
Gilgamesh, 35, 40
Gilligan, Andrew, 113

Global Carnival Against
    Capitalism, 222
Global Radio, 18
Global Research, 236, 245
Goldman Sachs, 184
Gomes, Ben, 245
Goodyear, 246
Google, 65, 116, 128, 205,
    207–209, 217, 233, 236,
    243–246
Goto Jogo, Kenji, 133
Graham Holdings Company, 228
Graves, Lisa, 259
Greenslade, Roy, 104
*Guardian*, 24, 142, 167, 179, 186,
    191, 198, 202, 209, 239,
    242
Gun, Katharine, 191

Hague, William, 154, 168
Hall, Justin, 225
Hallam, Dr Rola, 170, 171
Ham, Gen. Carter, 139
Han Dynasty, 40, 41
Hannan, Daniel, 49, 50
Harlow, Harry, 70, 71
Harmsworth, Jonathan, 18
Hartley, Aidan, 28
Harvey, Col. Derek, 126
Harvey, Nick, 149
HBO, 133, 228
Heer, Jeet, 224
Henry, David, 80
Heritage Foundation, 229, 237,
    243
Herridge, Catherine, 133
Hersant, Robert, 187

Hertz, 246
Herzl, Theodor, 59
Hewitt, Nicholas, 189
Higgins, Eliot, 60, 61
Hill & Knowlton, 120
Hilsum, Lindsey, 142, 152
History Channel, 59
History.com, 59
Hogg, Baroness, 184
Holmes, Anna, 224
Homer, 38
Hope, Bob, 92
HSBC, 24, 185
Huang-ti, Yellow Emperor, 40
*Huffington Post*, 208, 209, 227,
    229, 264
Huffington, Arianna, 227
Human Rights Watch, 118, 144,
    162
Hurt, Charles, 229
Hussein, Saddam, 95, 96, 113,
    118–120, 138, 160, 167,
    232–234
Hussein, Uday, 97
Hyndman, Henry, 56

i to i, 240
IAC/InteractiveCorp, 227
IAEA, 235
IBM, 91, 204, 241
IMF, 154
*Independent*, 24, 186, 198, 202,
    264
India, 24, 49, 50, 53–56, 109,
    183, 205, 207, 209
InfoWars, 209, 211, 261
Ingram, Adam, 110

Intel, 228
International Publishing
    Corporation, 104
Iraq, 10, 11, 21, 30, 34, 95–97,
    103, 107, 109–111,
    113–115, 117–130, 133,
    134, 138, 144, 146, 148,
    149, 160, 161, 163,
    165–167, 171, 219, 220,
    223, 224, 226, 232–234
Iraq Liberation Act [1998], 233
Iraqi Dream, 124
Iraqi National Congress, 120
Ireland, 29, 49, 51–54, 190
Irish Republican Army, 190
ISIS [also ISIL and Daesh], 10,
    114–119, 127–129,
    131–134, 138, 159, 161,
    164, 215, 218
Israel, 59, 108, 116, 163, 173,
    184, 204, 206, 224, 246,
    247, 252, 255, 262–265
Italy, 150, 187
Ivey, Bill, 33, 34

J. Sainsbury, 184
Jackson, Blanket, 93
Jackson, Michael, 92, 93
Jamail, Dahr, 226
James II, King, 51
Jarratt, Linwood, 236, 237
Jermy, Commodore Steve, 140,
    157
Jezebel, 224
John, Elton, 92
Johnson, John S., 227
Johnson, Lyndon B., 95

Johnson, Steve, 173
Johnston Press, 188
Johnston, Rotha, 185
Jones, Alex, 61, 211, 212, 229,
    237, 261
Jordan, 59, 125, 128, 130, 195
Julius Caesar, 42

Kangxi, 41
Kaszeta, Dan, 173
Katz, Rita, 116, 117
Kaus, Mickey, 224
Kay-Shuttleworth, Sir James, 65
Kekule, Alexander, 173
Kelley, Paul, 63, 68, 69
Kellogg, Brown & Root, 150
Kelly, Dr David, 113
Kennedy Dickson, William, 90
Kentucky Fried Chicken, 92
Kenya, 96, 179
Khan, Veryan, 132
Kherboga, 47, 48
Ki-moon, Ban, 166
*Kifaya*, 164, 223
Kim Jong-Il, 108
King, Cecil, 104
Kinsley, Michael, 228
Klein, Ezra, 223
Knight Foundation, 233
Koch Brothers, 260
Kosovo, 120, 149, 150
Koussa, Moussa, 154
Krueger, Brent T., 124
Kuehl, Daniel T., 94
Kuehl, Sheila, 91
Kuperman, Alan J., 144
Kurds, 128

Kushner, Jared, 230
Kuwait, 120, 153, 164

Lahav, Ori, 247
Lambert, Mary, 132, 133, 215
Lavender, Patrick M., 157
Law and Justice Party [Poland], 264
Lawson, Dominic, 106
le Carré, John, 105
Le Pen, Marine, 178, 179
Lebanon, 59, 163, 252
Lee, Brandon, 93
Lehman Brothers, 16
Leonie Industries, 124
Leslie, Mariot, 158
Libya, 9, 10, 12, 28, 36, 37, 46, 52, 60, 103, 107, 114, 132, 133, 137–158, 163–165, 171, 190, 191, 223, 232, 255, 256
Libyan Islamic Fighting Group, 151
Limbaugh, Rush, 26, 61, 195
Lincoln Group, 124
Lincoln, Abraham, 86
Lloyds, 16
Lobster Magazine, 254, 257
Lord, Geller, Federico, Einstein, 91
Lucent Technologies, 77
Luckey, Palmer, 179, 230
Ludlow Massacre [1914], 15
Lugosi, Bela, 91
Lumière Brothers, 87
Lyall Grant, Mark, 153, 157

MacDonald, Ramsay, 106
Macedonia, 219, 246
Macron, Emmanuel, 179
Maddow, Rachel, 245
Marketing Evaluations, 92
Marks, Gen. [Rt.] James, 123
Marr, Andrew, 138
Marwan II, Caliph, 44
May, Timothy C., 222
McCausland, Jeffrey, 123
McDonald's, 246
McInerney, Lt. Gen. [Rt.] Thomas, 123
McInnes, Gavin, 228, 229, 255
McNeil Technologies, 123
Media Ownership [Radio and Cross-media] Order [2011], 187
Méliès, Georges, 89
Mercer, Rebekah, 230
Mercer, Robert, 179, 225, 230, 241, 261
Merck, 82
Mercury, 216
Metabunk.org, 60, 133, 134, 210, 259
Metadate, 81
MI5, 103–106, 190, 191
Mid Staffordshire News, 188
Mikkelson, David, 231
Milburn, Alan, 17
Mill, John Stuart, 65
Miller, Judith, 120
Miller, Phil, 228, 255
Milošević, Slobodan, 150
Mir, Hamid, 97
Miranda, David, 190

Mirror Group Newspapers, 187
Modi, Narendra, 68, 109
MoJo, 223
Montvieux, 239
Moon, Madeleine, 157
Moran, Paul, 120
Morgan, Piers, 109, 110, 215
Morris, Errol, 86
Morsi, Mohamed, 165
Morten, Cyril, 105
Morton, Desmond, 106
Moussaoui, Zacarias, 130
Moynihan, Ray, 80
MSM, 210
MSNBC, 10, 34, 186, 208, 245
Mubarak, Hosni, 108, 163–165,
    223
Muhammad, 43, 44
Multilateral Agreement on
    Investment, 222
Muntada al-Ansar, 130
Murdoch, Rupert, 18, 194, 216

Narmer, 37
Nash, Capt. Charles T., 123
Nash, Gen. William L., 123
National Amusements, 186
National Endowment for
    Democracy, 163
National Security Agency, 38,
    213
Native Americans, 50, 51
NBC, 10, 34, 98, 124, 186, 208,
    219, 227, 245
NBCUniversal, 186, 227
Neil, Andrew, 113, 114, 117
New Republic, 224, 228, 238

New York Daily News, 241
New York Post, 229
New York State Economic
    Council, 66
New York Times, 115, 120, 122,
    123, 172, 179, 208, 209
New Yorker, 227
News Corporation, 186
News International, 187
Newsnight, 105, 194
Nightingale, Florence, 56
Norris, Woody, 95

Oath Inc., 228
Obama, Barack, 9, 13, 143, 148,
    149, 171, 179, 232, 238,
    260
Obokata, Haruko, 75
Oborne, Peter, 24
Office of the Federal
    Coordinator for
    Meteorology, 258, 259
Omaar, Rageh, 122
Oman, 164
Omnitec Solutions, 124
Onion, 27, 236
Operation Brother's Keeper, 262
Operation Cast Lead, 263
Operation Ellamy, 156
Operation Protective Edge, 263,
    264
Operation Unified Protector,
    156
Oppian, 38
Osborne, Ronald Lt. Col., 55
Outbrain, 247

P2T2 Solutions, 237, 238
Pakistan, 48, 96, 97, 127, 226
Palestine, 37, 59, 184, 262–264
Papcun, George, 94
Pascal Zanders, Dr Jean, 173
Pavitt, James, 97
Pavlov, Ivan, 68–71
Paxman, Jeremy, 105, 106
PayPal, 179, 205, 230
Peasants' Revolt [1381 and
    1524], 221
Peat, Jeremy, 184
Peretti, Jonah, 227
Pericles, 39
Peterloo Massacre [1819], 13
Petraeus, Gen. David, 152
Pfizer, 82
Phelan, James, 90
Philo, Greg, 11, 38, 186
Pike Committee [1978], 189
Piro, George, 234
PKK, 221
Podesta, John, 33
*Politico*, 227, 228
PolitiFact, 28, 233–235, 243
Porton Down, 167
Poynter Institute, 233
*Pravda*, 27
Procter and Gamble, 185, 186
Project Pandora, 95
Project Stormfury, 257
propaganda, 11, 15, 19–21, 27,
    30, 34–37, 39–46, 48,
    50–52, 56, 88, 95, 99,
    103, 107, 115, 120,
    122–124, 126, 129, 130,
    133, 134, 140, 144, 146,
    158, 160, 166–168, 171,
    172, 179, 189, 195, 201,
    205, 210, 216, 219, 221,
    226, 229, 230, 233, 253,
    256
  black, 20–22, 45
  grey, 20, 21, 45, 85
  white, 20
Proper Media, 231
Proyas, Alex, 94

Qin Shi Huang, 40

Račak Massacre, 150
racism, 145, 146, 191, 192, 220
Ralston, Gen. [Rt.] Joseph W.,
    124
Ramesses III, Pharaoh, 36
Ramsay, Robin, 103, 106, 254,
    255, 257
Raymond's of Derby, 188
RBS, 184
Reagan, Ronald, 96
Red Cross, 118
Reddit, 179, 207, 209, 230
Renaissance Technologies, 241
Rendon Group, 120
Revcontent, 247
Reynolds Journalism Institute,
    233
Ricardo, David, 65
Rice, Condoleezza, 163
Rifkin, Malcolm, 146, 154
RIKEN Institute, 75
Roberts, Kelly, 34
Robin, Corey, 225
Rockefeller, John D., 15, 16, 70

Rome [ancient], 42, 43
Rosenberg, Dan, 228, 264, 265
Rowell, Dr E., 79
RT, 27, 144, 173, 174
Ruder Finn, 120
Rumsfeld, Donald, 124, 125
Russel Wallace, Alfred, 55
Russell, James E., 70
Russia, 27, 30, 59, 60, 107, 134,
        161, 190, 210, 218, 264

Salon, 227, 228, 245
San Francisco Examiner, 228
Sanders, Bernie, 14, 91, 178, 179,
        219, 242, 259
Sargon I, 36
SAS, 28, 137, 158, 164, 190
Saudi Arabia, 29, 96, 125, 127,
        129, 130, 164, 165, 210
Scheffer, Jaap de Hoop, 149, 150
Scheuer, Michael, 61, 96
Schleicher, Andreas, 57
Scholey, David, 184
Schön, Jan Hendrik, 76, 77
SCIgen, 82
Scovill's, 78
Scudder, Billy, 91
Search for International
        Terrorist Entities, 116
Senusret III, Pharaoh, 37
Serbia, 46, 120, 150
Sethna, Zaab, 120
Shayler, David, 191
Shell, 139
Simpson, John, 105, 106, 130,
        131
Sinclair, Ian, 128, 260

Singolda, Adam, 246, 247
Sinn Féin, 190
Skinner, B.F., 68, 69, 71, 181
Sky, 185, 186, 257
Slate, 97, 223, 228
Smith, Adam, 63, 65
Smith, Albert E., 87, 90
Smith, Ben, 141, 151, 227
Smith, Shane, 228
Snopes, 12, 231, 232, 238, 243
Snowden, Edward, 38, 190
socialism, 65, 103, 104, 106, 107,
        160, 219, 245
Socrates-Plato, 38, 62
Sohn, Lydia, 77
Solinus, 43
Somalia, 28
Sontag, Susan, 86
SOS International, 124
SourceWatch, 128, 259, 260
Special Branch, 104, 105
Statoil, 139
Steiner, Gen. Carl W., 94
Strabo, 43
Sufyan, Abu, 44
Sullivan, Andrew, 66, 224
Summers, Lawrence, 225
Sun Tzu, 40
Sunday Pictorial, 104
Sunstein, Cass, 13, 39, 58
Swanson Foods, 160, 229
Syria, 10, 12, 44, 60, 61, 103,
        107, 118, 128–130, 133,
        137, 138, 159–174, 252,
        261
Syrian Observatory for Human
        Rights, 162

Taboola, 244, 246, 247
Talisman Energy, 139
Tampa Bay Times, 233
Tanzania, 96
Tea Party, 236, 237
Telegraph Media Group, 187
The Hill, 227
The Times (London), 19, 24,
    53–55, 131, 187, 190,
    217, 255
TheCanary.co, 253
Thiel, Peter, 179, 230
Third Reform Act [1884], 106
Thorndike, E.L., 70
Tippett, John D., 85
Tisdall, Sarah, 191
Tomlinson, Richard, 104
Toyota, 246
Transitional National Council
    [Libya], 139, 141, 147
Trilateral Commission, 16, 190
Trump, Donald, 9–11, 22, 27, 28,
    33, 34, 40, 159–162,
    177–179, 195, 201, 207,
    211, 212, 217, 230, 231,
    237–239, 241–245,
    250–252, 259–261
Trump, Ivanka, 230
Truth Squad, 233
Truthdig, 245
Tukulti-Ninurta I, 36
Tuner, Christian, 146
Turkey, 24, 89, 128, 164
Turner, Hugh, 97, 186, 216
Twitter, 10, 26, 194, 205, 206,
    209, 210, 214, 221, 223,
    224, 229, 237–239,

241–243

Ulster Defence Association, 190
United Nations, 145, 155–157,
    161, 168–170, 234
United Steel, 66
Universal Film Manufacturing
    Co., 85
UNMOVIC, 119
UNSCOM, 119
Ur-Nammu, 35, 40
Urban II, Pope, 46, 47
USA Today, 208, 209

Vallance, Chris, 226
Van Guysling, George E., 90
Vanity Fair, 227
Vanninen, Paula, 173
Venantius Fortunatus, 46
Verizon, 228, 246
Vernacular Papers Act [1878], 54
Viacom, 186, 228
Vimeo, 227
Vioxx, 82
Visa, 246
Vitagraph, 87, 88, 90
Vodafone, 184
Voice of America, 229
Vox, 58, 223
Vyvanse, 81

Walford, Cornelius, 56
Walker, David, 20, 105
Wall Street Journal, 208, 209
Wang Mang, 40
Washington Monthly, 223

*Washington Post*, 27, 94, 97, 125, 180, 208, 209, 223, 228, 233, 241
Watson, J.B., 69, 72, 196, 241
Wedderburn, Sir William, 56
Wells Fargo, 16
West, Mick, 60, 133, 134, 259
WHDH, 186
Wheeler, Marcy, 224
White, Adrian, 184
White's of Sheffield, 188
Wigmore, Andy, 242
Wikipedia, 195, 205, 207, 257–259
William of Orange, 51
Williams, Raymond, 116, 148, 191
Wilson, Harold, 103, 105, 196
Wilson, John, 184

Wood, Ed, 91
World Bank, 14, 154
World Socialist Web Site, 245
Wright, Peter, 104, 105, 191
WVC3 Group, 123

Yarbrough, Beau, 57
Yemen, 96, 164, 165, 167
Yglesias, 223
Young and Rubicam, 91
YouTube, 10, 94, 114, 133, 138, 144, 160, 161, 171, 172, 174, 191, 201, 205, 207, 214, 228, 238, 249
Yugoslavia, 150, 219
Yukawa, Haruna, 133

Zinoviev Letter, 106
Zionism, 59, 263
Zolof, 82

# About the author

T.J. Coles is a postdoctoral researcher at Plymouth University's Cognition Institute working on issues relating to blindness and visual impairment. His thesis *The Knotweed Factor* can be read online.

A columnist with AxisOfLogic.com, Coles has written about politics and human rights for a number of publications including *Counterpunch*, *Newsweek*, the *New Statesman* and *Truthout*. His books include *President Trump, Inc.*, and *Human Wrongs*.